SCOTT OF THE ANTARCTIC

SCOTT

of the Antarctic

———

REGINALD POUND

WORLD BOOKS : LONDON

FIRST PUBLISHED 1966
THIS EDITION PUBLISHED BY WORLD BOOKS 1968
BY ARRANGEMENT WITH CASSELL & COMPANY LIMITED
COPYRIGHT © REGINALD POUND 1966
MAPS COPYRIGHT © CASSELL & COMPANY LIMITED 1966

To

PETER SCOTT

PRINTED IN GREAT BRITAIN BY RICHARD CLAY (THE CHAUCER PRESS), LTD.,
BUNGAY, SUFFOLK

CONTENTS

MAPS

ILLUSTRATIONS

ACKNOWLEDGEMENTS

THIS is the first biography of Captain Scott to be based on extensive original research. Wholly new material for it has been found in his journals at the British Museum; in the archives of the Royal Society and the Royal Geographical Society; in the Kinsey Collection files at the Alexander Turnbull Library, Wellington, New Zealand; in the diaries kept by the late Lady Kennet (formerly Lady Scott); and in recently discovered family letters and other documents.

For the privilege of examining the historic journals, especially the last tragic pages, I am indebted to Mr Peter Scott, who, with his brother, Mr Wayland Young (Lord Kennet), also made available to me family correspondence at great biographical interest, together with their mother's diaries. This, with the necessary permission to quote, has been invaluable and, indeed, indispensable help. I can but hope that they will consider the result worthy of it.

Their handsome co-operation has been supplemented by the kindness of Miss Esther Ellison Macartney, Captain Scott's niece, who gave me access to the large collection of family letters handed on by her mother, the late Lady Ellison Macartney. I have been fortunate also in having the goodwill of other members of Captain Scott's family: Vice-Admiral A. C. Scott; Miss Stella Scott; Mr Robert Scott (of Manaccan, Cornwall); Mr John Ellison Macartney; and the Rev. T. R. D. Sharpe.

Recourse to the files of the Royal Society and the Royal Geographical Society was essential, for without the support of those two institutions Scott might never have been an explorer. I thank the officers and librarians of both Societies for facilities generously given. In the same category of appreciation, I include the Keeper of Manuscripts, British Museum; the Alexander Turnbull Library, Wellington, New Zealand; the Department of Scientific and Industrial Research, Antarctic Division (Mr L. B. Quartermain), Wellington, New Zealand; Ministry of Defence, Naval Library (Miss M. S. Heath); Scott Polar Research Institute, Cambridge; and the Public Record Office.

Mr Stanley Richards, B.Sc., Administrator & Keeper. The Royal Institution of South Wales, contributed helpful material concerning his heroic fellow countryman, Petty Officer Edgar Evans, and the visit to Cardiff in 1910 of Captain Scott's exploring ship *Terra Nova*. Mrs D. Irving-Bell, of Bristol, placed unreservedly at my disposal her store of Antarctic information, gathered over many years. Mrs Philip Dumas answered question arising out of her friendship with Captain Scott, showed me the unpublished diaries of her husband, the late Admiral Dumas, and lent me photographs. Lord Howard de Walden kindly found for me the letter quoted on page 268.

My grateful thanks are extended to Lord Mountevans; the Trustees of the late Sir Ernest Shackleton; Sir Charles Wright; Lady Simpson; Mr J. C. Sharp; Mrs Wayland Young (Lady Kennet); Miss Joan Flemington; Miss Molly Leeper and Miss V. A. Leeper; Mr C. H. Hare; Mr C. Reginald Ford; Dr Colin Bertram; Captain B. M. Peck, R.N. (Retd.); Mrs Sarah Owen; Sir Geoffrey Harmsworth; Miss Deirdre Clark; The Librarian, Britannia Royal Naval College, Dartmouth; Mr James K. Nesbitt; Mr F. Plumley and Miss Doris Plumley; Mr W. Hands; Miss A. C. Rees; Major C. R. Wolhuter; Mr A. V. Chamberlain; the City Librarian, Plymouth; Mr C. L. Quinlivan; Commander J. M. Palmer; Mrs Miriam M. Jones; Mr D. P. Bennett; Mr R. W. Richards; Mr John Fairfax; Lady Young; Mrs A. Rowan; and the editors of the following newspapers and other publications: *Sunday Times; Western Morning News; Western Mail; South Wales Evening Post; Melbourne Herald; Melbourne Age; Cape Argus; Cape Times; The Navy;* and the *Royal United Service Institution Journal*.

In response to the published notices of my intention to write a new biography of the man who inaugurated what has been called the heroic age of Antarctic exploration, I received a large number of letters from well-disposed correspondents, whose generous impulses are also gratefully acknowledged.

*London, W.*1.   R. P.

CHAPTER ONE

A PRIDE OF VENTURERS

AN aunt of Robert Falcon Scott, the polar explorer, was re-membered as 'a wonderful old lady, full of the family history, and very eager to repeat it'. She was Miss Charlotte Scott, who lived with his parents at Outlands, Milehouse, Devonport, where she died in 1890, aged ninety-six. One of her repetitious topics was the family's alleged kinship with Sir Walter Scott. She was proud to relate that as a very small girl she sat on his knee. Consanguinity was not stated but implied. No documentary warranty for it exists. The startling likeness to Sir Walter reproduced in the silhouette of Captain Scott cut by his Antarctic companion, Dr E. A. Wilson, recalls Hardy's lines: *I am the family face, Flesh perishes, I live on.* . . . If the stamp of Sir Walter Scott can be said to characterize the family face of the Scotts of Devonport, it lives on in Captain Scott's first cousin, Vice-Admiral A. C. Scott, R.N. (Retd.) and in Peter Scott, the explorer's son.

Some of the Devonport Scotts preserved a belief in their descent from the men of the Rough Clan, as their namesakes of the old no-man's-land between England and Scotland were collectively known in the eighteenth century. For untold years they kept the Border in a state of turmoil. According to Sir Walter Scott, they took to the Jacobite fighting as to the manner born. He encouraged the presumption that they were in the thick of it. One of them, John Scott, a sea captain, was captured and hanged.

A twentieth-century Garter Principal King-at-Arms, Sir Alfred Scott-Gatty (1847–1918), was said to be in direct descent from that victim of the hangman's rope. His nephew, Reginald Gatty (d. 1935), who had a professional connection with the Birmingham Repertory Theatre in Sir Barry Jackson's time, drew up a genealogical chart to support the romantic notion that the line was traceable to James, duke of Monmouth, 'and his mistress named Percy'. He was able to show more conclusively that Alexander John Scott (1768–1840), Lord Nelson's chaplain and private secretary, on board the *Victory*, was a collateral forebear.

Sir Alfred Scott-Gatty, at the College of Heralds, wrote to Captain Scott's eldest sister on 21 October 1908: 'My people claimed to be of the House of Buccleuch—so do your people. Both were out in the 1745 rising. So it looks as if there may be something in it. Of course the children of rebels would try and hide their identity lest the sins of the fathers should be visited on their children, and this is why we are so much at sea.'

No ancestor of Captain Scott has been traced with certainty beyond the third generation, all Devonshire born. In 1780, Robert Scott arrived from France to set up as a schoolmaster at Holbeton, a village of placid charm a few miles south-east of Plymouth, where Turner lingered during his climacteric painting tour of the West Country in 1812. That Scott was believed to have been a nephew of the Culloden rebel who was hanged. Old Miss Charlotte Scott had circumstantial stories to tell of his father's escape to France after the '45. What drew Robert Scott to Devonshire none of his descendants could say; possibly, his marriage to a woman twenty years younger than he, by then a middle-aged man. 'She never called him anything but Mr Scott to his dying day.'

The Holbeton schoolmaster had four sons, who took to the sea as by a natural law. The eldest, Robert, went into the Royal Navy as a midshipman and retired as a purser, having held the intermediate post of captain's clerk in different ships. Up to the nineteenth century the purser was in effect a purveyor of supplies and his ship's accountant, dual activities that were long a subject of cynical regard in the Service. Pursers were often implicated in forms of graft which hardened custom made it difficult even for honourable men to avoid. Towards the middle of the century a number of pursers petitioned the Admiralty for a change of name, 'because of the odium attaching to it'. The rank of paymaster superseded it from 1852.

Robert Scott left the Navy in 1826, after twenty-five years. He had for some time held a tenancy of Outlands, then a slate-hung cottage. He bought it about 1820 and added to it, enlarging it again in 1834, and making it an attractive property in two or three acres of garden and woodland. In 1826, he and his brother Edward bought the Hoegate Street Brewery, Plymouth, for £4,782, prize money they had gained in the war with France.

One of Edward Scott's sons, Major-General H. Y. D. Scott, of the Royal Engineers (1822–83), drew up the plans for and supervised the building of the Royal Albert Hall, London. He was the first to enter the Hall when the dome was completed, it was thought at some risk to himself. His sister Anne married William Courtney, of the Indian Civil Service, whose son, W. L. Courtney, M.A., LL.D, was for many years editor of the *Fortnightly Review*.

Robert Scott had eight children. The youngest, John, born 1830, was delicate and remained at home to be trained in the brewery business by his father. There was an understanding that he would inherit Outlands. When he was thirty-one he married Hannah Cuming, twenty-one, of 8 Lansdown Place, Plymouth, daughter of William Bennett Cuming, one of the eighty surveyors then employed by Lloyd's underwriters in the ports of the United Kingdom. The couple went to live with John Scott's parents at Outlands.

Both Scott parents died the following year, 1863. There were family ructions about Robert Scott's will. Made many years before, it disposed of funds that no longer existed. One of his sons, General Edwin Luddington Scott, of the Bombay Staff Corps—'he was mauled by a tiger, and cauterized the wound himself', the resident aunt used to say—persuaded two of his sisters, Mrs Preston and Mrs Harford, to join him in a lawsuit. As a consequence, Outlands was thrown into Chancery until William Cuming, the Lloyd's surveyor, came to the rescue and settled the property on his daughter, Hannah Scott (Captain Scott's mother), who sold it in 1924.

John and Hannah Scott had four girls and two boys, of whom Robert Falcon Scott, the explorer, was the third child, the elder son, and the fifth of his line to be given the name Robert. He was born on 6 June, 1868. Taught at first by governesses, when he was eight he went to a small private day school, Exmouth House, at Stoke Damerel, riding there and back each day on a pony. His father was a churchwarden, his mother a church worker, he a choirboy at St Mark's, Ford, a nearby parish. He was recalled in that role as late as 1965 by

11

William Hands, a retired naval outfitter, who sang in the choir with him on Sundays and went fishing with him during the holidays. Known in the family as Con (from his second name Falcon, his godparents' surname), at thirteen he was sent to Stubbington House, Fareham, Hampshire, to be coached for a cadetship in the Royal Navy.

As a boy, Scott was delicate, weak-chested, and shy. Before going to Stubbington House, he was examined by a Plymouth doctor, who gave the opinion that he lacked the physique to qualify for a naval career. An undefined malaise ran through his growing years, showing itself briefly in phases of lethargy that were later regarded by him as a weakness inherited from his father, who had the look and style of a squire of leisurely habits rather than of a man of business. Con Scott was untidy and absentminded. He would put off writing thank-you letters for Christmas presents until months had passed. He had a quick temper which required to be subdued as part of his long and ultimately triumphant campaign of self-restraint.

He shrank from suffering, human and animal. The sight of a trapped rabbit filled his eyes with tears. One of the first entries in the diary he started to keep when he was twenty lamented 'the ill-health, the sickness of heart', that he had to fight against.

*

To be born and brought up in that part of England was to receive the title-deeds of a splendid past. Devonshire had been the kingdom's foremost county, Plymouth its chief port, in the time of the first Elizabeth. 'If any person desired to see her English worthies,' wrote an old historian, 'Plymouth was the likeliest place to see them. All were in some fashion associated with the old town.' It was the cradle of England's maritime glory, a base of classic enterprise and discovery. Out of Plymouth Sir Humphrey Gilbert sailed for Newfoundland, Sir Richard Grenville for Virginia, Sir John Hawkins for the Bay of Mexico, Sir Martin Frobisher for the North West Passage, Sir Walter Raleigh for Guinea, Sir Francis Drake against the Armada, of which his captains 'got a full sight' on 20 July 1588, 'standing majestically on, the vessels drawn up in the form of a crescent, which, from horn to horn, measured some seven miles'.

One of the forgotten venturers, William Furneaux, is buried in Stoke Damerel church, where he was christened in 1735. Scott as a boy would certainly have known about his captaincy of Cook's second ship, the *Adventure*, in the great voyage of 1772–4 when the Antarctic Circle was crossed for the first time. He may have known, too, that the subsequently notorious Bligh was of the company.* Furneaux led another expedition that proved Tasmania to be an island.

In that context a boy's imagination was constantly on the wing; and to young Con Scott the horizon was more enticing than the typical red-and-green middle distances of the Devonshire landscape. Northward, there was mystery in the Dartmoor wasteland, strewn with the rocky debris of the ages, graveyard of kings and chieftains; not less awesome, its stone rows, cairns, and hut circles; far more so to a sensitive young mind, its gaunt-walled prison full of desperate men. Dartmoor could shiver the nerves; a spell easily broken by the magnetic pull southward, swinging the eye to the clustered masts of Plymouth Sound.

Down there, canvas was no longer being spread by the acre to catch the favourable winds. A Cunarder, the *Scotia*, was still threshing her way across the Atlantic by paddle-wheel, but the screw had already sent others like her to the breaker's yard. Five years before Scott was born, H.M.S. *Warrior*, first of the ironclads, had steamed up that coast to Portsmouth, a future First Sea Lord, 'Jacky' Fisher, on board as a lieutenant. Three years before, the Channel Fleet had anchored in Torbay, the admiral flying his flag in H.M.S. *Edgar*, a wooden two-decker of 3,094 tons, fitted with a screw propeller, 'but otherwise not unlike the ships of Nelson's time'.†

Almost any day Con Scott could see the smoke of the most significant phase of the industrial revolution smudging the Channel sky above Mount Edgcumbe and beyond. A greater change had come over the maritime scene in five decades than in a thousand years.

Had Scott been born a few years earlier he would not have needed to go to a 'crammer's' to qualify educationally for the Royal Navy. Boys with the ability 'to write English correctly

* The Bligh and Scott families were connected by marriage in the early nineteenth century.

† Cecil Torr: *Small Talk at Wreyland* (1926).

from dictation, and acquainted with the first four rules of arithmetic, reduction, and the rule of three', were eligible for nomination as cadets by the Admiralty or by ships' captains hoisting their pennants for the first time. They were sent to a receiving vessel moored in one of the naval ports, there to hang around in idleness, and sometimes in dissipation, until a chance came for them to be drafted to seagoing ships.

An examination system, introduced in the middle of the nineteenth century, was capable of farcical application. A memory of it survived to well past the Second World War. Captain J. E. Hunter, R.N. (Retd.) recalled his father taking him to Woolwich. 'My examination was to write out the Lord's Prayer, which I did. I was taken to the surgeon to be examined. He said, "Strip." I took off my coat. "Go on, strip." Then he examined me. He said: "Take that boy away, he will do." '

The system was changed in 1857, when the Admiralty inaugurated training ships through which every future cadet had to pass. It was a refinement that led to others, including a raising of the educational requirement. By Scott's time, a boy had to reach the equivalent of the fifth-form level of the public schools to pass into *Britannia*, which was in effect the Royal Navy's own public school. Hence the intensive course at Stubbington House, Fareham, or Foster's as it was familiarly known (from the proprietor's name). It was one of several similar establishments. Littlejohns' at Greenwich and Burney's Naval Academy at Gosport were equally well known. They were the forcing houses of careers that provided British naval leadership for more than a century.

The educational process finished as abruptly at thirteen for navy cadets as it did for the boys from the nation's elementary schools. Both types of boy had to learn thus early to stand on their own feet. Cadet training in *Britannia* largely neglected general education (including geography). Some French was taught, along with mathematics connected with navigation; the emphasis, otherwise, was on seamanship.

The training ship system originated during the Crimean War, when the two-decker *Illustrious* was used for training seamen for the Royal Navy. The superior type of sailor it produced encouraged an extension of the scheme to officer training, for which purpose the three-decker *Britannia*, lying near by in Hasler Creek, Portsmouth, was acquired as a sort of annexe. Moral objections to Portsmouth as a resort for cadets on shore leave eventually secured the removal of *Britannia* to Portland, where the social atmosphere was more congenial to parents if not consequently to their sons. Wind and tide compelled the final move to the sheltered waters of the River Dart in 1863.

Extra accommodation, necessitated by the increasing number of boys wanting to be naval officers, was provided by an old teak-built two-decker, the *Hindustani*, moored astern of *Britannia* and joined to her by a gangway. Some shore installations were added, mainly recreational. Then *Britannia* herself was replaced by a bigger ship taking the same name, the former *Prince of Wales*.

The new *Britannia* had her guns and two aft-masts removed. Her foremast with its topmast, and her big jib-boom and flying jib, were perhaps not specifically retained as a ready-made gymnasium. They served that unofficial purpose. First-term boys were expected to display their nerve by climbing to the foremast head. In their second term the test was more severe, performed a hundred and twenty feet above deck.

The valley of the Dart, where the *Britannia* lay, was the cradle of one of England's greatest Arctic navigators of the sixteenth century, John Davis, born at Sandridge, near Dartmouth. If his name was not known to Scott and his fellow cadets, they were certainly aware of the more recent repute of Vice-Admiral Sir George Nares, K.C.B., formerly a lieutenant in *Britannia*. He was in command of H.M.S. *Challenger* in 1874, when she crossed the Antarctic circle, the first steam-driven vessel to do so. The voyage, dedicated exclusively to science, was hailed as a national achievement. Nares became famous in the land. Despite its limited results, his *Challenger* expedition roused new curiosity about the problems waiting to be solved in the far South.

Whether it was subconsciously significant for Cadet R. F. Scott, for instance, cannot as fairly be surmised as that Nares's connection with *Britannia* was a source of pride among all ranks in the training ship. Eldorado talk was in the air, rumours of vast mineral wealth waiting to be prospected in an unknown, silent continent. There was the dream of adding new greatness to the globe-girdling British Empire.

During her voyage, *Challenger* lost her jib-boom in a collision with an iceberg. The accident prompted the expedition's scientific adviser, Professor Wyville Thomson, to suggest in a lecture that 'we can only anticipate disaster multiplied a hundred-fold should the South Pole ever become a goal of rivalry among the nations'.

At his final examination in *Britannia* in 1883, Scott obtained first-class certificates in mathematics and seamanship. His order of merit was seventh in a class of twenty-six. He was not among the sixteen cadets who were awarded prizes. 'Very Good' was filled in under the heading of 'Conduct' by Commander Edward S. Dugdale, signing for 'Captain on leave'. Scott had paid 'very much' attention to the various branches of study. He gained a first-class certificate in mathematics, a second-class in French and extra subjects, a first-class in seamanship, 'and can swim'.

He was rated a midshipman without examination. His midshipman years were 1883–7. In that period he served in four of Her Majesty's ships: *Boadicea, Lion, Monarch, Rover*.

CHAPTER TWO

PHASE OF ILL-FORTUNE

UNKNOWN to himself, before he was twenty, Scott's future was being mapped out for him by a noted British geographer, Sir Clements Markham, K.C.B., F.R.S. (1830–1916), secretary and later president of the Royal Geographical Society. Grandson of an archbishop of York, Markham had entered the Royal Navy as a midshipman and served in one of the ships that searched the Arctic in the 1850s for the fateful expedition led by Sir John Franklin. He left the sea, 'with no regret', to join the Civil Service. As a young India Office official, he was sent to the forests of the Eastern Andes to collect specimens of cinchona trees for acclimatization in India, ultimately to the benefit of malaria sufferers in large areas of the sub-continent. He resigned his post in 1877 to give his time and energy to furthering the authority and prestige of the Royal Geographical Society.

As a geographer, he had an unrivalled theoretical knowledge of the Antarctic, conceiving it as the proving ground of a great English venture dedicated to scientific exploration on a scale never before attempted. His long and obsessive preoccupation with the unknown southern continent that some thought unknowable and others, among them Captain Cook, probably not worth knowing, was that of an enthusiast who was also largely animated by patriotic zeal. Like many Englishmen of his class and time, he was beset by concern for the national honour.

The Union Jack was the pre-eminent symbol of sovereignty in the world. Clements Markham was one of those who hoped to see it unfurled in the loneliest latitudes on earth as renewed proof of the indomitable spirit of the race. As far back as 1870, he had sketched out a plan for an Antarctic expedition having for its main object 'the encouragement of maritime enterprise, and to afford opportunities for young naval officers to win distinction in times of peace'. The quotation is from Markham's own manuscript notes in which he surveyed the course of Antarctic exploration after Sir John Ross's expedition of 1839–42.

He was nominated a member of the Antarctic committee of the British Association meeting at Aberdeen in 1885. As a preliminary to campaigning for funds, the committee optimistically approached the Board of Trade 'respecting the trade of the Antarctic regions'. The official reply was unfavourable.

Markham met discouragement almost everywhere. Hardly anyone, not excluding the highest scientific circles, showed more than a passing interest. He refused to yield in his determination to organize an expedition, though it entailed working and waiting many more years. He was a man of admirable staunchness of character, if often of faulty judgement on the personal plane. At that distant time, when there was no obvious chance of launching an expedition to the Far South, he thought seriously about 'the most important question of a commander for the future expedition'. The candidate, he wrote, 'must be a naval officer, he must be in the regular line and not in the surveying branch, and he must be young. These are essentials.' He had no doubt, either, that 'such a commander should be of *a scientific turn of mind*' (his italics).

In 1887, Markham was with the training squadron of the West Indies station as a guest of the commodore, his cousin.

Each of the squadron's four ships carried about twelve midshipmen. Scott was one of them in H.M.S. *Rover*. With his Antarctic dream ever fresh in his thoughts, Markham noted that 'it would be a dozen years at least before an expedition could be actually on foot. The midshipmen of the Training Squadron were, therefore, the future gunnery and torpedo lieutenants from among whom an efficient commander of the expedition must be selected. I cultivated their acquaintance. Allowing for the changes wrought by a dozen years, I believed Tommy Smyth to be the best man in the *Active*, though wanting ballast, Hyde Parker in the *Volage*, and Robert F. Scott in the *Rover*.'

The lieutenants of the Training Squadron at St Kitts arranged a cutter race during Markham's visit. He described the event. 'The boats were to be at anchor with awnings spread. They were to get under way and make sail, beat up for a mile, round a buoy, down mast and sail, pull down to the original place anchor and spread awnings again. The race tried several qualities. For a long time it was a close thing between Hyde Parker and Scott; but Scott won the race.'

He was invited to dine with the commodore and his guest four nights later. 'Noel, his captain, who rarely praised anyone, spoke highly of Scott,' Markham wrote in his notes. 'He trusted him to keep officers' watch in the day time, with the ship under sail. My final conclusion was that Scott was the destined man to command the Antarctic expedition. He was then 18.'

Markham's sincere and touching faith in youth is fully apparent in those painstakingly kept manuscript notes of his. 'The fatal mistake, in selecting commanders for former polar expeditions, has been to seek for experience instead of youth. Both cannot be united, and youth is absolutely essential. Old men should supply information and the results of experience, and should stay at home, making room for the younger and therefore more efficient leaders.' He considered that Franklin, Ross, M'Clintock and Nares had all been too old for polar exploration in their day. 'Elderly men are not accessible to new ideas and have not the energy and capacity necessary to meet emergencies. How can novel forms of effort be expected from stiff old organisms hampered by experience!'

A little later, Markham compiled a list headed 'Possible Antarctic Leaders', all naval officers. In the first place, he put

Captain George Le C. Egerton, C.B., aged forty-six. 'The very best man for it, but too late.' Among the other names were Commander John De Robeck, 'about 38, hard as nails, lots of nerve, an excellent messmate'; Commander Murray J. Park, 'keen sportsman, hard as nails, very energetic, 37'; Commander Owen F. Gillett, 'age 37, overflowing with energy'; Commander James W. Combe, 'clever and full of resource'. Scott's name, with no qualifications added, is numbered 6 in the list of eleven names.

*

Commissioned as a sub-lieutenant on 14 August 1887, Scott was posted a year later to H.M.S. *Amphion* on the Pacific station. Reporting for duty in that ship, he had to travel alone by land and sea to Esquimault, British Columbia. Because of snowed-up railways, the last stage of the journey was by tramp steamer from San Francisco. The ship was taking Californian miners and their families to new diggings in Alaska. Scott shared a single cabin with three unattractive characters from San Francisco and another Englishman, Courtauld Thomson.*

A full gale produced indescribable conditions. Top-deck hamper was swept away. Water poured into the cabins. Scott took charge of a chaotic situation in the saloon, where seasick passengers sprawled in misery on the floor. Forming a volunteer group, with Thomson and another, he dressed the mothers, washed the children, fed the babies, nursed the sick, and performed every imaginable service for all hands. The same eyewitness saw Scott use his fists to separate others who were using theirs in private feuds.

In British Columbia he was welcomed into the home of Judge Peter O'Reilly, of Victoria, described to him by a brother officer, Commander George Warrender, R.N.,† as 'a type of the finest men the colony possesses'. Scott showed more than a casual interest in the judge's daughter Kathleen. He corresponded with her up to 1906. The language was hardly that of romance, though in a letter written in August 1899 he referred to his 'ever-fresh memories of good times', presumably in her company. He showed more ardour when she visited London. 'Please don't let me miss the opportunity of seeing

* Later Lord Courtauld-Thomson (1865–1954), British Red Cross administrator.

† Later Vice-Admiral Sir George Warrender, K.C.B. (1860–1917).

you if it can possibly be seized—there is always such a lot to be talked about that my wretched pen can't express.'

In his diary he was noting 'the daily round of petty annoyances ... this slow sickness which holds one for weeks; how can I bear it? I write of the future, of hopes of being more worthy, but shall I ever be? Can I alone, poor weak wretch that I am, bear up against it all? How can I fight against it all? No one will ever see these words, therefore I may freely write: What does it all mean?'

In spite of his sickly introspection, the evidence was of his being in better physical shape than he had ever been before. To his sister Grace ('Monsie') it seemed that he had 'greatly developed'. She thought him more 'awake and alert'. He had come home in 1891. His passing certificates for the rank of lieutenant show that he gained the highest marks of his year for seamanship, and that he was first in a class of nineteen in his subsequent examination at the Royal Naval College, Greenwich. He spent the next three years at the torpedo school at Plymouth. It meant frequent weekend leave at Outlands.

One of the regular visitors there during that period was his first cousin, Bertie Scott, a future vice-admiral, who welcomed the opportunity of escaping from his mother's excessive anxiety about the state of his soul. 'She and my father were P.Bs [Plymouth Brethren] ... My mother was for ever asking me: "Are you saved? Are you *sure* you are saved?" ' She thought that the Outlands branch of the family was hell bound, 'I suppose because of the brewery.'

Admiral Scott remembered (1965) that Scott himself never spoke of God—'always of Providence'. He recalled Scott, home on leave, telling him: 'I don't feel the cold,' and meeting him in London, 'on a bitter March morning, the only person I saw that day who wasn't muffled up to the eyes. He hadn't even an overcoat on.' He remembered hearing at Outlands that his cousin had forced himself to go to a local slaughterhouse to overcome the nausea that always afflicted him at the sight of blood.

There was bad news for Scott in the early 'nineties. His father had sold the brewery and had kept the family going on the proceeds until he ran out of funds. He had given his two boys the education required for their careers in the Services and had supplemented their meagre pay, neglecting the education of his daughters to do so. Literally, there was no money left. It meant giving up Outlands, while Scott, senior, looked for a job as a brewery manager.

The information was given almost casually in a letter in which John Scott professed to be more immediately interested in the new torpedo device that his son was helping to perfect. It was left to Scott's mother to fill in the details of their financial plight. Admiral Scott well remembers that period of the family history. 'Con was deeply worried and distressed. All of us Scotts at that time were poverty stricken.'

Scott now had to manage on his lieutenant's pay of £182 10s. a year. He liked the companionship of the wardroom, but 'forking out' in the name of conviviality was not for him. His uniforms became shabby, the epaulettes tarnished. He was sensitive to personal appearance, his own and other people's: 'perhaps too much so', he conjectured in a letter.

Poverty was not simply an economic misfortune. It was a social blemish. It obliged him to be circumspect in his dealings with the young women who attracted him. He could not afford the most modest hospitality or present-giving. According to his sister 'Monsie', his temperament did not much expose him to extravagance, but 'he was very impressionable'. She spoke of his being 'wildly in the throes of his first love', when he was eighteen, 'and longing to rush off to his charmer, who had a very short-tempered husband'.

His sister believed that his feelings were more genuinely engaged by 'a girlhood friend of ours who later married but who was always in the background of his affections. She remained so, I think, until he met his wife.' One of his colleagues of later days thought that Scott had 'only a slender knowledge of women. Their subtleties were perhaps beyond him. But he enjoyed their company if they were pretty, and more so if they also appeared to be intelligent.'*

*

Outlands was let to J. B. Love, a Devonport linen draper and alderman, who cherished the house and its associations and behaved with becoming deference to members of the Scott family calling at long intervals to see their old home. For the time being, they moved into a farmhouse lodgings in Somerset,

* L. C. Bernacchi: *Saga of the 'Discovery'*.

while John Scott cast about for employment. He was given the management of a small brewery in the Bath district, and moved his family to Holcombe House, near Shepton Mallet. Described as 'a substantial Georgian residence', it had once been the manor house. In some notes drawn up by Con Scott for a family budget, the rent was put down at £30 a year.

Acknowledging the receipt of a 'note of hand' (a written promise to repay money), Con Scott assured his father: 'I have great faith that you will pull matters straight in quite a short time' (13 October 1896). 'My dearest Mother,' he wrote a week later, 'it is delightful to hear such cheery news of the way things are going at Holcombe and to feel that there is a prospect that fortune will smile again.'

Ettie, the eldest Scott daughter, chose the stage as a career. She had taken part in amateur theatricals with some success. Following a course of training at the Sarah Thorne Academy in London, she took the name of Ettie Scott-Damer for professional use, and joined a touring company in which Irene Vanbrugh was the leading lady.

Scott to his mother:

H.M.S. *Empress of India*,
Arosa Bay,
November 22nd 1896.

My dearest Mother,—I'm so afraid that you must be grieving over Ettie's absence very much but think, dear, what it means to her, what prospects of independence. I hate to think that you did not go and see her before she left. I hate to think that I did not have the forethought of writing to urge you to go. That you should have studied economy in such a matter makes me feel very bitter. Promise you won't do it again. But you really shan't, for when she comes back I am determined you shall go and see her act and shall yourself see the life. I can't forgive my own want of forethought in not writing about it.

Your affectionate son,
ROBERT F. SCOTT

Another of the daughters, Rose, trained as a nurse at St Bartholomew's Hospital, London, and chose to work in a hospital on the Gold Coast, where her personal expenses were minimal, enabling her to send money home to the family. The other two girls, Kitty and 'Monsie', went into the dressmaking business. Trade was still an unhallowed province for genteel young women.

Cheerfully oblivious of the social implications, the Scott sisters took rooms over a milliner's shop (Mrs Rust) at 80 Queen's Road (now Royal Hospital Road, Chelsea). They spent a preliminary interval in Paris, studying the newest trends of fashion. They then opened their own shop in Beauchamp Place, Brompton Road, London, S.W., aided by a life insurance policy, and trading under the name of Kate Grace. When Kitty became Mrs Brownlow, wife of a Henley-on-Thames surgeon, 'Monsie' retained the business and moved to 81 Chester Square, S.W., using the name of Kate Grace & Co., up to the 1930s.

The Scotts were always a united family; never more so than in their reduced circumstances. The two brothers were the mainstay. Con Scott, absorbed in mastering the changed tactical theories resulting from the development of the torpedo, disregarded the possible detriment to his future by transferring to a depot ship at Devonport, so that he might be nearer his parents in their time of trouble. He was a dedicated naval officer in that he was more ardent for the honour and glory of the Service than for the advancement of his own fortunes in it. He wrote letters of many pages to his father about the specialized studies he was pursuing and what he hoped for as the outcome of them, recognition as 'a competent torpedo man'. After that, his highest ambition was to shine 'in general service duties'.

He was not looking for self-fulfilment elsewhere. Though not by nature thrustful, he was prepared to join 'the ranks of the advancers', as he put it, and to fit himself for such responsibilities as might come his way. He wrote to Kathleen O'Reilly in British Columbia: 'At present I have neither rest nor peace to pursue anything but promotion. It is doubtful sometimes whether the game is worth a candle.'

Concerning promotion, he aspired to an unspecified post, telling his father: 'Next to my name in the Navy List you will find Stanley—Michael Culme-Seymour*—and Goodenough.† Stanley is a godson of the Queen, son of the Earl of Derby, a nice chap, popular, and has war service (though only Egyptian).

---

* Vice-Admiral Sir Michael Culme-Seymour, Bt., K.C.B., Second Sea Lord (1867–1925).

† Admiral Sir William Goodenough, K.C.B. (1867–1945).

Michael Seymour is of course the son of the Admiral, which is saying a great deal as by the time of selection his father will be at Portsmouth in command, after a unique succession of employment and popularity. Goodenough is very well connected, has many personal friends in high places, war service, and altogether an excellent chance. Mike Seymour tells me all these people will try for the billet—so you see I fear there is a very poor chance for me.' (8 November 1896)

His brother Archie, a subaltern of the Royal Artillery, applied for service with the Houssa Force, a West African regiment, in which the allowances were higher and the mess bills lower than at home, so that he, too, might contribute to the family's support. Con Scott wrote to his sister Kate: 'I have taken steps to give regular financial assistance and have written Arch to do the same. The joint amount will not be very great, but it will, I hope, make it easier. Poor dear Mater, doesn't it seem hard that these eternal worries should fall on her?' He undertook to contribute £70 a year; his brother £120.

It can be imagined as a frustrating period for the brothers, naturally eager to relish the pleasures of youth. They were warmly attached to each other. 'Isn't Arch just splendid?' Con Scott wrote to their mother, on hearing that his brother had been appointed A.D.C. to the Governor of the Gold Coast. 'He is so absolutely full of life and enjoyment and at the same time so keen on his job. Dear old chap, he deserves to be a success.'

*

The great climacteric decade, the dazzling 'nineties, held all too little glamour for Scott. The family's financial misfortunes were followed by the health breakdown of his father. Scott wrote to him at Holcombe, Somerset, from H.M.S. *Majestic* in Spanish waters on 8 October 1897: 'Well, old chap, I do hope you will buck up and get rid of your weaknesses, so that we can stroll round once more when I get home.' The family had been medically warned that his recovery was unlikely—'a great shock to us all', Scott told Kathleen O'Reilly in a letter in which he acknowledged Christmas greetings received eight months before.

John Scott died on 27 October 1897: certified cause of death, 'heart disease and dropsy'. He was sixty-six. The Country Brewers' Society, holding their annual banquet in London a week later, reserved their condolences for the royal family, in mourning for the Duchess of Teck. Nor did the *Brewers' Journal* include John Scott in its obituaries of the month. He left £1,550, which may have been exhausted by outstanding liabilities, as Con Scott referred in a letter to £50 being put at his mother's disposal by a family friend.

After two years on the stage, Ettie Scott married, in 1897, William Ellison Macartney, Unionist M.P. for South Antrim and later deputy master of the Royal Mint, and Governor of Tasmania. Scott's mother went to live with her two younger daughters in the rooms in Royal Hospital Road. Judging by a letter Scott wrote to her, the family uprooting had advantages for his sisters. 'The difference in them since they have been about, meeting all manner of people, and relying on themselves, is so very plain to me. They have gained in a hundred points, not to mention in appearance and smartness. I honestly think we shall some day be grateful to fortune for lifting us out of the "sleepy hollow" of the old Plymouth life. I am longing to see old Arch and to tell him how hopeful I think it all.'

A month after that was written, Archie Scott, home on leave from his new regiment, went to play golf at Hythe, Kent. He was taken ill with typhoid fever. In less than a week he was dead.

Scott was at sea as torpedo lieutenant of H.M.S. *Majestic*, flagship of the Channel Squadron. Receiving news that must have struck him to the heart, he replied from Gibraltar at once to his mother, whose letter was full of self-reproaches. She feared that she was responsible for her younger son's death by encouraging him to change to the regiment stationed in West Africa with its bad health record. Scott begged her to discard any such notion. 'It hurts to hear you blaming yourself.' He assured her that 'Archie was never anything but glad' to forsake the routine of garrison duty with the Royal Artillery. 'If ever children had cause to worship their mother we feel we have, dear; you can never be a burden, but only the bond that keeps us all closer together—the fine example that will guide us all our lives.' There was the final injunction: 'Don't be bitter, dear.' To his sister Ettie, he wrote:

My dearest Girl,—It is good to hear there was no pain and it is easy to understand that he died like a man. All his life, wherever he went, people felt the better for his coming. I don't think he ever did an unkind thing and no form of meanness was in him. It is a strange chance that has taken him who perhaps of all of us found the keenest pleasure in life, who was always content and never grumbled. Of course, now we know he never ought to have gone to West Africa. After watching him carefully, I saw that despite his health he was not strong and I meant to have a long talk with you on the subject. Too late—doesn't it always seem the ending of our wretched little mortal plans? Good God, it is past all understanding. He and you and I were very close together, weren't we? I know what your loss is, knowing my own. As we are returning so soon, I will not discuss the money question....

Scott was glad to acknowledge that his mother had brought up him and his brother 'in a way that made us gentlemen', but for him there was no snobbish significance in that. Life had been rough on him in his twenty-two years, and he already saw the hollowness of social pretensions, that the gentleman concept is centred not in a class but in a type, a quintessential quality to be found, and saluted, in all ranks.

He had by no means yet attained the self-command that was one of his strongest aspirations and perhaps his final ideal. When his sister Ettie was having her first child, he went with another sister to call at the house, 4 Walton Street, Knightsbridge, S.W., where the event was imminent. The birth was a long and difficult one. Scott was so overwrought with anxiety that he swooned on the front steps as they waited for the bell to be answered.

CHAPTER THREE

CLASH WITH THE SCIENTISTS

SCOTT had 'no predilection' (his words) for Polar exploration. He regarded his appearance on that scene as accidental, showing 'how curiously the course of one's life may be turned'.*

* Scott: *The Voyage of the 'Discovery'*.

He had no reason to know that the good opinion Sir Clements Markham had formed of him after the cutter race in the West Indies in 1887 was confirmed ten years later at Gibraltar, when Scott was torpedo lieutenant in the *Empress of India*. 'We were thrown together again. I was more than ever impressed by his evident vocation for such a command,' Markham wrote.

It seems that something akin to an occult force was at work in Scott's favour, for his sponsor never defined his qualifications for leadership except in a generalizing way. True, Markham noted with satisfaction that Scott had 'written a complete section of the *Torpedo Manual*', and had a firm grasp, too, of 'the principles of surveying'.

The subjective element entered strongly into Markham's judgement of men. Travelling down to Greenhithe in a river steamer, he saw on board 'a young Conway cadet who bore a remarkable resemblance to Wyatt Rawson, the gallant Arctic officer in the expedition of 1875-6'. The cadet, Charles Royds, 'turned out to be his nephew', a sufficient reason for Markham to enrol him, when the time came, as a member of the National Antarctic Expedition. Considering candidates to man the Expedition relief ship, Markham struck out the name of a young officer because his upper lip was too short.

Sir Clements was prominent at a memorable meeting convened by the Royal Society at Burlington House, London, on 26 February 1898, when leading physical scientists discussed the zone of exploration, 'south of the Pacific', assigned to Great Britain at the International Geographical Congress held in London three years before. That meeting set up a record in the domestic history of the Royal Society by continuing to nearly midnight. From it came an impetus that resulted in the National Antarctic Expedition of 1901-4. By then, Markham had no doubt that ships had reached their limit of usefulness in exploring the region. The next great advances, he foresaw, would have to be made overland.

After months of discussion, dispute, negotiation, the Royal Society agreed to join the Royal Geographical Society in promoting an expedition. 'A serious mistake,' was Markham's private verdict when he afterwards reviewed the arrangement; 'in fact, a fatal error. The coalition has been a source of worry, delays, friction, and danger; and no good whatever.'

A committee of the two Societies considered an approach to

27

the Government for a grant to enable the project of a National Antarctic Expedition to go forward. Giving a lead, the Royal Geographical Society headed a subscription list with £5,000. Alfred Harmsworth, the young founder of the *Daily Mail* (1896), promised another £5,000. But Markham soon found that 'raising funds was desperately uphill work'. He secured a further £4,000 or so, at which point 'some influential people said I should get no more, and advised me to return it. I replied that I would do nothing of the kind.' Instead, he 'kept on writing letters to rich people'.

In response to and perhaps in admiration of his tenacity, Llewellyn Wood Longstaff, F.R.G.S., of Ridgelands, Wimbledon, a director of the paint manufacturing firm of Blundell, Spence, Ltd., wrote to inquire whether 'the sum of £25,000 would enable an expedition to start'. Longstaff's entry in *Who's Who* gave the information that he was a colonel of volunteers. To that modest distinction he was therefore able to add, right up to his death in 1918, that 'his support made practicable the National Antarctic Expedition'. One of its immediate results was to ensure royal patronage of the fund, a valuable asset to the organizers. As Markham put it, 'this noble conduct altered the whole posture of affairs'.

Above all, it evoked a show of interest from the Government. 'Mr Balfour, the First Lord of the Admiralty, was induced to consider the question and, being favourable to scientific researches, he thought a grant might be made.' Sir Francis Mowatt, the Secretary of the Treasury, and later one of Winston Churchill's acknowledged mentors in the art of government, was also well disposed. Rejoicing in the turn of events, Sir Clements introduced a deputation—it included Lord Kelvin and Sir Joseph Hooker—to Balfour, who received them at the Foreign Office. 'Mr Balfour said that expeditions towards the poles of the earth were eminently desirable.' He indicated that the Chancellor of the Exchequer was sympathetic.

In July 1899, the Treasury made a grant of £45,000, subject to a similar sum coming from other sources. Markham's little triumph was clouded. 'So there is a condition attached.' In response to his eloquent appeal, the Royal Geographical Society provided cash to enable the Government grant to be claimed at once. Markham's relief still exudes from the notes he made recording that happy climax of his efforts.

By then aged seventy, he threw himself into the business of organizing the expedition as the crowning work not only of his presidency of the Royal Geographical Society but of his life. With accelerated zest, he drafted circular appeals, gave lectures, sought interviews, wrote innumerable letters by hand. Dauntless, indefatigable, proud, he achieved the resounding total of £93,000. It was the largest amount ever raised for such a purpose.

The Admiralty lent scientific instruments and, more important, allowed a number of officers and other ranks to volunteer for service with the expedition at full naval pay. In that matter, indispensable help was given by Admiral Sir Anthony Hoskins, whose widow afterwards wrote to Scott: 'He did more for you (your cause) than you or anyone will ever know.'

Markham went to Norway for a well-deserved rest. His ruling passion would not be denied. He gave up every hour of his holiday to 'a very detailed examination of all previous voyages and of all that is known of the Antarctic regions'. Studying the charts, he divided the Antarctic into four quadrants, naming them Victoria, Ross, Enderby, Weddell. The two first-named, he decided, were to be reserved for British enterprise.

*

Lieutenant Scott had gone back to sea in H.M.S. *Majestic*, flagship of the Channel Squadron, in which he served three years, from July 1897 to September 1900. During that period he transmitted, 'through the usual channels', observations made by him of the electrical equipment of the German warship *Aegir*, presumably noted during a courtesy visit. His report was read by the Lords Commissioners 'with much interest'. The signatory to the letter of acknowledgement was commanded to state that 'reports of this nature are always useful, and should be obtained whenever practicable'. Scott suggested in a follow-up report that fuller use of electric power in ships of the Royal Navy 'must come, and come soon', and that his fellow officers 'would welcome the day when there will be no far reaching and leaking steam pipes, no distant engines needing to be warmed through, or raising a noisy clatter when running'.

As for the Antarctic expedition, he knew nothing of it until one day in June 1899 he crossed, by chance, Sir Clements

Markham's path again. The old gentleman was passing Victoria Station, London, on his way home to 21 Eccleston Square, close by. Scott happened to be walking in the opposite direction on the other side of the street. Seeing Sir Clements, he stepped over to join him in his homeward stride.

'That afternoon I learned for the first time that there was such a thing as a prospective Antarctic expedition. Two days later I wrote applying to command it,' doubtless with Markham's earnest approval. 'A year after that I was officially appointed.'* His application was endorsed by Viscount Goschen, sometime First Lord of the Admiralty, who deplored the possibility that Scott would be 'relinquishing a brilliant naval career'; Admiral Lord William Kerr, senior naval lord of the Admiralty Board; and Captain (later Sir George) Egerton, commanding the Channel Squadron. For all the imposing support, there was 'much tedious opposition' to the appointment. Markham had to champion Scott through joint committees, special committees, sub-committees, 'and all the complicated apparatus which our junction with the Royal Society involved, harder to force a way through than the most impenetrable of ice-packs'.†

The Royal Society desired that a scientist should lead the expedition. Markham, for the Royal Geographical Society, opposed that view. He believed, strenuously, that a civilian leadership could not impart the necessary discipline. An equally vigorous objector to Scott's appointment was Admiral Mostyn Field, of the Admiralty hydrography department, whom Scott specially named in a letter as 'a partisan in the bitter controversies that preceded the departure of the Expedition'.

The argument swayed for months over the council tables of the two Societies, 'until we got through', Markham wrote, 'and I had the pleasure of signing Scott's appointment on 9 June 1900'. Scott's admiration for Markham's 'unique, unconquerable personality' never wavered.

In the same month, Scott received his promotion to the rank of Commander, R.N. In another month his service with the flagship *Majestic* ceased. By the grace of their lordships of the Board of Admiralty, he was free to assume, temporarily on half pay, his intimidating new responsibility of trying to solve one of the last and greatest of the earth's geographical mysteries.

* *The Voyage of the 'Discovery'.*
† Sir Clements Markham: *The Lands of Silence* (1921).

He preferred to speak of it less ponderously as 'novel and important work'.

Scott to the President of the Royal Society and the President of the Royal Geographical Society:

United Service Club,
June 11th, 1900.

My Lord and Sir,—I have the honour to acknowledge your communication of June 9th, acquainting me with my appointment as Commander of the National Antarctic Expedition.

I am keenly alive to the great honour done me in this selection, and sincerely hope that the trust reposed in me may be justified by my conduct of the enterprise, and by my earnest wish to further its great scientific aims.

I am grateful for your kindness in the applications you have made on my behalf to the Lords Commissioners of the Admiralty, and feel that whilst in your service I can confidently leave in your hands my interests in a profession to which I am devotedly attached.

I have the honour to be,
Your obedient servant,
ROBERT F. SCOTT

Hearing from Markham that a strong undercurrent of antagonism to his appointment was still running at Burlington House, headquarters of the Royal Society, he wrote a letter, dated 24 June, setting forth the terms on which he consented to take charge of the Expedition. Its tone suggested that he was not disposed to further argument. Having defined what he conceived to be the scope of his authority, he concluded: 'I am ready to insist upon these conditions to the point of resignation if, in my opinion, their refusal imperils the success of the undertaking.'

Markham confided his satisfaction to his notebook. 'When Scott wrote this he was still serving on board the *Majestic*. It gave me the greatest confidence in his firmness and clear insight.'

*

Scott lodged with his mother and sisters in Royal Hospital Road, S.W. From there, most mornings, he set forth for the

Expedition office at 1 Savile Row, *via* The Green Park. His choice of parks was deliberate. Entering the gates, he would drop the style of the staid City-goer and break into a quick sprint. Exercise was important, deep-breathing an obsession, activated by his disdain of London's vitiated air.

Since the Franklin expedition of fifty years before, England had lost many of the skills that her Arctic explorers had perfected, including the secret of making good pemmican, then a staple food in the cold latitudes. In 1900, an inferior make of it had to be ordered from the Chicago meat factories; later, a better quality was supplied from Copenhagen. The sledge-making craft had declined; so had the building of wooden ships. There were few replies when tenders were invited for the National Antarctic Expedition ship; and only one from a shipbuilder with recent experience of that kind of construction.

Because of those deficiencies, and as a first step in his Polar education, Scott accompanied Markham to Lysaker in Norway to meet Fridtjof Nansen, a towering figure among contemporary explorers. Nansen was listened to with deference on Polar ship design, personal equipment, sledge-building, and diet. He insisted, and reiterated, that preparation was the hardest part of any expedition.

From the beginning of the visit Scott sensed uncomfortably that they were trespassing on Nansen's time, generous though he was in his attention to them. 'He is quite a great man,' Scott wrote home to his mother, 'absolutely straightforward and wholly practical.' Nansen remembered Scott's 'tight, wary figure, his intelligent, handsome face'.

Leaving Christiania (now Oslo), Scott went to Berlin to consult with Baron von Richtofen, and Professor Erik von Drygalski, a scientist who was to lead a German expedition to the far south the following year. He was shown 'the greatest kindness and consideration'. The Germans proposed 'co-operative action'. They were so well ahead with their plans that he hurried home after three days 'in considerable alarm'.

The national rivalries that the chief scientist of the *Challenger* expedition of 1874 feared would bedevil the South Polar scene were already set in motion. As part of the international programme of Antarctic research, the Admiralty was being asked for coaling facilities at Sydney for the German expedition. Similar facilities at the Falkland Islands were sought by a Swedish Antarctic Expedition under Otto Nordenskjöld. A request to the Admiralty for the loan of scientific instruments was about to be made on behalf of a Scottish Antarctic Expedition under Dr W. S. Bruce.

Startled by the extent and efficiency of the German preparations, Scott was the more dismayed at finding, on his return, how little progress was being made with the British plans. The only considerable satisfaction for him at that stage was the news that the keel of the expedition ship had been laid at Dundee. Soon he was battling with delays in that quarter too. His mother remembered that for him it was a time of 'the greatest stress'. He sent a memorandum to the Royal Society and the Royal Geographical Society: 'Sirs,—I have the honour to bring to your notice that the work of equipping the Antarctic Expedition is very backward; in some details, no advance at all has been made.'

Dealing with the various committees was exasperating to one who was used to giving orders. The members were mostly men with other and wider interests that precluded regular attendance at meetings. Dr H. R. Mill, for many years librarian of the Royal Geographical Society, wrote of 'the tangle of jealousies, misconceptions, and mistakes which clouded these preparations'.* Scott considered resigning. Curbing his low flash-point temper added to the strain. A stage was reached at which he was prepared to nominate his successor.

Sir Clements Markham, who conducted his correspondence in miniscule script that showed him to be one of the last users of the long 's', was weighed down by office routine as well as policy worries. Cyril Longhurst, a Belgravia doctor's son, aged twenty, who was the Expedition's £2-a-week secretary, fell ill from scarlet fever. Recording that misfortune, Markham added: 'Hodge, our typewriter, has got epileptic fits. I have been working single-handed with only an office-boy four feet high. Bills pouring in.' The often lively letter exchanges between the two Societies went into broad black-edged mourning in February 1901, marking the death of Queen Victoria.

With Markham's forthright backing, which was reinforced by the powerful moral support of the venerable scientist, Sir Joseph Hooker, O.M. (1817–1911), Scott was given full execu-

* Hugh Robert Mill: *An Autobiography* (Longmans, Green, 1951).

tive power, answerable only to a finance committee. From then on his headquarters address was University Building, Burlington House, where he worked twelve hours a day, six days a week, for £32 5s. a month, paid from the Expedition funds. He was also receiving naval pay (£1 a day). He had never been so well off.

Callers found him in a room that exhibited the temperamental untidiness which his years of naval training had not eradicated. It was cluttered with samples of tinned food, polar clothing (including socks made of human hair), wolf skins, medical supplies, models of sledge parts, and cooking equipment. A similar disarray filled a small adjoining room.

When he rose up out of the confusion, visitors saw before them a wide-chested, narrow-hipped man of five feet nine whose personality conveyed an unmistakable assurance of integrity, and who looked at them with deep-blue eyes over a faintly tip-tilted nose and inquired their business in a tone that combined authority with charm.

He looked mature beyond his thirty-three years. Nature had modelled his pale-complexioned face with bold eyebrows, slightly flared nostrils, a strongly indented upper lip, and a delicately rounded chin. His brown hair was thinning in front, accentuating his good forehead, 'the brow of a man of a science', as one observer said. In his civilian role he habitually appeared in a well-worn herringbone tweed suit, with the high starched double collar popularized at Marienbad by the new monarch, King Edward VII. He did not require uniform to give him his air of a commander.

He was apt to be thought autocratic because of the cold reserve that he was capable of displaying in uncongenial company. He was socially sensitive; and never of the gregarious majority. It was easy for him to retreat into solitariness, though if he seemed to be oblivious of others it was not because he was excessively aware of himself.

He was no exponent of nautical heartiness. His smile could be frank and warming; he was equally capable of suggesting that pleasure did not matter. Deviousness was alien to him. His handshake was that of an entirely trustworthy man. He had a temperamental bias towards the sombre side of things, as if at some formative stage he had learnt to be suspicious of life. He was given to brooding on the mystery of existence. 'What is it

34

all about?' he would ask when perplexities crowded in upon him.

*

Every member of the Expedition received a letter on joining, intimating that articles of clothing for use in cold climates would be supplied free. 'The cloth garments are being made at the Civil Service Supply Association, Ltd., of Chandos Street, Strand. The woollen clothing and boots are being made by Dr Jaeger's Sanitary Woollen System Company, Ltd., 125 Regent Street, W. You are desired to call at each of the above establishments at your earliest convenience, in order that your measurements may be taken.' Fur clothing ('made in Norway') would also be a free issue. Each letter was signed by Scott.

The logistics side of the work was daunting. It made him self-conscious about his 'want of practical experience'. Retrospectively, he spoke of 'the busy year of preparation, when on my own inexperienced shoulders alone rested the responsibility of every department of the undertaking'. He authorized bulk purchases of tinned meat, and of Norwegian dried fish, without adequate safeguards. The consequences for the Expedition could have been serious. Danish butter was loaded in London, whereas fresher supplies were available in New Zealand.

The 'great liberality' of several leading manufacturers eased his task in some particulars and earned his gratitude: Cadbury's, who gave 3,500 lb. of 'excellent cocoa and chocolate—all that we needed of these articles, in fact'; Bird's Custard Powder, who supplied eight hundredweight of their product; Colman's of Norwich, who gave nine tons of flour and all the mustard the Expedition would be likely to use.

He soon came into collision with the chief scientist of the Expedition, Professor J. W. Gregory, F.R.S., a geologist, who had been appointed (at £10 a week) some months before Scott was named as the leader. Gregory obtained leave of absence from temporary duty at Melbourne University and travelled to Dundee to meet Scott and Markham in December 1900.

There he learnt that he and his scientific staff were expected to accept Scott's overriding authority. In a letter to the Royal Society's representatives on the joint committee of the two institutions, Gregory expressed the fear that 'there would be no guarantee to prevent the scientific work from being sub-

35

ordinated to naval adventure—an object admirable in itself, but not the one for which I understood the Expedition is to be organized'.

Then Gregory lodged a formal complaint about 'an act of thoughtlessness on Captain Scott's part' in ordering scientific equipment without consulting him. Sir Michael Foster, F.R.S., a physiologist who was also member of Parliament for London University, noted privately: 'The Gregory–Scott imbroglio is very serious.'

On 2 April 1901 Markham wrote, 'Privately and Confidentially', to Sir William Huggins, O.M., K.C.B., F.R.S., an astronomer who had been president of the British Association: 'My impression is that Dr Gregory is very reckless and impulsive, and of an exceedingly nervous temperament. His health has been impaired by tropical fevers. I consider him unfit to have charge of the lives and safety of men for a long period under exceedingly difficult and trying conditions.'

Refusing to play second fiddle to Scott, Gregory resigned. Two members of the joint committee resigned in sympathy with him.

Clashes between individuals precipitated the possibility of a rift between the two Societies. The Royal Geographical Society held fast to the opinion that the commander of the Expedition must be free to use his judgement about wintering in the ice. The Royal Society insisted that he was to be 'stringently instructed' not to winter in the ice if it could be avoided. It was recorded by Markham that 'this difference of opinion was so acute that it was evident to the President and Officers of the Royal Society that unless it could be arranged by arbitration an open rupture between the two Societies was inevitable'.

A small arbitration committee of six Fellows of the two Societies dealt with the difficulty. They reported complete concurrence in the proposition that 'it is for the commander of the Expedition to decide as to wintering, after careful consideration of local conditions'.

*

One of Scott's appointments to the commissariat side had to be peremptorily terminated, a procedure in which he showed a sufficiently ruthless hand. He was on surer ground in signing on Lieutenant Albert B. Armitage, R.N.R., aged thirty-seven, a *Worcester* trained officer of the P & O Line, as his navigator and second-in-command. Armitage was the son of a Scarborough physician. He had spent three winters in the Arctic with the Jackson–Harmsworth Expedition of 1894–7, gaining the Murchison Award for scientific observations. Markham wrote of him: 'Without any particular cleverness, he possesses one of the soundest judgements I ever met with.'

In making his executive appointments, Scott had to decide at an early stage whether the Expedition would require an ice-master. Ice-masters had served in all the Arctic expedition ships between 1817 and 1848, and some of them, such as Tom Abernethy of Peterhead, who sailed with Ross, were famous figures among the seamen of the time. They were signed on as 'Greenland Masters', having the same status as Masters in the Royal Navy and, like them, wearing uniform. Their work consisted of 'conning' ships through the pack-ice. They had a reputation for being over-cautious. Scott came to the conclusion that Armitage would provide the necessary experience and skill. 'He is as good an ice-man as any.'

Scott would have manned the Expedition entirely from the Royal Navy (except for the scientists) had the Admiralty been compliant. 'I had grave doubts as to my ability to deal with any other class of man.'* Merchant seamen were not subject to the Naval Discipline Act. They had their own governing code, 'adequate for commercial purposes', Scott agreed, but not, in his opinion, a sufficient guarantee of strict obedience and good behaviour. Above all, he could say with his hand on his heart that what mattered most to him was the honour of the Service to which he was always proud to belong. He fervently desired that the National Antarctic Expedition would embellish it.

The Royal Navy representation in the Expedition totalled thirty-eight officers, non-commissioned officers, and men, in a company of forty-seven, including the scientists. By a special Admiralty dispensation, they were allowed to wear uniform while serving with the Expedition, 'providing that the regulations are strictly adhered to'. (Scott could be counted on to see that they were.) In the wardroom, besides Armitage, were Lieutenant Charles W. Rawson Royds, R.N., aged twenty-five, from Rochdale, Lancashire, 'an excellent officer', Markham wrote, 'the right man in the right place'; Lieutenant Michael

* *The Voyage of the 'Discovery'.*

Barne, R.N., aged twenty-three, from Sotterley, Suffolk, who vowed that he would sacrifice his commission rather than forego the chance of joining the Expedition; Sub-Lieutenant Ernest H. Shackleton, R.N.R., aged twenty-six, an Irishman of Yorkshire descent, who at sixteen went into the Merchant Service from Dulwich College; 'a marvel of intelligent energy' (Markham); and Engineer-Lieutenant Reginald Skelton, R.N., aged twenty-eight, from Long Sutton, Lincolnshire, 'a general favourite', and, also by Markham's testimony, 'a man of inventive genius'. Barne and Skelton had been shipmates of Scott in the *Majestic*.

As 'the father of the Expedition', Sir Clements Markham made copious notes about practically every member of it. In the case of the officers, he examined and recorded their family pedigrees. His industry in that respect showed that he himself had a distant family connection with both Scott and Barne.

His page of notes headed 'Appointment of Shackleton' shows curious later revisions. Its opening sentence: 'Scott was fortunate in finding such an excellent and zealous officer for third Lieutenant,' was struck out to read: 'Scott appointed Ernest Shackleton to be third executive officer.' A sentence further down the page originally read: 'He is a steady, high-principled young man.' It was altered to: 'He seemed a steady young man.' The comment that he was 'remarkably well informed, considering the rough life he has led', was allowed to stand. 'He takes an interest in many subjects.'

*

On the scientific side were two men with medical qualifications: Reginald Koettlitz, M.R.C.S., L.R.C.P., aged forty, and Edward A. Wilson, M.B., aged twenty-eight. Both were trained at London hospitals, Koettlitz at Guy's, Wilson at St George's. Koettlitz (nickname, 'Cutlets') was of German extraction. He gave up his medical practice at Dover to join the Jackson–Harmsworth Expedition to Franz-Joseph Land in 1894. His scientific studies included bacteriology and botany. He wrote a paper for *Guy's Hospital Gazette* (March 1901) suggesting that scurvy, the bane of polar expeditions, was due to 'the continuous ingestion of foods which have undergone putrefaction.' That wide-of-the-mark speculation was accepted by Scott, among others. Markham's high opinion of Koettlitz's professional abilities was tempered by the reflection that he was 'exceedingly short of common sense'. He also lacked humour and was much chaffed because of it, 'but takes it all in good part' (Markham).

Wilson, the son of Dr E. T. Wilson, consulting physician to Cheltenham General Hospital, had been placed in the first class in the Natural Science Tripos of 1891, and came down from Cambridge intending to practise medicine. He was handicapped by ill-health, diagnosed as latent phthisis. He spent several months in a Continental sanatorium. Applying for the post of assistant surgeon to the Expedition, he sent specimens of his drawings of birds, fish, and Alpine scenery, 'all showing a masterly hand', wrote Markham, who added to his notes the conviction that 'Wilson will do great things some day. He has quite the keenest intellect, and a marvellous capacity for work.'

The post of marine biologist was given to Thomas Hodgson, aged thirty-seven, from Harborne, Birmingham. He was curator of the Plymouth Museum. 'Young to be so bald-headed,' Markham wrote of him, 'and quite the most careless, untidy individual it is possible to imagine. However, I think we shall get him all right in time.' As geologist, Scott appointed Hartley Ferrar, aged twenty-two, of Windsor Avenue, Belfast, an oarsman and athlete, newly down from Cambridge with Natural Science Tripos honours, 'but very unfledged and rather lazy' (Markham).

The team of specialists was later strengthened by the appointment of Louis C. Bernacchi, F.R.G.S., aged twenty-five, a Tasmanian-born physicist trained at Melbourne Observatory. He had served with the *Southern Cross* Expedition of 1898, financed by Sir George Newnes, the London publisher. A man of considerable ability, Bernacchi was to be in charge of the magnetic observations that had a high priority in the scientific programme of the National Antarctic Expedition.

Scott received £10 a week from the Expedition fund, in addition to his Royal Navy pay of £1 a day. His second-in-command and navigator, Armitage, was paid £9 a week. Royds and Barne, the two lieutenants, received £3 a week each, plus £3 10s. a week from the Navy. Skelton, the engineer, was paid £5 a week, and Shackleton the same. Koettlitz, the doctor, received £8 a week, Wilson, his assistant, £4 a week. Hodgson, the biologist, and Ferrar, the geologist, were paid £4 a week each, Bernacchi, the physicist, £5 a week. Warrant Officers (2) received £4 8s. 10d. a month from the Expedition fund; Petty Officers (6) £3 8s. 5d. a month; Stokers (5) £3 8s. 5d.; and Able Seamen (13), £2 5s. 7d. a month.

At that early stage, Scott appeared to have few doubts about the competence of his professional associates. He more than once stressed the harmony that prevailed from the beginning, as if it guaranteed proficiency. His reliance on the ability of his naval colleagues, in particular, to make scientific observations and deductions on the basis of the brief training given them before leaving England was in some instances misplaced.

*

The Expedition ship, building on the Tay, was the sixth *Discovery* in the annals of British exploration. The decision to perpetuate the name was decided on at a meeting of the council of the Royal Geographical Society on 6 June 1900. It was formally conferred by Lady Markham on 21 March 1901, when the ship was launched at Dundee.

Like the old whalers before her, the *Discovery* was built for her purpose down to the last plank. Her designer was W. E. Smith, one of the Chief Constructors at the Admiralty. Nearly all his working life had been spent in building wooden ships. He was one of the last two men in the Service of whom that could be said. The *Discovery*'s frame of solid English oak, twenty-six inches thick, was made to resist tremendous side stresses. Her bows were fortified to a degree beyond anything known in wooden ship construction. Some of her bolts were eight feet long, running entirely through wood. She was considered a masterpiece of specialized shipbuilding, a verdict that time was to modify.

Her overhung stem ensured that when she charged into pack ice it was lifted two or three feet until the ship's weight acted with a downward force that cracked the floe and made a passage for her to move forward to the next obstacle. There was less enthusiasm among the shipyard critics at Dundee for her peculiar stern, intended to buffer the rudder in heavy ice. Some were prepared to bet that it would collapse under stress; in fact, it served the vessel well in several seaward crises.

An unrecorded accident that occurred on 30 May 1901 while the ship was on the stocks at Dundee was like an early warning of the fatalistic element that seemed to underlay Scott's career as an expedition commander. The gear for raising the propeller was being tested. A wire cable snapped and a massive pulley crashed down into the narrow propeller well where he was standing. It missed him by no more than an inch or two: 'a very narrow escape', said Markham who was standing close by.

Early in June 1901, the *Discovery* was towed to London to be berthed in the East India Dock. Sir Evelyn Wrench remembers going aboard on sailing day to see Scott, who during their meeting, anxiously patted his breast pocket, then his side pockets, and his breast pocket again. 'He had forgotten his handkerchief,' a characteristic lapse. 'Mine was a clean one, so I gave it to him.'

Visitors to the ship who asked Scott to face their box Kodaks observed that he liked his pet terrier Scamp to be in the picture. Scamp was sailing with him. No such favour was shown to the East End cats that had taken up quarters in the ship. A last-hour count revealed the number to be thirty-two. It was reduced to one by a ruthless concerted drive organized by the stewards.

There were sore mouths in the ship's company that week. By medical decree, all officers and men were examined by dental surgeons from Guy's Hospital. A total of 92 teeth was extracted, and 178 filled. The bill came to £62 4s.

A letter in the handwriting of extreme infirmity arrived on Scott's desk on 4 July. It was from Sir Erasmus Ommanney (1814–1904), a great and honoured name in British seafaring annals. 'I am very desirous to visit the *Discovery*. Being very much advanced in age, I would be obliged if you will take me under your escort. I understand you start from your office every day for the ship.' Sir Erasmus had served in the Antarctic long ago with Ross and Crozier. 'I have ever since advocated the very interesting service now entrusted to you, and which I pray will be most successful.'

On 15 July, the Bishop of London addressed the members of the Expedition, and their relatives and friends, assembled on the mess deck of the *Discovery*. He took his theme from the text: *Behold how good and how pleasant it is for brethren to dwell together in unity*.—Psalm cxxxiii, 1. Heads were bowed as, with upraised hand, he blessed the ship and all who were to sail in her. At Scott's request, he afterwards composed 'a prayer for daily use during the voyage'. Scott took care to send a copy of the prayer to his mother, who had a Victorian regard for bishops.

He put a foot wrong when, on hearing that certain Fellows of the Royal Society were planning a farewell dinner for him and his officers at the Athenaeum, Pall Mall, on 23 July, he asked that the Expedition secretary, Cyril Longhurst, should be included in the guest list in recognition of his services. The suggestion was thought improper by some of the Fellows, who exchanged letters of annoyance about it.

The evening was a successful one. Armitage, the second-in-command, remembered long after 'the venerable, white-haired President who for once came down from the stellar regions; the great physiologist and the equally great physicist; the man responsible for the safe navigation of the world's waters and the one who had revolutionized surgical practice, to say nothing of others. There they stand, all smiles, glasses uplifted: "For they are jolly good fellows, and so say all of us. Hip-hip-hooray!" I believe it was the first dinner of its kind ever given in the famous club.'*

Sir Joseph Hooker, O.M., F.R.S., to Scott:

> The Camp,
> Sunningdale.
> July 17, 1901.

Dear Captain Scott,—I took a cursory view of the 'Discovery' last week and was exceedingly interested in what I saw.

I do hope that the balloon will be obtained. I feel sure that without a balloon the Expedition will be heavily handicapped in many ways. I am writing to Markham, urging it most strongly, authorizing his using my name if he thinks proper in stating that without this instrument the Expedition may lose half its means of accomplishing its end.

I have suggested to Markham that he might state that the idea of a balloon originated with me.

> Ever sincerely yours,
> J. HOOKER

That veteran scientist believed that 'an ascent on a clear day might yield not only geographical discovery but information of immense importance to the plans and safety of the Expedition'. Pursuing the theme, Scott appealed through *The Times* for

* Albert B. Armitage: *Cadet to Commodore* (Cassell, 1925).

help in procuring a balloon 'of sufficient dimensions to carry an observer to the height of 500–1,000 feet'. He received donations amounting to £80, leaving the Expedition finance committee to find the balance of £1,300 needed to pay for a suitable balloon supplied by the War Office.

*

By 1 August 1901 the *Discovery* was at Spithead, being 'swung' for compass tests. All her clock dials were inscribed '*Discovery* leads to discovery'. The King had assented to a request from Sir Clements Markham that she should be allowed to fly the White Ensign. The Admiralty objected. Scott was thereupon made a member of the Harwich Yacht Club, entitling him to fly the Blue Ensign, and the club's blue burgee with a yellow lion rampant. The *Discovery* also hoisted the azure swallow-tailed house flag of the Royal Geographical Society, bearing the Cross of St George and the Society's badge.

In her registration papers, issued by the London Customs House, the Royal Geographical Society was formally named 'the Owner', and Sir Clements Markham 'Managing Owner'. She was to sail under the Merchant Shipping Act.

On 5 August she steamed into Cowes, which was filled with a concourse of vessels for the annual regatta that was one of the last events of 'the season'. She had hardly moored when a white and gold launch appeared smartly alongside to point out that she had committed the *gaffe* of making fast to one of the buoys of the royal yacht. The launch brought polite admonition and gracious permission.

Scott needed no reminding of his ship's ungainliness in that scene of 'delicate beauty'—his description. Her black hull, stubby masts, long spars, and her big barrel of a crow's nest, were in crude contrast with the butterfly daintiness of so many of the ships around her.

That same day, King Edward VII and Queen Alexandra, not yet crowned, paid a visit of inspection and farewell. The Queen was particularly attentive to the bunks, pressing the mattresses with her knuckles, and asking Scott whether he was *quite sure* they would be comfortable. There was a flurry when one of her Pekinese, scuffling about the deck, slipped under the guard rail and fell overboard, to be loyally rescued by a member of the crew, who dived in fully clad.

The King, in admiral's uniform, addressed the ship's company. 'Captain Scott, officers, and crew of the *Discovery*, it has often been my lot to bid goodbye to an expedition going away on warlike service. It gives me great pleasure to wish goodbye and good luck to an expedition going away on service from which the whole world will benefit. I wish you goodbye, good luck—and God speed.'

His Majesty then took a silk-lined case from his pocket and invested Scott with membership of the Royal Victorian Order, fourth class, a mark of personal esteem. Scott's mother was one of the guests on board. By a happy thought, she was asked to pin the ribbon of the Order to her son's tunic.

On holiday with her daughter Grace ('Monsie'), she wrote to tell Scott of her deep pleasure in being presented to the King and Queen. 'People here like hearing about them. I never *begin* the subject, but of course if I'm asked I am only too pleased to tell them and recall my time of triumph in my son, for, after all, it is only the very few who actually shake hands with Royalty. Apart from that, I like to think of the sweet sympathetic face that looked at me and smiled such interest in all she was looking at. And now, dear, one word of thanks for the holiday you are giving us both, and then good-bye. God bless, keep and preserve you, my best of sons.'

Scott had been handed a printed document headed 'Instructions to the Commander of the Expedition from the Royal Society and the Royal Geographical Society.' It consisted of twenty-seven numbered clauses. The last of them reads like an extract from a script of destiny:

'The *Discovery* is the first ship that has ever been built expressly for scientific purposes in these kingdoms. It is an honour to receive the command of her; but we are impressed with the difficulty of the enterprise which has been entrusted to you, and with the serious character of your responsibility. The Expedition is an undertaking of national importance; and science cannot fail to benefit from the efforts of those engaged in it.'

At 11.50 a.m. on 6 August 1901, the *Discovery* slipped away from her buoy at Cowes and moved decorously through the white-winged throng towards the Needles and what lay beyond. She was well under way when she was chased by a steam launch with whistle blowing shrilly. The launch carried Lord Sel-

44

borne, First Lord of the Admiralty. The *Discovery* was stopped at a right angle across the track of a crowd of small yachts whose skippers, forgetting her imposing mission, 'let her have it good and strong', in the words of an eyewitness, who said that 'each yacht crew excelled the one before it in picturesque language'.

Typically, Scott pondered the 'burden of sadness' on those who had waved their farewells from ship and shore. 'We thought much of the grim possibilities of our voyage. Ever present before us was the unpleasant reflection that we might start off with a flourish of trumpets and return with failure.'

It was Sir Clements Markham, not Scott, who had Ulysses' 'joy of the journey'. He bade the Expedition good-bye with the wholehearted conviction that 'no finer set of men ever left these shores, nor were men ever led by a finer captain.'*

CHAPTER FOUR

VOYAGE OF THE *DISCOVERY*

Scott wrote a 'Letter of Proceeding' to the Royal Geographical Society dated 15 August 1901. It reported the departure from Cowes, conveyed the disappointing information that the *Discovery* was 'unlikely to average more than $6\frac{3}{4}$ knots', slower than was expected, and 'likely to mean delays'. He mentioned weaknesses in the ship's ironwork, and the 'possibilities of serious results' arising from it.

He blamed the Dundee shipbuilders for carelessness, confirmed later when an examination of the ship's bottom revealed 'not a few defects which should have been remedied before the ship was launched'. Dictating the formal document he went on to ruminate: 'Amongst the many skilled workmen whose united labour had produced the solid structure of the *Discovery*'s hull, had been one who had scamped his task, knowing full well that he was free from all chance of detection, and for this we were condemned to suffer throughout our voyage.'

His long-distance planning was upset by the ship's sluggish

* Sir Clements Markham: *The Lands of Silence.*

behaviour at sea. 'This proved a most serious drawback.' He had anticipated having 'ample opportunities' for carrying out necessary and valuable experimental work with sounding and dredging devices while they were still in the temperate zone. 'Some of these devices were new, and with all we were unfamiliar; and the fact that we were unable to practise with them during our outward voyage was severely felt when they came to be used afterwards in the Antarctic regions.'*

Unlike a fully powered vessel, the *Discovery*'s course could not be set from port direct to port. Conserving coal was vital; hence they had to depend largely on the ship's sailing capability, 'which we found to our chagrin exceedingly poor'. The need to take advantage of favourable winds and currents meant detours of hundreds of miles and the loss of many days in the sailing schedule.

Scott's worries were deepened by the elusive 'Dundee leak', which defied all attempts then, and later, at location and remedy. 'It became as much a part of the ship as the ancestral ghost in an old castle,'† giving them 'many anxious hours, many hours of unnecessary back-breaking toil'. It also ruined a quantity of supplies in provision cases packed close down in the hold.

He was seen constantly poring over maps and charts, thinking ahead to the time when they would move into the icy remoteness of the Far South. He asked Dr H. R. Mill, the Royal Geographical Society's frail and learned librarian, who had gallantly undertaken to sail with them to South Africa, to set out in writing his suggestions 'as to the best way of penetrating to the interior of Antarctica'. Mill, who was also an oceanographer and meteorologist of repute, retired to Scott's cabin, and for three hours was 'oblivious to everything', he wrote, 'but the intensity of my own concentration'.

He emerged from his self-communion with the advice that a landing 'be attempted at the head of McMurdo Bay on the ground that, where the south-running mountains of Victoria Land met the coast running east from Mount Erebus, there was sure to be an important valley to serve as access to the interior'. The oracular voice had spoken. Its message was respectfully heard and acted on, with results that, though immediately

* *The Voyage of the 'Discovery'*.
† L. C. Bernacchi: *Saga of the 'Discovery'*

46

advantageous, were thought by some to have limited the scope of the Expedition in exploring the polar plateau.

Scott to his mother:

Discovery Antarctic Expedition,
Madeira.

My own dearest Mother,—It is so nice to get your brave letter, but indeed I don't think there is the least cause for anxiety. All you have to do is to take the greatest care of yourself and be ready for all sorts of good times when we come home.

The ship is a magnificent sea boat, smooth and easy in every movement, a positive cradle on the deep. We only sigh for more sails. Ours are made for tempestuous seas, so they look rather like pocket handkerchiefs in a light Trade; they are so small that even in a hurricane they couldn't capsize the ship. I'm a little disappointed with her speed. We want very favourable conditions to keep up 7 knots.

The fellows in the wardroom are beginning to get on splendidly and we have very cheerful times at meals. Of course it is all yachting and comfort so far. The trying conditions are not yet arrived.

I like Wilson more and more. *Entre nous* his, Skelton's and Barne's are the three characters that attract me more than any other on board. Wilson is a little more serious than the others.

Scamp* is distinguishing himself on all sides. He was landed for the first time yesterday and his enjoyment was the delight of all beholders.

My dearest, I do hope you will have a nice quiet holiday. You certainly have earned it, for I fear my affairs gave you a good deal too much to do before we left.

Best of love, dear.

Your affect. son,
CON

On holiday in Normandy, his mother wrote to him on 28 August: 'It is quite impossible for me to describe the delight of getting your letter.' It was so good of him, she wrote, to describe the ship, 'and so sweet of you to tell me of the small

* His dog.

47

sails and the safety of these in high winds. I prize *every* detail and read and re-read what you say, all of which is *most* interesting, and comfort beyond words to me.' She was not surprised by what he confided about his best-liked companions. Mrs Wilson, she said, was wisely going on with her teaching while her husband was away. 'As for me, dear, you have surrounded me with all the comfort that I can possibly want, and I have the constant knowledge of your great love.'

Calling at the Cape for coal and magnetic instrument setting, they were gratified by the warmth of the attention shown to them by a populace in the throes of the South African war. Martial law was in force in Cape Town. To Scott, 'the termination of hostilities seemed very remote; officials and residents,' he wrote, 'took a gloomy view of the outlook.' Some of the officers were shown over a camp for Boer prisoners. 'One blond giant, captured at Paadeberg, said he wished he could go South with us to see the world.' (Armitage)

Scott's second 'Letter of Proceedings', dated 29 September, 1901, reported 'grave delays due to head winds. We had to use steam and to over-drive our engines.' The stokehold temperature was 140 degrees, hard on 'the inexperienced hands down there'. The interior heat plus the tropical sun opened the ship's planking, letting two feet of water into the hold. Lieutenant Shackleton had been put in charge of the catering, with 'an appreciated improvement' in that department. One of the crew was found to have 'contracted syphilis in London', and was 'exchanged at Simon's Bay'. Another merchant seaman had been troublesome and was discharged. 'I found it necessary to advance £140 for the men's wages on account,' presumably for spending ashore at the Cape. There was some annoyance in London at his having drawn a bill at Cape Town for a further £200, 'without notice'.

More signs of discord appeared when the temporary director of the Expedition's scientific staff, George Murray, Keeper of the Botany Department at the Natural History Museum, South Kensington, left the ship prematurely at Cape Town, after having undertaken to accompany it to Melbourne. 'He bade us farewell, much to our regret,' appears in Scott's book;* but in a report Scott made to Sir Clements Markham he suggested that Murray's appointment was a serious mistake.

* *The Voyage of the 'Discovery'*.

'I have had to take the whole direction of the scientific work into my own hands,' he told Markham. His ready assumption of that added responsibility won him the esteem of Dr Mill, who wrote to Scott's mother: 'Captain Scott has shown a power that, I must own, surprised me in mastering the details of all the scientific work which is being arranged.'

*

In the Roaring Forties the *Discovery* showed seaworthy qualities that soon regained for her the respect she had lost earlier in the voyage. 'She rose like a cork to the mountainous seas that now followed,' and frequently exceeded 200 miles in a day by sail power alone. Once, 'we flew under bare spars before a terrific gale' (Bernacchi). Her extended whaling-ship stern that the wiseacres on the quay at Dundee had jeered at gave her a buoyancy and liveliness that made it hard to keep her on course. '*Discovery* became another word for perpetual motion' (Armitage).

She rolled alarmingly, once completely eluding the skill of young Barne, on duty as helmsman, wrenching the wheel from his grasp with enough force to send him sprawling. A huge wave came over as the ship broached-to. Scott was on the bridge with Wilson, who wrote of the experience: 'We were simply deluged, and I burst out laughing at the Skipper who was gasping for breath. The whole of the upper deck was afloat.' Scott noted that 'spray dashed as high as our upper topsails. A great deal of water found its way below, flooding the wardroom and many of the cabins.'

As they approached New Zealand, most of the ship's company wrote letters to their people at home, for soon the *Discovery* would be beyond postal range. Wilson, the doctor, confided to his wife in Cheltenham the opinions he had formed of Scott during the ninety-days' voyage thus far. He admired Scott greatly, 'all but his temper. He is quick-tempered and very impatient', but was none the less 'a really nice fellow, very generous and ready to help us all'.

The quick temper was more usually provoked by the easy-going response of the Merchant Navy men. Charles Hare, who was the captain's steward, did not consider Scott 'bad-tempered in the ordinary sense of the term. He was over-sensitive and allowed himself to get worked up if things did not go as planned.'* Some of the scientists thought he was too touchy about discipline. When a merchant seaman accosted him on deck with a complaint about the lower-deck issue of cake, he took it as a personal affront and ordered the man below to await his displeasure, which was severe.

He allowed no slackness in the customary etiquette of the wardroom, whatever latitude they were in. Each officer took his weekly turn as mess president, with a gavel as the symbol of his authority and the right to impose fines for bad language, betting, contradicting the president, recourse to reference books. Grace and the loyal toast were observed as rigidly when the ship was iced in as when she was in calm waters.

Wilson referred in his letter to Scott's firmness of mind. 'He is very definite about everything; nothing is left vague or indeterminate.' In argument, Wilson reported, 'he goes straight for the main point, and always knows what he is driving at'. The doctor assured his wife that under the leadership of such a man there was 'no fear of our wandering aimlessly about in the Southern regions'.

Scott wrote to Mrs Wilson, communicating his regard for her husband. 'There is one thing he will not have told you, and that is what a fine fellow we all think him. His intellect and ability will one day win him a great name, of that I feel sure.' It was to Wilson that Scott turned in a renewed effort to overcome his continuing aversion from the sight of blood. He forced himself to watch Wilson skinning and dissecting seals and sea-birds.

The first ice of the voyage appeared almost immediately after the *Discovery* crossed the 60th parallel on 16 November 1901. Only three of the company had seen it before in high latitudes. Scott said that it was an occasion for 'much excitement'. The *Discovery*'s real ice baptism came later in the day with the appearance of heavier floes. He recorded his impression of the scene after nightfall. 'The wind had died away; what light remained was reflected in a ghostly glimmer from the white surface of the pack ... for the first time we felt something of the solemnity of these great Southern solitudes.'

*

After apprehensive hours to windward of the Auckland Islands,

* In a letter to the biographer, 1965.

in the course of which the ship rolled to an angle of 55 degrees, the Expedition arrived in the harbour of Lyttelton, New Zealand, on 29 November 1901. From that hour they were enveloped in the heartfelt hospitality of a people more sensitive to their ties with the Mother Country than any of the other British communities spread around the world. They were made to feel like new-found kith and kin.

The New Zealand Government made a grant of £1,000 towards the expenses of the Expedition. Harbour dues were remitted, 'a very large saving' (Scott). Railway companies provided free travel, hotels free accommodation. The Christchurch Magnetic Observatory opened its doors to the scientists. The farmers of New Zealand gave a flock of sheep. Scott wrote that 'on every side we were accorded the most generous terms by the firms or individuals with whom we had to deal in business matters.'

Even so, he had to cable to London for ready cash. 'This morning,' the Royal Geographical Society's treasurer, Edward Somers Cocks, of the banking firm of Cocks, Biddulph & Co., of Charing Cross, London, wrote to the secretary of the Royal Society on 6 December 1901, 'my firm have had a telegram as under from Scott from Lyttelton: *Wire additional £500. I* suppose we must send it but I do so with regret.'

On December 19, another protest was registered in the same quarter when a request from Scott for further funds came through Markham. 'He wants £400 more! ! to cover advances. Under the circumstances, I see nothing for it but to send it and to hope for the best.'

A final resolute attempt was made to stop the now notorious 'Dundee leak'. The *Discovery* was dry-docked, inspected inch by inch, scraped, caulked. Scott informed the president of the Royal Geographical Society: 'Unfortunately the wages of workmen here are ruinously high, and the account is in consequence grievously heavy.'

When the ship was afloat again, crowds of sightseers from all parts of the colony trod her decks. 'It was impossible not to accede to their requests to see the ship' (Scott), but it was often a highly inconvenient invasion. There was general surprise at the fresh-faced youthfulness of the crew, among whom the average age was twenty-five. Local newspapers referred to them as 'the Babes in the Wood'.

While the *Discovery* was sailing out to New Zealand, plans had been going forward at home for the relief ship which Sir Clements Markham considered an indispensable adjunct of polar exploration. He made a public statement in October 1901. 'In the case of all great Arctic expeditions, except that of Franklin in the *Erebus* and the *Terror* (which ended in complete disaster), a second ship was sent out in the second year.* It would be criminal to omit such a precaution in the case of the *Discovery*, which has gone to a region where, in case of disaster, escape is impossible except in a relief ship.'

Captain R. F. Scott to the Presidents of the Royal Society and the Royal Geographical Society:

> 'The Discovery',
> Lyttelton.
> 17th December, 1901.

Gentlemen,—It is with great satisfaction I learn that it is intended to send a relief ship to the Antarctic regions in the Southern summer of 1902–3.

I had contemplated writing most urgently to you on this subject, knowing how absolutely our retreat would otherwise be cut off, should any accident result in the loss of the *Discovery*.

The conditions which surround the Antarctic lands with a belt of tempestuous ocean have always impressed me with their difference to those existing in Higher Northern Lands, and I have felt that since our retreat by boats to any civilised spot is a practical impossibility, our movements and the risks we could rightfully take must be greatly limited, if the loss of the ship of necessity implied the loss of all on board.

... It will be a great relief and satisfaction to me to leave Lyttelton, confident that such efforts will be successful and that a line of retreat is practically assured to us.

> I have the honour to be, Gentlemen,
> Yours faithfully
> (signed) R. F. SCOTT †

He wrote a note of deep private feeling to his sister Ettie

* A memorandum in the National Antarctic Expedition files of the Royal Society states that 'at least 9 ships on Arctic expeditions had worked without relief'.

† Scott makes no reference to this letter in his book, *The Voyage of the 'Discovery'*.

that day. 'My dearest of girls,—Just a line of farewell. I really haven't a moment. It is worse than London. But I must tell you how often my thoughts will be with you all. My dear girl, you know what you have been to me and what you always will be to your loving brother CON.'

By the time the *Discovery* was ready to sail again, on 21 December, 1901, she was so deeply laden as to be a cause for worry. A heavy new load of stores had been stowed away in her holds and piled on her decks. 'One could reflect that it would have been impossible to have got more into her,' Scott wrote, and he did not 'look forward with pleasure to crossing the stormiest ocean in the world. We could only trust that Providence would vouchsafe us an easy passage to the South.'

The quartermaster at the wheel was jostled by an agitated huddle of forty-five sheep occupying the after-deck. In a smaller space close by, enclosed by sacks of food, were twenty-three imported huskies, excited by their release from quarantine. Not caring to expose his dog Scamp to the rigours of the Antarctic, Scott found him a good home with a Christchurch family.

Special trains crowded Lyttelton with well-wishers as the hour of the *Discovery's* departure grew near. Wharves were packed, bands played, farewell speeches made. The Bishop of Christchurch blessed the explorers at the end of the short service held on the mess deck. As the ship moved out into the roads, cheer after cheer echoed over the water. Bunting-gay pleasure boats fell into line on unofficial escort duty. Two Royal Navy frigates led the procession. A myriad handkerchiefs fluttered along the quayside.

Some of the crew, waving their good-byes from the rigging, sent their caps spinning into the crowd on the jetty as souvenirs. A smart and popular young sailor, Charles Bonner, climbed above the crow's nest to the top of the mainmast, cheering with the rest. A lurch of the ship unbalanced him. He fell headlong, his wild despairing cry stifling the cheers from below as completely as if a shroud had been thrown over the ship. Within minutes his body lay on the stern gratings under a Union Jack. Signals were sent to the two leading ships not to cheer the *Discovery* when they parted company with her. 'Sadness and gloom descended on the ship,' Scott wrote, 'and damped for the time all thought of our future in the South.'

CHAPTER FIVE

ANTARCTIC MISERIES AND MARVELS

THEY sighted their first iceberg in latitude $65\frac{1}{2}$ S, with more bergs swinging into view as they crossed the Antarctic circle on 3 January 1902. They saw far-off peaks lighted by the midnight sun. Then came fog that sealed them off from the world, a depressing effect accentuated by the sudden withdrawal of all bird life. Scott felt it as 'a curious sense of desertion'. It was a temporary phenomenon, unlike the 'Dundee leak,' malignantly seeping again and now to be accepted as a permanent liability. Bernacchi, the physicist, recorded that the engine-room was awash when the pumps became frozen.

The *Discovery* was being handled with almost abject care, the total concern of the officer of the watch, alert with minute-to-minute orders to the helmsman and dependent on the expert 'conning' of the ship from the crow's-nest. Often making no more than a mile and a half an hour in the thickening pack ice, the ship moved as if doom awaited the slightest incaution at the wheel. It was terribly monotonous work, rewarded by a reversion to sail in the clear open water of the Ross Sea and, presently, by a magnificent prospect of the blue summits of Mounts Sabine, Minto, and Adam in the Admiralty Range, still a hundred miles away.

The great distances over which naked-eye visibility was effective in that rarified atmosphere were astonishing. Scott saw Mount Erebus, a lazily smoking volcano, from a hundred and forty miles. Coulman Island, some days, was in sight at a hundred and sixty-five miles. Refraction and mirages could play tricks with the visual faculty. Bernacchi: 'Whole ranges, higher than the Alps, are transported in vision hundreds of miles from their true position.' Scott noted later having seen a series of recognizable landmarks 'in an included range of vision of 240 geographic miles'.

To signpost the relief ship, he proposed to leave messages in red-painted tubular canisters nailed to posts at Cape Adare; on Possession Island and Coulman Island; at Wood Bay; on Franklin Island; and at Cape Crozier, all conspicuous points of call. At Cape Adare in Robertson Bay, Victoria Land, where the

Southern Cross expedition wintered in 1898, the little wooden hut put up on the landing beach then was still intact. It contained well-preserved provisions.

Notes on their progress thus far, and indications of their future direction, were left in the hut, the door of which was then made fast. Having stretched their legs after the cramping days at sea, the shore party pulled back to the ship, Scott reflecting poetically that 'there is always something sad in contemplating the deserted dwellings of mankind, under whatever conditions the inhabitants may have left'.

When Bernacchi spoke of the fate of Hanson, the zoologist of the *Southern Cross* expedition, Scott could not forbear writing in his diary: 'He recalled the past and told us of the unhappy death of Hanson, now lying buried on the hilltop 1,000 feet above our heads. The dying man had requested that he should rest there, and slowly and laboriously his body was borne up the steep hillside to the chosen spot. So there rest the remains of the only human being who has found burial on this great Southern Continent, and above his body still stands, in touching memorial, a plain wooden cross.' He returned to the melancholy subject the following day: 'Bernacchi and some others landed again to visit once more the grave of poor Hanson; and to see that all was well with it.'

His moods of abstraction were carried into that new and distant environment. His steward, Charles Hare, remembers 'one day when Captain Scott put milk on his curry. He was going to add sugar, only I stopped him and changed his plate.'*

He kept diligently to the daily regime with which he had begun the voyage. Hare roused him each morning with the call: 'Captain Scott, *sir*, your bath water is ready.' The bath was a shallow galvanized tub filled with hot water that, in the high latitudes, was got from ice melted on the galley stove. Stripped, he was seen by a fellow officer to be 'well-built with a good chest and rather narrow hips'. He never appeared in the wardroom unshaven. He did his own clothes-washing—'and made a very poor job of it' (Diary).

He saw to it that every man in the ship was answerable for personal cleanliness. He was a heavy pipe smoker; and warned Hare against becoming one. 'He said that at my age it would stop my growth.' He ate heartily and was appreciative of well-

* Letter, 25 June, 1965.

cooked food. Hare remembers that 'he had a very happy smile when pleased'.

*

Leaving Cape Adare, the *Discovery* ran into conditions that taught Scott 'not to underrate the enemy', by which he meant 'the elements with their icy weapons'. The ship was borne along by the increasing pace of the heavy ice-pack towards a chain of grounded table-topped icebergs, against which the floes were piling up with menacing turbulence. 'For the first time, we faced the dangers of the pack, and became aware of its mighty powers.'

Twisting and turning, they could make no real advance and were often halted in their track, the ship quivering with each unavoidable impact. 'Progress was so slow that it looked almost inevitable that we should be carried down amongst the bergs. It was one of those hours which impress themselves for ever on the memory.'

Only he and Armitage and the officer of the watch knew the peril they were in. The others were 'resting from their labours of the previous night, happily unconscious ...' (Scott). The drama was being enacted in a setting that belied it: 'brilliant sunlight, cloudless sky, smooth water, gloriously keen air'. Beneath them there ran 'a mighty current, bearing the ship on to possible destruction'. Against that relentless force the *Discovery*'s panting engines could not prevail.

Pacing his tiny planked bridge, Scott thought it incredible that they were 'so completely impotent—it seemed so desperately unreal'. Imperceptibly, the tidal pull slackened. Soon they were making for open water and safety. 'For me,' Scott wrote in his diary, 'the lesson had been a sharp and, I have no doubt, salutary one.'

Coulman Island, described by Lieutenant Evans as 'a sinister-looking blob', cast a deceptive black shadow that kept the *Discovery* standing clear by a mile or so more than was necessary. Aiming to make a landing, the ship hit an iceberg broadside on, trying to avoid collision with another. 'It sent us reeling round.' (Scott) A boat was got away to steep rocks that were a vantage point for another canister post, which the relief ship of the following year missed.

'Like looking for a needle in a haystack,' was the simile used by those who were given the mission of tracking Scott down in those unexplored immensities. He himself was fully aware of the slender chances of his red canisters being found. At Cape Crozier, 'we proposed to keep our chain of records, and had brought with us a post, a tin cylinder containing an account of our doings, and the necessary implements for erecting them. In spite of all our efforts to mark the place, at a few hundred yards it was almost impossible to distinguish it, and one could not help thinking that, should disaster come to the expedition, what a poor reed was this on which alone we could trust to afford our friends a clue to our whereabouts.' * It is not straining the imagination to see more than prudence in his reiterated references to the possibility of disaster.

One of his deepest sensibilities was touched when they reached the ice-filled bay named after the wife of Sir George Newnes, the London publisher, who financed the *Southern Cross* expedition. The sight of a large colony of seals basking in the sun was a reminder of the wisdom of laying in a good supply of fresh meat for winter use. 'It seemed a terrible desecration to come to this quiet spot only to murder its innocent inhabitants and stain the white snow with blood.... Some of us were glad to get away on our ski.' He had already given an order than no seabird was to be shot unless it was required for a scientific collection.

Lady Newnes Bay was choked with ice of enormous thickness, some of the formations rising 150 feet above the surface. 'We felt that we were gazing on a phenomenon unlike anything else reported elsewhere.' Behind the bay, glaciers swept down to the sea edge in gigantic scimitar curves that gleamed like polished steel in the sunlight. Away to the north and north-west were high peaks among 'bewildering clusters of lesser summits'. The Antarctic scene being revealed to them was one of illimitable desolation redeemed by the magical colour effects that inspired many of Dr Wilson's paintings.

'I wish to God I could lay it all before you,' Wilson wrote to his wife. 'I long to do as much as I can that others may share the joy I find in feasting my eyes on the colours of this wonderful place, and the vastness of it all. "The works of the Lord *are* great and very worthy to be praised and had in honour," but I do wish you could see them here.'

* The Voyage of the 'Discovery'.

A lower-deck member of the Expedition, Frank Plumley, asked in 1965 what he specially remembered, replied at once: 'Why, the colours—you wouldn't believe them!' Not after more than sixty years had he lost his awe of *Aurora Australis*, which stirred Scott to write that 'there is something very weird and awe-inspiring in a phenomenon so fleeting, so intangible, and so difficult to describe'.*

*

Climbing the 1,350 feet of one of the nearer volcanic cones Scott, Wilson, and Royds had their first look at the Great Ice Barrier, its white, opaque frontal cliffs towering in places to 200 feet above sea level, an eighth wonder of the world, extending for 400 miles east and west in about latitude 78°. 'You could put the United Kingdom down on it and have room to spare' (Evans), a claim disapproved by geographers but indicating the effect of the Great Ice Barrier on undisciplined imaginations. When it was seen first by Ross in 1841, one of his men aboard the *Erebus* was impelled to celebrate the spectacle in the lines: *Awful and sublime, magnificent and rare, No earthly with object the Barrier can compare!* Scientists had suggested that, better than any glacier in Greenland, it illustrates conditions existing in Europe and North America during the Ice Age.

Coming down from the volcano cone, Scott more prosaically observed that 'it was an impressive sight'. Shortly afterwards, he was noting that 'the heaviest battleship would have shattered itself ineffectually against the Barrier'. He saw 'a million-ton iceberg' brought to a standstill at its edge.

Ross had called it the Barrier† because it stopped him in his southward course. He sailed along it eastward for 250 miles and, still not coming to its end, had to be content with achieving the deepest penetration up to that time, as far as 78° S. Sixty years after, Scott wrote 'that perhaps of all the problems which lay before us in the South, we were most keenly interested in solving the mysteries of this great ice-mass', e.g., does it rest on land or water? (It is now held to rest on water.) Having entered McMurdo Bay, which he found to be not a bay

---

* *The Voyage of the 'Discovery'*.
† It is known to glaciologists as the Ice Shelf.

but a Sound,* which it was thereafter designated, on 21 January 1902, he took the *Discovery* on a survey voyage along the Barrier, measuring its wall-like face, which reached 280 feet at its maximum height, and obtaining numerous photographs and frequent soundings, the latter consistently showing depths of 300–400 fathoms. Scott wrote:

'For days we steamed along the white ice cliffs, whiter than the cliffs of Dover. From time to time great masses calved off to float away as ice-bergs. Here was the great mother of the Antarctic bergs which floated Northward in majestic silence, often as much as ten miles in length.'

In places, the Barrier ice had split to form deep caverns with arched openings, like a series of Aladdin's caves. The light effects within were sometimes breathtakingly lovely, ranging from translucent blue to the deepest sapphire. Almost they gave credence to the romantic novelists' concept of the Ice Barrier as the cold wall of a warm country inhabited by supremely beautiful beings.

On 25 January 1902 the *Discovery* look-outs noted a dramatic change in the Barrier height, that it fell abruptly to 30 feet, rose again to 80 feet, then dipped to as little as 15 feet, rising gradually to 100 feet again. Heavy currents slowed the ship down to what for Scott was 'negative progress: one requires' (he wrote) 'a great deal of patience for this sort of work'. On 29 January, they passed the farthest point reached by Sir James Ross in 1842. He had reported from that position 'a strong appearance of land to the south-east'. The men in the *Discovery* were eager to confirm his findings.

After intense searching with binoculars and telescopes, they decided that Ross had been a victim of one of the optical illusions common to the region. Scott was almost fanatically determined not to be similarly misled. 'Many an eager face peered over the side,' he wrote. 'Now and then a more imaginative individual would find some grand discovery in the cloud-forms that fringed the horizon, but even as he reported it in excited tones the image would fade and he would be forced to sink again into crestfallen silence.'

*

* 'Narrow passage of water connecting two seas or sea with lake, etc.'— *Concise Oxford Dictionary*.

Late on 30 January 1902 Scott graduated from the ranks of the explorers to the more exclusive company of the discoverers. They had come to the eastern extremity of the Great Ice Barrier, where no man had been before. Nine miles ahead of them they saw through their glasses a new prospect, a long coast line in which bare rock showed through the surrounding glaciation. Soundings at 88 fathoms indicated thick brown mud. As those on deck were going below for the evening meal, the officer of the watch, Shackleton, called their attention to black patches showing above the horizon. 'All glasses were levelled; assertions and contradictions were numerous ... until all agreed that at last we were looking at real live rock.'

Closer examination convinced Scott that they were seeing for the first time 'a country of considerable altitude and extent. We gazed for hours, endeavouring to drink in every detail of this distant view.' Shackleton scribbled exuberantly in his diary: 'It is a unique sort of feeling to look on lands that have never been seen by human eye before.'

Speculation about the discoveries awaiting the first explorers of *Terra Incognita* were as old as literate man. The Antarctic was postulated as part of a symmetrical antithesis by the Greeks, who considered that another habitable world would be found there. The Sieur de Kerguelen, who sailed south from Brittany in 1772, reported his belief that from 'the central mass of the Antarctic continent' would come new life for the trade of France: 'no doubt wood, minerals, diamonds, rubies, and marble.' He conceived it as the home of a people 'living in their primitive manner, ignorant alike of offence or remorse, knowing nothing of the artifices of civilized society'.

Alexander Dalrymple, Captain Cook's jealous contemporary, thought that the Antarctic continent would be found to contain fifty million inhabitants, and dreamed of trading with them, 'thus maintaining the power, dominion, and sovereignty of Britain'. Much later, the fascination of the Antarctic was such that twenty-eight stowaways were found on a Dundee whaler that was preparing to sail thither in the early 'nineties.

The new region discovered by Scott was named King Edward VII Land. He charted a hundred and fifty miles of its coast, and afterwards wished that they had 'made a dash towards the distant hills'. The plan was hardly feasible. A landing on that icy shore would have meant risks and delays. 'Such are the disadvantages of inexperience,' he wrote, regretting their unreadiness, especially with sledges.

He had found the eastern limit of the Great Ice Barrier, that it was not, as some thought, a glacier that had poured down to the sea, but a floating ice mass that joined Victoria Land in the west to the new-found territory in the east. It was entirely new information for geographers, and for his rival explorers in the years to come.

CHAPTER SIX

WOES OF THE INEXPERIENCED

ON 2 February 1902 the *Discovery* steamed into an inlet that breached the Great Ice Barrier not far from its eastern end. The surrounding ice was at deck level where she anchored. They could step straight off the ship on to the snow surface. Scott proposed to make a balloon ascent early the next morning; meanwhile, he looked forward to a quiet night's rest.

A strong undercurrent moved some of the bigger floes at the opening of the inlet, making a passage for two or three small but still formidable icebergs. One of them bore down on the ship. 'It gave the *Discovery* a squeeze which caused every frame to groan, and brought all hands on deck with scared faces. Had it met us fair and square the consequences might have been more serious.'

To his diary note Scott added that 'it is difficult to realize what an overwhelming force even a small berg may represent, until one remembers that it is, perhaps, barely one-sixth of its mass that is visible, and that there must always be thousands of tons submerged to support the hundreds which are seen'. He had now learnt, he wrote, that 'an iceberg of any dimensions is not to be trifled with'. It is an obsessive theme of the two volumes of his book about the *Discovery* voyage.

For two days, working westward, the ship was surrounded by 'mighty masses of ice'. Some of the bergs were immense. One, 'we estimated as at least six miles in one direction, and as probably more in another'.

A memory remains of Scott standing on his little bridge, 'tight-lipped, looking hard to leeward', in one of the unaccountable southerly gales of the Antarctic. The *Discovery* had a rudder defect. They were in imminent danger from icebergs. All hands were piped on deck, to stand by to throw the yards back and so bring the ship to a standstill. Their faces upturned towards him, the men awaited his orders. The *Discovery* steward, C. Reginald Ford, said: .'It gave us the utmost confidence just to see him there, piloting us out of trouble. We never doubted he would do it, and he did.'

Pack-ice blocked the channels between the bergs. 'Though our hearts sank at the thought of so much obstruction, we could afford to admire such a majestic and impressive ice scene. Under a dark, threatening sky the pack-ice showed intensely white in an inky sea, whilst the towering walls of the icebergs frowned over us, shaded from the palest to the most intense blue.' (Scott)

The balloon ascent was made on 4 February. Unlike five members of the Expedition who, at his instigation, had been given some preliminary training at the Royal Engineers balloon department at Aldershot, Scott had not been up before. He wrote afterwards that, 'perhaps somewhat selfishly', he seized the chance of 'being the first aeronaut to make an ascent in the Antarctic Regions'. It was no doubt also true that he was conforming to his rule of never asking others to do what he would not himself do. A lower-deck survivor of the Expedition recalls it as one of Scott's most appreciated characteristics as a leader.

Swaying in the one-man basket at the end of five hundred feet of wire rope he endured a few bad minutes when, impulsively, he flung all his ballast overboard and, as a result, shot up another three hundred feet. 'Thoughtless inexperience', was his phrase for it. No one before him had seen so much of the Great Ice Barrier or the wave-like undulations running from east to west across its otherwise featureless surface. Shackleton went up next and took photographs that proved to be of value chiefly as illustrations for *The Voyage of the 'Discovery'*.

For expedition purposes, the balloon ascents, originating in the suggestion made by Sir Joseph Hooker, were a waste of effort. Wilson considered them 'an exceedingly dangerous amusement'. Scott was soon persuaded that the balloon equipment, including fifty hydrogen gas cylinders, was not worth its space in the ship. He disposed of the subject of Antarctic ballooning summarily in his book on the Expedition.

*

During the night of 8 February 1902 the *Discovery* anchored in a small bay at the Southern end of a narrow peninsula jutting out from the foot of Mount Erebus (13,270 feet), the active volcano overlooking McMurdo Sound, and 'in some particulars the most remarkable mountain in the world'.* Shackleton described it as 'standing like a sentinel at the gate of the Great Ice Barrier'. It is visible from a hundred miles in any direction. Close by is Mount Terror (11,290 feet), an extinct volcano. 'A scene of more awful grandeur could hardly be imagined. At first its magnificence appealed to me, and often during the following two years did I gaze around me filled with delight at the splendid view; but more often still the deadly isolation of this lifeless land filled me with a feeling of nothingness hard to shake off.' †

For the moment, Scott cast pessimism aside. 'The scene is wonderfully beautiful at times; the most characteristic feature is a soft pink light, that tinges the snow-slopes and ice-foot and fades into the purple outline of the distant mountains. Here and there a high peak is radiantly gilded by a shaft of sunlight.' The effect was 'of sunset or sunrise for many hours together'.‡

A site for a bungalow-style prefabricated hut was chosen; it was thereafter charted as Hut Point. Armitage considered that 'it was more suitable for a colonial shooting-lodge than for a Polar dwelling'. Alongside it were erected asbestos shacks for the scientists to work in. A little apart kennels were built for the sledge dogs; according to Bernacchi, useless toil, for 'the dogs despised them and preferred to curl up in the snow'.

Scott was making ready to lead a sledge party to Cape Crozier for the purpose of leaving records there for the relief ship. He sprained a knee tendon in a ski-ing fall and was disabled for several days. Ford, the steward, broke a leg out on the ice. Royds, the engineer lieutenant, fell overboard late one night and was lucky to get back into the ship unaided—'a very

* J. Gordon Hayes: *Antarctica* (1928).
† Armitage: *Two Years in the Antarctic* (1905).
‡ *The Voyage of the 'Discovery'*.

63

narrow shave' (Scott). That the emergency potential had not been reduced by their more settled situation was shatteringly demonstrated on 11 March 1902, 'one of our blackest days in the Antarctic'.

The sledge party for Cape Crozier went out under the leadership of Royds, taking Scott's place. It consisted of three officers, one scientist, and eight men. A blizzard swept over them as they were descending an icy slope near the prominence known as Castle Rock, one of the familiar landmarks in the McMurdo Sound area, 'looking like a great boulder dropped from the skies' (Scott).

Those who were wearing fur boots had great difficulty in keeping a foothold. Three of the men, with Petty Officer Edgar Evans, whose name was later to be linked imperishably with Scott's, shot helplessly downward until they were checked by soft snow at the very edge of a cliff with a sheer 200 ft. face. A fourth man, Able Seaman George T. Vince, unable to get a grip, flashed past the others, flung up his arms, and disappeared into the icy sea below. With him went one of the dogs. At the same time, it was realized that Hare, the young steward, had lost touch with the rest of the party during the blizzard. He was not within sight or call.

Frank Plumley, who was with the party, has never forgotten the horror of that day. 'It cast a gloom over the whole lot of us.' He has a vivid and still terrifying memory of 'the furious way' in which they used their jackknives to cut footholds on a surface that was as smooth and hard as glass. Clambering back to safety from the cliff edge was 'like a nightmare'.

A whaleboat under Shackleton went off to search the shore line. Search parties overland returned exhausted without news of Hare. Scott had steam raised in the ship, so that she might send syren blasts as signals that echoed weirdly over the scene.

Armitage wrote that Scott was 'terribly agitated'. The elegiac note recurred in Scott's diary. 'We have now finally and sadly resigned ourselves to the loss of our shipmate (Vince), and the thought was grievous to us all.... Life was a bright thing to him, and it is something to think that death must have come quickly in that icy sea.'

Two days afterwards he was writing in the diary: 'A very extraordinary thing has happened,' and gave an account of the return of Hare, missing for two days. 'He must have lain under the snow for thirty-six hours. I cannot but believe that his preservation is unique, and almost miraculous. The boy, who is only eighteen, has been forty hours without food, and sixty without warm food; he must possess great stamina to have come through without hurt.'

Hare himself has written: 'I shall never forget the welcome when I got back safely, unaided.' * If his shipmates' cheers were muted by the recent tragedy, they were fervent enough to register not only relief at his deliverance but a heightened awareness of the imminence of dangers common to them all. Scott's reaction was noted by Wilson. 'He looked as though he thought the dead was really walking in.'

A funeral service for Vince was held in the hut the following Sunday evening. Armitage recalled that 'the Captain alluded to the tragedy, and endeavoured to impress on the men's minds the absolute necessity there was for them to exercise their individual intelligences for their own safety.'

His admonition was repeated more forcefully after a misadventure in which Bernacchi and Skelton might have lost their lives within shouting distance of help. Tired of the din in the hut, they set out to return to the ship, no more than two hundred yards away. Stepping into the night, they were overwhelmed by a blizzard. Soon they were completely lost, wandering in circles for an hour and a half, while the snow piled up around them.

Badly frost-bitten, they eventually made themselves heard and were brought in by a search party. Recording that they were rescued 'in the nick of time', Scott observed in his diary that 'it is the most convincing lesson on the blinding, bewildering effect of a blizzard that we have had', and he confessed to 'a lurking anxiety' about excursions from the ship during the winter months.

'Danger is rife,' Shackleton wrote in his diary. 'I say it without wishing to unduly exaggerate these sort of things ... more than once the escapes have been narrow ... and of course it is all part of the game. We didn't expect a feather bed down here.'

Again and again in *The Voyage of the 'Discovery'* Scott stressed their lack of experience. The deficiency count in that respect is sufficiently indicated by such diary entries as 'the

* Letter, 21 June 1965.

woes of the inexperienced sledger' (page 226); 'our ignorance was deplorable' (page 229); 'again we erred for want of experience' (page 255); 'a severe shock to our inexperience' (page 271); 'we had to buy our experience sadly' (page 286).

'Whoever selected the Polar library for the *Discovery* was determined that members of the Expedition should not greatly counteract their inexperience by reading.' * Scott admitted his own 'woeful ignorance' of Arctic literature. Disbelief in dogs; belief in man-hauling; ill-judged food allowances, were points of more fully considered criticism, the sum of which was that the Expedition was hampered by ineffectual land transport and inadequate rations. Scott agreed that 'amid the general ignorance that prevailed the lack of system was painfully apparent in everything'. Even so, the Expedition was the greatest pioneering achievement of Antarctic exploration.

*

The days were drawing in. Soon darkness would enclose seventeen of the diurnal twenty-four hours, and that for the next four months. The temperature was falling fast. On Easter Sunday, 1902, it was appropriately noted by Bernacchi that 'there were ice-flowers on the newly-frozen sea, waxen white formations, with radiant prismatic colours where the low-hung sun's rays touched them.'

The sun showed briefly on 23 April, then withdrew from the sky, which was thereafter dominated by the slow curling vapours of Mount Erebus. Their first Antarctic winter was upon them. They were utterly cut off from the world. Scott wrote:

'The ice about the ship had been firmly fixed for nearly a month, and there seemed little reason to suppose that the heaviest gale could move it before the following summer. For good or ill we were now a fixture, destined to spend our winter nearly 500 miles beyond the point at which any other human beings had wintered, and therefore about to face conditions at which we could only guess.'†

* J. Gordon Hayes: *Antarctica*. The *Discovery* library contained books covering a wide range of subjects, including Arctic exploration. 'By some oversight those which would have been of the most assistance were not included.' (Bernacchi: *Saga of the 'Discovery'*.)
† *The Voyage of the 'Discovery'*.

Would their health and spirits survive the sunless months? Armitage felt that 'some vitalizing force had been withdrawn from our lives'. What were the risks of temperamental clashes during the long winter confinement? They were largely averted by the propinquity of the ship, in which the officers had their own quarters, and the men theirs.

A well-ordered daily routine provided scope for mental and physical recreation. Shackleton produced *The South Polar Times*, a magazine that gave opportunities for self-expression to a variety of pent-up talents, literary and graphic. Debates, concert parties, minstrel shows, chess, card games, were other outlets.

The physicist, Bernacchi, wrote that 'the friction of conflicting tastes was eliminated from the beginning', a statement modified by Wilson, who told his wife in a letter: 'God knows it is just about as much as I can stand at times, and there is absolutely no escape. I have never had my temper so tried as it is every day now, but I don't intend to give way.... We have had *very* few rows, but friction is continual in some parties.'

Bernacchi had his 'one and only experience' of what seemed to him 'an unreasonable side' of Scott's temper when he made suggestions concerning the winter disposal of the ship's boats. 'I was told, in no uncertain terms, to attend to my own speciality.' Scott's decision in that matter had unfortunate results in that they nearly lost the boats.

Shackleton and Scott established a good working partnership that never touched cordiality and later deteriorated. Armitage did not see eye to eye with Scott in certain technical matters, sledge loading among them. For the time being, he could agree that 'the great depression felt by some Polar explorers was certainly not developed during our stay in the Antarctic; nevertheless, there was a slight amount of it, as well as a tendency to irritation'.

Later, Armitage disclosed personal grievances against Scott, a circumstance that provoked a postscript from one of the Expedition's survivors in 1965: 'I could never understand it, because I knew that at one time Scott was very good to Armitage. I also think that Armitage himself was a good chap.' *

*C. Reginald Ford, F.R.I.B.A., in a letter, 14 September 1965.

In one of his letters home, Wilson mentioned Royds's exemplary patience, 'which takes any amount of snubbing from his superiors'.

For all the tensions, hidden and otherwise, Bernacchi believed that 'the comparative formality of meals, and more especially dinner, helped to preserve an atmosphere of civilized tolerance such as has seldom been found in polar expeditions'. * He had no doubt that naval traditions, 'which in some things might have proved a disadvantage', had a favourable effect in preserving surface harmony.

On Sundays, under orders, they changed their clothes, a disciplinary decree that meant little alteration in the appearance of individuals. At 9.30 a.m. the men fell in on deck for inspection. Scott, followed by his officers, passed along the ranks, lighted ahead by the boatswain's lantern. 'Front rank, one pace forward—march!' It was one of the only two naval orders of the week; the other, 'Dis-miss!'

Then came church parade, heralded by the tolling of the ship's bell. Scott took the service from the Book of Common Prayer, Koettlitz read the lessons, Royds accompanied the hymns on the ship's harmonium. A deep-throated rendering of the sailors' hymn, *Eternal Father, strong to save*, sounding through the ship, marked the end of the parade.

Scott was weightily preoccupied by planning the sledge journeys that were to warrant the Expedition's existence as a scientific enterprise. Recovered from his leg injury, he took out a party consisting of Armitage, Wilson, Koettlitz, and eight men, with eighteen dogs. It was a trial run, partly to discipline the dogs. Apparently affected adversely by a sudden temperature fall, they pulled badly. Those that lagged were called 'sooners'. because they would 'sooner do anything than pull'. †
After no more than three days out, Scott gave the order to turn back, as it was obvious that the dogs were failing. At once, aware that they were homeward bound, they pulled so well that they had to be restrained.

As Scott quickly found, sledge dog behaviour produced unforeseen problems for the Expedition. He was shocked by its more primitive manifestations. Individual dogs that were petted, or shown special favour, were liable to be exposed to

* L. C. Bernacchi: *Saga of the 'Discovery'*.
† E. A. Wilson: Diary.

the venom of others in the pack. Scott recorded an instance of the savagery that could ensue.

'It was on March 15 that we witnessed the first attack. There was a growl, a wild rush, a heap of heaving, snarling forms, and the horrid deed was done. We shouted and whistled, but might just as well have held our breath.' A lifeless form lay on the snow when the pack dispersed. The following day a similar tragedy was enacted. Punishment followed at the hands of the men; but, Scott reflected, 'you cannot change dog nature'. The victims were two 'quiet, harmless animals' that had been chosen for a trial sledge run.

None in the Expedition knew that the Siberian sledge dog had a habit of treating as strangers, and sometimes as enemies, any dogs that had been separated from the pack, however briefly. It was not apparent at the beginning that an inferior type of Siberian dog had been supplied to the Expedition. They were capable of pulling only the lighter loads. It had also been overlooked that as a Northern breed they would shed their heavy coats just as winter came on in the Antarctic.

Soon, too, it was discovered that sledge dogs suffer from their own form of ennui when facing endless miles of unrelieved white snow and that the only remedy was for men to march ahead of them. 'This monotony tells on the spirits of dogs, perhaps more than on men, and it is quite pitiful to see how a team raises ears and tails if there is some shadow ahead which might turn out to be a man or a penguin, only to drop it again when it turns out to be an illusion.'*

There were eerie moments on moonlit nights when, suddenly, a dog would uncurl itself from the sleeping mass and lift its head to give forth a long and dismal howl that echoed far over the snows. As the sound died away, another dog would stir to take up the cry; and so on, through the pack. That insensate baying rarely failed to wake every sleeping man. After one such night, Scott wrote: 'What lingering instinct of bygone ages can impel them to this extraordinary custom is beyond guessing.... As an accompaniment to the vast desolation without, it touches the lowest depths of sadness.'

Wilson, who made few comments of a personal nature in the diary he was keeping, wrote on 3 May 1902 that Scott was

* Frank Debenham, O.B.E., M.A.: *Antarctica: The Story of a Continent* (1959).

'an excellent man for this job, full of theories and ingenuity—and always thinking'.

*

Trial sledge runs were made in September and October 1902 to test harness, dog-handling, and loading, minor rehearsals for the bigger ventures to come. Royds and six men, Armitage with five, were sent away on reconnaissance missions westward. Scott took a party ninety miles out to lay a depot of supplies for his coming southward journey, during which he would attempt to reach a higher latitude than anyone before him.

That initial foray was a hardening experience. They spent a day and a half clinging to the flaps of their tent, in danger of being torn away by a blizzard. Scott wrote: 'Without exception, this was the most miserable day I've ever spent.' On the return march, their clothes froze on them. 'My trousers might have been cut out of sheet iron.'

They had their first encounter with a menace that was to become all too familiar. 'I heard a shout behind, and looking round, saw to my horror that the boatswain had disappeared; there stood the dog-team and sledges, but no leader. I hurried back and saw that the trace disappeared down a formidable crevasse and to my relief the boatswain was at the end of the trace. He had a pretty close call.'

Pertaining to that part of the journey, Scott wrote afterwards: 'I cannot but think our procedure was extremely rash. I have not the least doubt now that this region was a very dangerous one and the fact that we essayed to cross it in this light-hearted fashion can only be ascribed to our ignorance.'

Those apprentice marches had their virtue in proving the inefficiency of the Expedition in a number of technical aspects; for instance, in making camp in adverse conditions. It was agreed that some of the hours spent in debates, sing-songs, and midnight football, might have been more usefully employed in 'the acquisition of wisdom', as Scott put it.

Back in winter quarters there were grumblings about the food, especially about the pemmican, which the men said tasted like 'a mixture of tow and sawdust'. Scurvy symptoms appeared: swollen legs, inflamed gums, loosening teeth. A decade was to pass before the organic compounds known as vitamins were revealed to the bio-chemists (1912), though Arctic ex-

70

perience had taught the value of fruit, vegetables, and cod liver oil; and 156 gallons of lime juice were included in the Expedition's supplies. An American commentator on Scott's expedition brusquely observed that 'in modern polar exploration, scurvy is unknown except among Englishmen, who hate to avail themselves of the lessons learned by other nations'.* Scott's prejudice against the slaughter of seals meant too great a reliance on tinned meat.

Koettlitz, the doctor, grew prophylactic mustard-and-cress in boxes of Antarctic soil scraped up by the spoonful from under the snow and placed high up under the ship's wardroom skylight. Studying the symptoms in the doctor's text books, Scott noted that the worst stage of the disease produced conditions 'from which death is a merciful release'.

His own belief was that scurvy resulted from food poisoning. He suspected the tinned meat brought out from England. Writing his account of the Expedition, he considered the risk of libel involved in publishing the name of the suppliers. 'A pity he was not more explicit,' remarked a reviewer in *The Times Literary Supplement* (13 October 1905), 'though it is not difficult to read between the lines.'

The Times in 1904 reported that some medical authorities considered mental depression to be a contributory cause, rather than an effect, of scurvy. 'The theory now most in vogue is that it is due to ptomaines developed in poisoned meat. Unfortunately, nobody knows what ptomaines rightly are or how they get there. The old faith in vegetable acids is exploded.'

CHAPTER SEVEN

WHEN SHACKLETON WEPT

IN June 1902 Scott was completing arrangements for the sledge journeys that were to bring lustre to his first Antarctic expedition. Armitage and Royds were to lead teams beyond their previous westward tracks. Scott intended to make the south his goal; not the Pole but the farthest point reachable by a sledge party of two.

* *The Bookman* (U.S.A.), May 1906.

In England, the redoubtable Sir Clements Markham, as President of the Royal Geographical Society, was organizing the dispatch of the ship that was to take out provisions and mail, 'bring back any invalids, and afford relief and the means of return if anything had happened to the *Discovery*.' After the months of silence, he had peremptorily decided that 'there was no time to be lost'.

He went to Norway and, after tough bargaining, secured an option on an old barque-rigged whaling ship for £3,880, returning to England to undertake the familiarly dispiriting task of raising funds. The King headed a public subscription list with £100. Llewellyn Longstaff dipped into his pocket again and produced £5,000. Edger Speyer, a City financier of German origin who later figured more prominently in Scott's affairs, gave £1,000. 'With these exceptions,' Markham wrote, 'very rich people refused to help'. Five City companies and the Stock Exchange contributed generously.

Slowly, money came in from Royal Navy wardrooms, regimental messes at home and abroad, and public schools. The total amount raised was £22,640. Markham had the Norwegian whaling ship renamed the *Morning*. Her hull was black and, by his orders, a band of white was painted along her sides as a reminder of the barque *Assistance* in which he had sailed to the Arctic nearly fifty years before.

Tireless and perennially keen, he interviewed and chose the relief ship officers and crew, bought her supplies, supervised her loading. He begrudged neither time nor energy in organizing the help that he conceived might by then be urgently awaited by Scott in the *Discovery*.

At the Royal Society it was suspected that he had clandestinely sounded the Treasury about the possibility of an additional grant. A draft memorandum in the Royal Society's files states that 'if such an appeal has been made by Sir C. Markham, it was made not only without the connivance but the knowledge of the Royal Society', which was sensitive about its good standing with the Government.

The *Morning* sailed from London docks on 6 July 1902 with a crew of twenty-nine. She was registered with the Royal Corinthian Yacht Club and commanded by Lieutenant William Colbeck, R.N.R., chief officer of the *Montebello*, of the Wilson Steamship Line, Hull. Her second officer was

Lieutenant E. R. G. Evans, R.N., who was to go down in naval annals as 'Evans of the Broke'.

'How strange it all is!' Scott was entering up his diary, a fortnight after the relief ship sailed. 'For countless ages the great sombre mountains above us have loomed through the gloomy polar night with never an eye to mark their grandeur, and for countless ages the wind-swept snow has drifted over these great deserts with never a footprint to break its white surface.' He was oppressed by the transience of their human invasion of 'the eternal solitudes'. Soon, he wrote, 'all must be surrendered again to the desolation of the ages'.

In the same ruminative phase, it struck him as 'fascinating to consider the moneyless condition in which we live. With absence of wealth, community of interest, and a free sharing of comforts and hardships, we must realize much that is socialistically ideal, yet in recognition of rank and supremacy of command the government must be considered an autocracy.'

He did not know that the relief ship was coming out. More important to him was the sledge journey by which he hoped 'to solve the mysteries in a southerly direction'. All his attention was centred in that project. He planned to make a major advance in geographic knowledge, a march that would take him nearer to the Pole than men had ever been.

Five sledges bore a total load of 1,850 lb.: nine weeks' supply of food for men and dogs, plus clothing, cooking equipment, skis, tool, and a tent. Extra provisions laid at a depot by a supporting party would see them through a further four weeks, if necessary.

There were no illusions about what lay before them. Wilson's diary, kept for his wife, shows it. 'If anything happens to me so that you can't see me again in this life, and you want to hear about me from those who do get home, will you please make a point of seeing the Captain and Royds in preference to anyone else.... Don't give way to despair.'

Shackleton left a letter to the young woman whom he wished to marry. 'Beloved I hope you may never have to read this but darling loved one if it comes to you you will know that your lover left this world with all his heart yours....'

Scott's mood was laconically expressed in a diary note: 'We have just been gazing with anxious eyes on the road to the south.' A champagne party was held in the wardroom on the night of 1 November 1902. The following day, he wrote: 'We are off at last.' With Wilson and Shackleton and a team of nineteen dogs, he set out on the great sledge journey that inaugurated what has since been flamboyantly described as 'the heroic age of Antarctic exploration'.

*

Scott originally meant to make the southward thrust with only one companion. It would have saved weight and food. Wilson argued him out of it by emphasizing the hazards of an unknown terrain and the risk of sickness, in which event the burden might prove to be too heavy for one man alone. Scott then agreed that the party should consist of Shackleton, Barne, and himself. Severe frost-bite put Barne out of the running. Wilson was asked to take his place. He welcomed the chance.

As a medical man, he had private doubts about Shackleton's stamina. 'For some reason, I don't think he is fitted for the job. The Captain is strong and hard as a bulldog, but Shackleton hasn't the legs that the job wants. He is so keen to go, however, that he will carry it through.'

In the same diary note, Wilson reflected that 'when Polar exploration becomes possible to any form of motor transport or flying machine its attraction to most people would be finished, and would interest an entirely different mind'. It was a perceptive glance forward from 1902, when the internal combustion revolution had hardly begun and no aeroplane had appeared in the sky.

Five of their first days out were spent cooped up in the tent because of blizzards. Yet Scott's diary indicates what for him was almost a euphoric state of mind as they entered the second week of the march. 'We are already beyond the utmost limit to which man has attained; each footstep will be a fresh conquest of the great unknown. Confident in ourselves, confident in our equipment, and confident in our dog team, we can but feel elated with the prospect that is before us.'

The same day, 15 November, they covered only three miles, a depressingly poor performance in that scene of overwhelming distances. 'To the north,' he noted, 'the land has become dim, to the west we have the same prospect of detached snow-plain.' They pressed endlessly on, little black silhouettes moving jerkily forward through the engulfing whiteness.

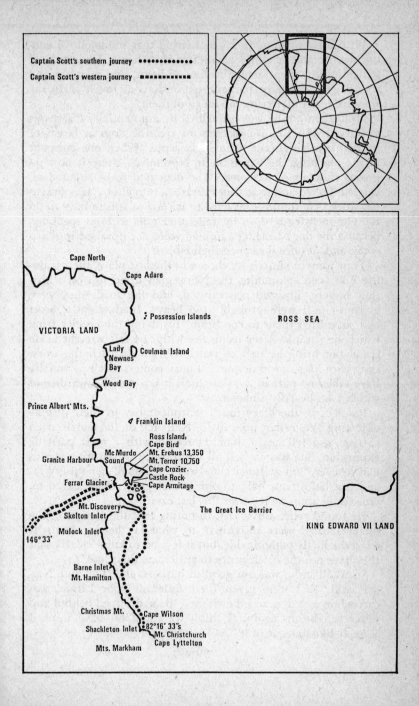

Captain Scott's southern journey ●●●●●●●●●●●●
Captain Scott's western journey ■■■■■■■■■■■■

Cape North

Cape Adare

⁞ Possession Islands

ROSS SEA

VICTORIA LAND

Lady
Newnes
Bay

◻ Coulman Island

Wood Bay

Prince Albert' Mts.

⊲ Franklin Island

Ross Island:
Cape Bird
Granite Harbour   Mc Murdo   Mt. Erebus 13,350
                   Sound   Mt. Terror 10,750
                               Cape Crozier.
Ferrar Glacier   Castle Rock
                               Cape Armitage

Mt. Discovery
Skelton Inlet   The Great Ice Barrier

Mulock Inlet   KING EDWARD VII LAND

146° 33'

Barne Inlet
Mt. Hamilton

Christmas Mt.   Cape Wilson
                     82° 16' 33" s
Shackleton Inlet   Mt. Christchurch
                     Cape Lyttelton
Mts. Markham

Within twenty-four hours of writing that testament of confidence, he was ruefully amending it. 'After a few yards of struggling the dogs seemed to lose all heart, and many looked round with the most pathetic expressions as much as to say we were really expecting too much of them.'

From then on, he was bedevilled by a potentially disastrous sentiment. His English distaste for treating dogs as beasts of burden became almost torturingly acute. 'When one goes out in the morning,' he wrote on 19 November, 'there is now no joyous clamour of welcome.' The dogs had to be shouted at, cajoled, lashed and sometimes thrashed into effort. 'It is sickening work.' He found it 'as hard to witness as it is to have to do it'. The men trudged on for mile after mile without speaking, because the dogs, hearing a human voice not upraised in sharp command, at once slackened their efforts.

They were too hurriedly chosen in the first place, their training had been spasmodic, the Norwegian dried fish on which they largely subsisted was tainted, and the loads they were given to pull were probably too heavy. Inadvertently, Scott had submitted them to conditions involving the cruelty from which he shrank. After using the whip, he felt wretched. He could not bring himself to watch Wilson dispatch the worst cases with his surgical deftness. 'I must confess that I personally have taken no part in the slaughter; it is a moral cowardice of which I am heartily ashamed.'

Passages in the diary touch sentimentality in their display of feeling. 'Yesterday, poor little "Nell" fell on the march, tried to rise, and fell again, looking round with a most pathetic expression. She was carried all night, but this morning was as bad as ever, and at lunch-time was put out of her misery ... and just before our halt, to our greater grief, "Kid" caved in. One could almost weep over this last case.'

He found relief, obviously, in noting that the victims of the mercy killings were insensitive to what lay before them. 'It has a distinctly pathetic side, but it is good to know clearly that they have not the intelligence to anticipate their fate.'

So 'Wolf', who was not good in harness, and 'Joe' and 'Nigger' and 'Jim' were given their quietus, 'poor Birdie' was carried on a sledge, and 'Lewis' and 'Boss' dropped behind and never caught up again. 'I think we could all have wept. I scarcely like to write of it.'

He wrote too late for his own profit that 'the lesson to future travellers in the South is obvious in that they should safeguard their dogs as securely as they do their men.' When early in the New Year the last of the dogs died, he almost rejoiced. 'No more clearing of tangled traces, no more whip.'

An American reviewer of Scott's book on the Expedition could 'but note with admiration that those heavily burdened men, amidst a wilderness of snow, not sure of fighting their way back to the ship, not believing in dogs, nevertheless loaded the weak animals on sledges, hoping to save them. Such humanity is unprecedented, I think, in the annals of Pole exploration.'*

Relaying their sledge load, man-hauling half forward and returning for the other half, was the only answer to the failure of the dogs. It meant a sterile addition to their mileage, and an unlooked-for tax on their energies. 'For one-and-thirty awful days we have been at it,' and Scott doubted whether human endurance 'could have stood much more'.

As for dogs, out of his recent experience came a dictum that was admired more for its sentiment than for its logic. 'No journey ever made with dogs can approach the height of that fine conception which is realized when a party of men go forth to meet hardships, dangers, and difficulties with their own un-aided efforts, and by days and weeks of hard physical labour succeed in solving some problems of the great unknown.'

*

New and formidable perspectives came up over the horizon. 'This morning we sighted further land to the south-west, and like the rest it appears as a detached fragment. We now see three distinct gaps between the several land masses, and the distance is too great for us to make out any detail of the latter; to the south and round through east to the north we have still the unbroken snow horizon.'

By 21 November 1902 he felt that their chance of reaching the highest latitudes was 'melting away'. Little had been said about the Pole as an objective, though Shackleton hoped that they might make 'a dash' for it, and Wilson had noted it as a possibility in his diary for 12 June 1902. Scott's main purpose

* *The Bookman* (U.S.A.), vol. 23, p. 292.

was to travel as far south as was commensurate with his role of scientific explorer.

Now they were beginning to know the real rigours of the journey. Even where the going was firm and level, every step was as if they were climbing a steep hill. Breathing was harshly audible, noses and lips were chapped. Licking their cracked lips was an added discomfort. It was painful to drink out of hot pannikins. Wearing goggles was not an infallible preventive of eye inflammation. Wilson became a barometer of lowering temperatures; he was crippled by rheumatism when blizzards approached. Through it all they stuck as long as they could to a morning routine of washing, shaving, teeth brushing.

On 25 November 1902 they crossed the 80th parallel. 'This compensates for a lot of trouble' (Scott). It was a physical achievement in more ways than one; geographically, a notable advance. 'Slowly but surely we are finding out the secrets of this wonderful place,' Shackleton wrote in his diary that week.

On 29 November they saw a solar manifestation that compelled their admiration. The sun's rays, thrown back from thin clouds of ice crystals, projected into the heavens a series of bisected circles and curves that looked like mathematical symbols chalked above the distant blue horizon. Double haloes, fog bows, prismatic rings, mock suns, iridescent clouds, appeared overhead 'the most striking atmospheric phenomenon we have as yet seen in these regions'. And again: 'We have never been privileged to witness a display that approaches in splendour that of today.' Scott wrote as if they had been uplifted.

The gods, at their old business of discouraging *hubris*, contrived what he called 'rather a scare' a few hours afterwards by shrouding the party with sudden night fog. He and Wilson were relaying some way ahead of Shackleton, who had been left in charge of food and personal equipment. They groped for the rearward track like blind men, not knowing whether their direction was right or wrong. 'The incident set us thinking,' Scott wrote in a note conjecturing what their fate might have been had the fog thickened still further.

Another sort of perversity gave him 'rather a shock—it was so unexpected', when the ice crust around them cracked with a succession of reports as loud as pistol shots, followed by a weird 'long-drawn sigh' as the exploded areas subsided. The result was 'an instantaneous feeling of insecurity which was not pleasant'.

The going became still harder. 'We now find difficulty in gaining even four miles a day.' There was compensatory pleasure in the spectacle of ice-crystals shimmering in the light of the midnight sun, like feathery six-pointed stars, 'sometimes as large as a shilling: the effect of these *en masse* is wonderful. One realizes that the simile of a gem-strewn carpet could never be more aptly employed. It sparkles with a myriad points of hollow light, comprehensive of every colour the rainbow can show and is so realistic and near that it often seems one has but to stoop to pick up some glistening jewel.'

They were encased in stupendous silences. Wilson described them as uncanny. 'One could imagine oneself on a dead planet. Everything was so still and cold and dead and unearthly.' On 17 December, they came to 'a yawning gulf' of a crevasse, bridged by snow. Unaware of the danger, they 'unconsciously passed within an ace of destruction. It certainly had been a very close shave.'

Scott had reckoned that 28·6 ounces of food per man per day was adequate, including only $7\frac{1}{2}$ ounces of meat. In the third week of December hunger pangs seized them. 'We talked of little else but food.' Their sleep was disturbed by 'active gnawing sensations'. Wilson and Shackleton had 'very bad food dreams', a regular topic of breakfast hour conversation. Scott thought it 'a sort of nightmare'. They sat at well-spread tables with their arms tied, reached out for dishes that were snatched away by unseen hands, lifted 'dainty morsels' to their mouths only to fall headlong into crevasses.

Wilson's diary mentions 'dreams of ball-suppers—but one shouts at waiters who won't bring a plate of anything. One rarely gets a feed in one's sleep'. Shackleton taunted himself by making a list of meals he longed to enjoy as a change from seal meat stew. 'Duck with crisp fried bread and thick bread soaked in golden syrup' figured in it.

Scott's smoking, for him one of life's lasting consolations, was reduced to two pipes a day, which he still believed gave him an advantage denied his two non-smoking companions. Hoarding his supply of Player's Navy Cut, he experimented with dried tea leaves, finding them 'nothing less than horrid'.

*

Every day reaffirmed the esteem in which Wilson was held by the leader, who had referred to him in a letter to Sir Clements Markham as 'an excellent fellow all round'. Scott predicted that 'Wilson will do great things one day'. No one appreciated his character and mental quality more, or his 'remarkable capacity for hard work'. Yet Wilson had joined the Expedition as a bad life insurance risk.

The antiseptic air of the high latitudes had apparently conquered his enemy, the bacillus of what was then commonly known as consumption (tuberculosis), a scourge of early twentieth-century civilization. As a doctor, he would have been aware of the more favourable prognosis; as a human being, he must have rejoiced in his heart at the lifting of an ominous shadow from his life. Banished also was the nervous instability that formerly plagued him in 'alternations of abject misery,' almost suicidal [his own words], 'with feelings of extraordinary freedom and happiness.' There had been a time when he had to sedate himself before facing a social or personal ordeal.

He was now able to work as steadily as any man in the Expedition, and for as long a day. Most evenings, when they pitched camp and the weather was right, he would squat outside the tent to sketch and paint the scene before him. Turner was his master, an old, unyielding devotion, expressed tentatively and delicately in his studies of the atmospheric phenomena of the Antarctic. His pencil and brush were ungrudgingly at the service of his colleagues who wanted graphic records of their scientific labours. It was calculated that for a set of drawings recording one of the sledge journeys in which he took part he used over a hundred feet of watercolour paper.

Wilson's sincerity, rooted in the Christian faith, was a radiant force. When Scott felt impelled to state his feelings about the man who most intimately shared with him the ardours of a unique and daring enterprise, he wrote in heartfelt terms. 'Words must always fail me when I talk of Bill Wilson. I believe he really is the finest character I ever met.'

Wilson told his wife, in a letter written during the outward voyage, that he and Scott understood one another 'better than anyone else in the ship, I think'. He had already noted that they 'agreed to differ' about religion. His diary reference to his having 'had it out with Scott' was thought to have been provoked by tensions between Scott and Shackleton.

The interplay of their personalities was not basically sympathetic. There was always the possibility of a clash of will between them. Protocol may have subtly asserted itself even in their hazardous circumstances. Shackleton was the junior partner in the team, besides belonging to the Merchant Marine. In temperament he tended to be an egotist, no commendation to Scott, trained in a service not conducive to self-assertion. There are fewer references to Shackleton than to Wilson in Scott's *Discovery* volumes.

Shackleton's cast of mind was optimistic, truculent, bantering; it was he who conferred most of the nicknames current in the Expedition. He was widely read, particularly among the English poets. Browning was his laureate. An admirer thought him 'an incarnation of the poet's virile faith and optimism'.* Seeking a personal favour, he was given to adopting a wheedling tone, ascribed by some to the Irish strain in his ancestry.

As with Scott, in the first place the Antarctic had no irresistible lure for him. Fame, plus adventure, was his spur, Dr H. R. Mill, the geographer, wrote that besides having 'no natural affinity for the polar regions', Shackleton had no genius for scientific research.

*

On 26 December 1902 Wilson was stricken with snow-blindness, 'writhing in horrible agony' (Scott). The symptoms were 'seeing double, a sensation of hot grit in the eyes, persistent watering, and increasing pain'. Cocaine, ice, zinc ointment, brought no relief. 'It is distressing to know that one can do nothing to help.' Wilson had to march with bandaged eyes: 'luckily I only fell twice' (Diary).

Scott described to him the surrounding scene as they travelled. 'On the near side is a bold snow-covered cape, and all day we have been drawing abreast of it.' The prominence seemed to roll aside as they advanced, 'like some vast sliding gate'. Wilson, meanwhile, was having 'the strangest thoughts or daydreams' as he trudged forward in his darkness. 'Sometimes I was in beech woods, sometimes in fir woods.'

Slowly there came into view a glorious panorama. There was excitement in Scott's voice as he told Wilson that towering 15,000 feet above distant red-tinted ridges was a splendid twin-

* H. R. Mill: *The Life of Sir Ernest Shackleton* (1923).

peaked eminence, more imposing than any other they had seen in the Antarctic. 'Pelion piled on Ossa!'

Solemnly that night they decreed that the new mountain should be named after the founding father of the Expedition, Sir Clements Markham. Scott then added two more names to the map. The 'snow-covered cape' was to be known as Cape Wilson. An inlet beside it was to bear Shackleton's name. Scott carefully refrained from adding his own name to any feature of the natural scene.

Unknown to him, that had been done for him by others in the same Christmas week of 1902. The relief ship *Morning* sighted an uncharted island just after crossing the Antarctic circle on Christmas Day. According to Lieutenant Evans's recollection, her captain, William Colbeck, went ashore with his officers to take possession in the name of King Edward VII. Running up the Union Jack, he named the island after Scott. Colbeck himself, in his report to the Royal Geographical Society, made no reference to that small ceremony, which Scott had deemed 'a great honour'.

Two days after Chrismas, Scott, Wilson, and Shackleton crossed the 82nd parallel and pressed on beyond it. Pitching camp in 82 degrees 16′ 33″, the 'farthest south' by more than three hundred miles, was an occasion to be marked by flying their individual sledge flags. 'We have almost shot our bolt,' Scott wrote. They were 420 miles from the South Pole.

'If this compares poorly with our hopes and expectations on leaving the ship, it is a more favourable result than we anticipated when those hopes were first blighted by the failure of the dog team.' The undertone of disappointment is like the first intimation of a symphonic theme committed to a sombre, far-off climax. It was momentarily absorbed in the affirmation that 'even as it is we have made a greater advance towards a pole of the earth than has ever yet been achieved by a sledge party'.

The theme reappears in Scott's notes of five days later, on 31 December. A formidable chasm opened up in their path. Beyond it, a mile away, was a gentle slope that would have made comparatively easy going. They had narrow escapes amid a network of crevasses, mostly deceptively snow covered. Their progress was finally stopped by a fifty-foot ice face. 'We were reluctantly forced to confess that all our trouble had been in vain. It was a great disappointment.'

The scene, photographed by Shackleton, is like a vast relic of ancient cosmic disturbance. There is nothing for the eye to rest on but primeval chaos blanketed by snow. A small figure stands alone amid the terrible desolation. It is Scott, contemplating the chasm that has finally frustrated them on their southward march.

They turned in their tracks on New Year's Day 1903 after having been out eight weeks, famished, exhausted, dispirited. 'We are positively ravenous' (7 January. 'It is impossible to avoid a sense of being lost' (11 January). 'We are approaching a very critical time' (12 January). 'I am now writing in the tent, and, I am bound to say, in no very cheerful frame of mind. Shackleton was terribly done up' (13 January).

Their faces were haggard with privation and blackened from exposure to the daylight glare. They now grew beards that still further occluded their identities. Weird vagabonds, they shambled on towards the food depot that they feared never to find: 'a load of anxiety' (Scott). Having found it, seen at first as a speck through Scott's telescope, and expressing their relief by giving 'a wild cheer', they could laugh at each other for looking like 'terrible ruffians', and press on to the next depot, a hundred and thirty miles away, each pulling a weight of 170 lb.

Signs that all was not well with Shackleton became disturbingly clear. He breathed laboriously, coughed through the nights and spat blood. His gums were angry-looking, his ankles swollen, scurvy symptoms which Wilson then diagnosed in a less aggravated form in Scott. Discussing Shackleton furtively, Wilson confided to Scott that he was alarmed. 'He did not know that the breakdown would come at once, but he felt sure that it was not far removed.'

Scott had to use the voice of authority. He ordered Shackleton to do no more tent pitching, sledge pulling, or camp work. Supposing he collapsed and had to be pulled? Scott seriously doubted his own and Wilson's capacity to meet that emergency, the more so as Wilson had 'vainly attempted to disguise a limp, caused by scurvy. It looks as though life for the next week or two is not going to be pleasant for any of us.' Scott and Wilson were now each pulling a load of nearly 250 lb.

That Shackleton did not take kindly to the rules imposed on him is clear from Scott's later note that 'we try to make him do as little as possible'. Twice he fell and, having helped him to his feet, the other two had to wait for him to recover. Hands on knees, he stooped with the pain of breathing. He had more coughing spasms and more haemorrhages.

'It is all very dreadful to watch,' Scott wrote at the end of the day. In due time he paid public tribute to Shackleton's 'extraordinary pluck and endurance'. Humiliated by the failure of his physique, Shackleton was determined to show that his will power remained unimpaired.

Pride and courage drove him on beyond his strength. 'Tonight matters are serious with him again. We were forced back to camp in a hurry.' Scott observed that Shackleton did not complain. 'There is no doubt he is suffering badly,' and on 24 January 1903: 'He is having a cruel time.'

Somewhere along their dolorous route relations worsened between Scott and Shackleton. Armitage wrote in confidence many years after to Dr Mill, the Royal Geographical Society's librarian, who was engaged on a life of Shackleton, alleging that 'bad feeling' had arisen between the two men during the southern journey. It could have been caused by Shackleton's dogged reluctance to be treated as an invalid.

Hodgson, the marine biologist, wrote that 'only three know the inner history of the Southern Sledge Journey, but it was pretty broadly whispered that Wilson was the backbone of that trip, which but for him would have been briefer.' The implication there seems to be that a situation had been reached in which Scott and Shackleton would not have gone on together. That Wilson thought it necessary to 'have it out' with Scott suggests that the leader's patience was severely tried.

On 29 January, Scott noted that 'Shackleton is extremely ill; his breathing has become more sterterous and laboured, his face looks pinched and worn, his strength is very much reduced, and for the first time he has lost his spirit and grown despondent. Wilson thinks matters are very critical.'

On 30 January, after a blizzard and a night broken by paroxysms of coughing, he was 'livid and speechless'. His strength had waned to a degree at which he was persuaded to be a passenger. His pride held out, even then, for it appears that he sat on the sledge, refusing to lie prone, his humiliation tempered by the hoisting of a sail to catch a following wind that eased the strain of pulling.

He was the youngest of the three, twenty-eight to Scott's thirty-five and Wilson's thirty-one. The blanks in his diary of that phase of the journey are eloquent of more than physical distress. Nowhere in its pages did he write words of grievance or dismay. Typical of his spirit is the phrase with which he began the entries for some of his worst days: 'The same old game again. . . .'

Scott's diary for 30 January 1903 tells us that Shackleton was exhausted and had to be sledge borne. Wilson's diary for that day says the same thing. A grossly exaggerated report was corrected by Scott in a letter to the *Daily Mail* of 7 November 1904. 'The facts were that though Mr Shackleton was extremely ill, and caused us great anxiety, he displayed the most extraordinary pluck and endurance, and managed to struggle on beside the sledge without adding his weight to our burden.'

Yet Scott's diary note, 'our invalid ... was so exhausted that we thought it wiser that he should sit on the sledge, where for the remainder of the forenoon, with the help of our sail, we carried him,' was left unamended in *The Voyage of the 'Discovery'* (1905). Sir Clements Markham repeated it in his *Lands of Silence* (1920), 'to the grief and indignation of Shackleton', whose first biographer, Dr Mill, denied that Shackleton was 'carried on the sledge, as rumour declared'.

A more recent and equally authoritative biography of Shackleton* refers to the 'unfortunate phrasing' of Scott's diary entry and surmises that it 'cannot have made matters easier for Shackleton when the two men met'. Shackleton's breakdown on the march, with its sequel of a discomfited ego, may perhaps be rightly seen as a dynamic factor in his subsequent achievements as an explorer.

*

They reached journey's end on 3 February 1903. The ship was gaily 'dressed' with bunting for their return. Her sides gleamed with new paint. Tons of frozen snow had been shovelled from her deck. Cheers rang out from her as the three men drew near, Wilson and Shackleton on skis, Scott hobbling in with badly swollen legs. Dirty strips of sticking plaster hung from his cracked lips. Shackleton, the chief casualty, kept his head

* *Shackleton*, by Margery and James Fisher (Barrie, 1957).

covered. The other two uncovered in response to the salutations of their friends. Several of the men in the welcoming party had put on neckties, a customary civility of those Antarctic reunions.

They had been away ninety-three days and had marched 960 miles, including the tedious relays. From latitude 82° 17′ S., which was nearer to the South Pole than man had been before, they saw mountains in latitude 83°, thus ascertaining the chief physical aspect of the western boundary of the Great Ice Barrier. In enlarging the world's scanty knowledge of its most forbidding region, they had tested themselves to a limit at which Scott could claim: 'We had striven and endured with all our might.'

Shackleton was at once put to bed. Wilson retired voluntarily to rest for ten days, stirring himself at intervals to make notes of observations outside his range as vertebrate zoologist, e.g., that there were cases of lumbago and muscular rheumatism in the Expedition, but no anaemia, and that in the colder temperatures the taste for alcohol diminished. Scott was 'the least affected' of the three, though senior in years. In his case, reaction came in the form of 'extreme lassitude' that lasted several days.

On the night of their return, he had a visitor. He was taking his first bath in three months—'delicious!'—when his steward came to tell him: 'Captain Colbeck of the *Morning* to see you, sir.' Colbeck had walked over the ten miles of ice that separated the ships in McMurdo Sound.

Colbeck told Scott that he had almost despaired of finding the *Discovery*. 'He was desperately wondering what to do next,' when the guide post at Cape Crozier, with its red canister containing news of the *Discovery*'s whereabouts, was sighted sticking up out of a large penguin rookery. Colbeck's report states: 'At 11.40 p.m. on January 23rd we had the pleasure of sighting the masts of the *Discovery*. Rockets were fired and we exchanged colours shortly after midnight.'

Colbeck brought mail from England and with it instructions for Scott from the Presidents of the Royal Society and the Royal Geographical Society. Scott was informed that with the arrival of the *Morning*, 'you will be in command of the two ships, and you are to take what you require from the *Morning*, and extricate yourself from your winter quarters with as little loss of time as possible.... You will return to Lyttelton in March or

April, 1903.' If funds permitted, it was considered desirable that he should resume his work of exploration and scientific observation during a third navigable season.

Scott did not find the energy to visit the *Morning* until nearly a fortnight after Colbeck's call on him. When he made the effort to cross the ice on 18 February 1903 he found it 'an awful grind'. Lieutenant Evans, second officer of the relief ship, was impressed by Scott's manner of arriving, calling out from the gangway in his commander's tone: 'Is Captain Colbeck on board?' Evans said that 'he might have been paying a routine visit to a ship of the Home Fleet'.

Both captains were worried by the lateness of the pack-ice in breaking up. There was no sign of it. In a week, the *Morning* had drawn less than a quarter of a mile nearer to the *Discovery*. Fourteen tons of stores were man-hauled between the ships, back-breaking work. A sledge party from the *Morning* made two trips a day to a half-way flag, where they met the *Discovery*'s men, who took over the load. It was essential that the *Morning* should get away by the first week in March 1903; otherwise, with her weak engine power, she too might be held in the pack. Explosive charges fractured the ice ineffectively.

As for the *Discovery*, she was securely ice-locked, with a poor prospect of release. The need for economy dictated a reduction of numbers in the ship's company; a chance, too, to get rid of 'the one or two undesirables that we possess'. Scott hinted in his diary at grievances 'fanned and exaggerated by a minority'. He called for the names of those who preferred to sail back to New Zealand in the *Morning*.

'The result is curiously satisfactory,' he noted. 'I had decided to reduce our number by eight, and there are eight names on the list, and not only that, but these names are precisely those which I should have placed there had I undertaken the selection myself.'

His published references to the men who chose to return were considered 'a most unfair' reflection on one or two of those concerned who were in no sense malcontents. To the list he added Shackleton's name. 'He ought not to risk further hardships in his present state of health.'

Armitage, the second-in-command, allegedly disagreed, and resented the decision. Scott's private feelings may or may not have entered into it. In any case, he was supported by the two doctors. Wilson wrote in his diary that it was 'certainly wise for him to go home'. Koettlitz told Scott in writing: 'I cannot say that he would be fit to undergo hardships and exposure in this climate.' To replace Shackleton, Scott retained the services of the naval sub-lieutenant of the *Morning*, G. F. A. Mulock, a nephew of Alfred Austin, the Poet Laureate.

Lieut. Albert A. Armitage to Alfred Harmsworth: *

Discovery Antarctic Expedition 1901
Winter Quarters
77    $50\frac{1}{4}$ S.
166   42 E.
27th February 1903

... We proceeded east, along the Great Barrier. Passed its eastern extreme and discovered new land. Stopped by close pack, the formation of bay ice, and the lateness of the season (having to find good winter quarters), we turned in 76 $01\frac{1}{4}$ S, 152 $26\frac{1}{4}$ W, and proceeded to McMurdo Strait, now open. Steamed up to it to our present quarters on February 8th.

Scientific observations of all kinds have gone on during the year. The collections, especially the biological ones, are in many cases new to science, and most interesting.

One fatality occurred soon after arrival, when a party was away sledging.

A slight attack of scurvy attacked the ship's company, nothing serious, now eradicated.

Capt. Scott, with Dr Wilson and Lieut. Shackleton and 19 dogs, sledged to 82 17 S. over the Barrier. All the dogs succumbed. They discovered that Victoria Land extends south to at least 83 20 S., high and mountainous. They were absent 92 days.

Lieuts. Royds and Barne, and Dr Koettlitz with the other members of the scientific staff, have made very good sledge journeys.

Mr Skelton, R.N. and 10 men accompanied me on a 52 days' sledge journey to the interior of Victoria Land. Found a pass, at an altitude of 4000 feet, by a steep descent to a typical glacier, which lay 2000 feet below us. Tobogganed on loaded sledges for 900 feet.

Ascended the glacier between high, bare granite moun-

* Later Lord Northcliffe.

tains. Grand scenery! Gained the summit of the inland ice
cap, after ascending many crevassed ice slopes at an altitude
of 9000 feet. Had to camp half my party at 8000 feet, owing
to their difficulty in breathing at such an altitude, and to
the total collapse of one man, who was carried most of the
way home.

Skelton, 4 men, and I, pushed on to the summit, which we
found at 116 miles (geographical) west from the ship, which
lies 29 miles, west, from the main coast line. We were, then,
38 days out. Returned in 14 days.

The *Morning* arrived on the 23rd January, 1903. She
leaves on the 2nd March.

This is a hard season. We are ice-bound: water five miles
dist., season well advanced, so may have to stay another year.
I have not given up hopes of our freedom yet, however.

We are, all, very fit.

*

The relief ship *Morning* sailed for Lyttelton, New Zealand, that
port of hearty welcome for Antarctic navigators, on 2 March.
As her sails were hoisted, great chunks of frozen snow
thundered to the deck. Salvoes of cheers echoed over the floes
as she moved slowly out. Not until she was a distant speck did
the shore party turn to face the long hard walk back to the
Discovery, eight miles up the Sound. Lieutenant Evans, of the
Morning, remembered the little group of men, huddled like
castaways at the edge of the frozen sea. Scott stood in front of
them, waving. Shackleton wept.

'Mr E. H. Shackleton, who returns much to my regret, should
prove of the greatest use in explaining the details of our
position and our requirements for the future.' Scott was addressing a foolscap memorandum, dated 26 February 1903, jointly
to the Presidents of the Royal Society and the Royal Geographical Society, adding, as if it pleased him nostalgically, 'of
England', though it was not part of the official designation
of either. He 'earnestly begged' them to inform the Admiralty of
his hope that the Service prospects of those officers and men
of the Royal Navy who had chosen to stay on in the *Discovery*
'may in no manner suffer by their prolonged absence'.

He referred to the defective rations supplied by Messrs. ——.
'I do not think the Presidents can take any steps in this matter

but I hope on the return of the Expedition some compensation will be required for such a scandalous breach of faith.' He urged an amendment of the salaries of Hodgson, the marine biologist, and Wilson, whom he thought were 'both seriously underpaid'.

Years after, Armitage stated in print that Scott had proposed that he, too, should go home in the *Morning* on the ground that he would be united with his wife, who, it was understood, had objected to his joining the Expedition. Armitage believed that, *vis-à-vis* Scott, he was at a disadvantage as a Merchant Service officer, that Scott and Markham were jealous, above all, for the good name of the Royal Navy. Armitage did not know that Scott had received in the mail brought by the *Morning* information that led him to suppose that Armitage would welcome an opportunity of returning home for private and personal reasons, unconnected with his rank or status.

Scott's relief at getting rid of the eight volunteers, of whom six were merchant seamen, is fairly obvious from his diary. Markham noted in a letter of 24 April 1902, that is, after the *Morning* had begun her return voyage, that the *Discovery* company consisted of thirty-seven, 'of whom 30 are naval officers and men and 7 other British subjects,' namely, the scientists. He listed the names of the recalcitrants under the general heading of 'Idlers'.

As soon as the *Morning* reached the outposts of civilization again, her captain cabled news of the Expedition to London. The world heard of the great endurance feat of Scott, Wilson and Shackleton, and of the fine performance of the western party under Armitage, whose discovery of a practicable route into the interior of Victoria Land paved the way for Scott's next important journey, later in 1903.

Among the letters taken home by the *Morning* was one from Wilson to Scott's mother at 80 Royal Hospital Road, Chelsea. 'You will hear that I was privileged to accompany your son on his long sledge journey southwards—and during those three months we naturally saw a good deal of each other. I am sure he will bear me out in saying that although we got to know each other very well, we were better friends at the end of the journey even than before. He stood the journey better than either Shackleton or myself, indeed he seems as strong as any here, and fit for any amount of exertion and exposure.'

Scott wrote to his sister Ettie (Mrs Ellison Macartney) on 23 February 1903 telling her that they were 'perfectly resigned' to sticking it out for another winter, and that 'having got rid of some undesirable characters', he himself would have less to worry about. He assured her: 'On the whole, the time has been gorgeous, though there have been bad moments.' Shackleton, he explained, was leaving 'only on account of his health. He is an excellent chap.' If his sister was asked what presents to send out to them, he suggested that she should answer, '*pâté de fois gras*, caviar, anchovies, sweetmeats, liqueurs, and current literature of the higher class.'

The following day he wrote a letter of many pages to his mother. It is a revealing document in the annals of the Expedition of 1901–4, written three weeks after his return from the Southern Journey that gave him his title to inclusion in the roll of great explorers.

> For myself, I have enjoyed the whole thing amazingly, and have remained throughout in better physical condition than even I expected. I had expected the sledging to be hard work, but I confess I did not fully appreciate the strain it would bring and the test it must be of a man's constitution.
>
> Our own journey to the South was, of course, the severest, the distance travelled was the longest, the time longest, and our food allowance the least. For Wilson and myself, saddled as we were with an invalid for three weeks at the end, it was especially trying. After our return, Wilson was in bed for 10 days, but as to myself, after the first day or two, when the reaction set in and I felt a bit done, I was quite myself again. I hope this will banish from your mind all fears for my health or fitness to stand another winter.

He urged her not to take too seriously 'any rumours' that may have reached her about the incidence of scurvy among the shore party. They had all had 'a touch of it'. He did not doubt that it was the cause of Shackleton's breakdown. It was never a cause for alarm. He hoped that his mother would be consoled by knowing that his own symptoms were milder than those of others living in the same conditions and sharing the same food.

'I have gone on with this rather dull subject because I can see excellently intentioned persons gathering about you with gruesome tales and prognostications until you may be led to regard us as a number of sickly persons, imprisoned in great discomfort and desperately dreading the prospect of another winter.' That, he begged her to believe, was ludicrous. 'All the "crocks" I am sending away, and am much relieved to be rid of. Except Shackleton, who is a very good fellow and only fails from the constitutional point of view.' He proceeded to discuss the qualities of other members of the Expedition.

Royds has improved wonderfully. His bumptiousness has entirely vanished, and the really solid good nature of the man has come up to the top, for which I take to myself much credit. Michael Barne is always in the front rank in health and spirits. Nothing daunts him, nothing dispirits him, and the more work he gets the better he seems pleased. When we spent 36 hours together holding on to the corner of a tent in a temperature of minus 40 degrees, whilst his fingers were being badly frostbitten, he was quite in his most cheerful frame of mind.

Wilson is another splendid fellow. Our Southern trip naturally brought us very close together and as we got into some pretty tight places I know there is no bottom to his pluck and endurance.

Skelton is an all-round sportsman, just the man for this sort of work, which he thoroughly enjoys, always ready to do or to make anything. He is also something of an epicure and we have to thank him for dishes which we might very well have missed. For instance, there is a brown gull which visits us at this season called a skua. We regarded him somewhat askance as being a carrion bird, but Skelton boldly put him in the pot and now we appreciate a skua to about the same extent as anyone at home does a pheasant. Skelton also first introduced us to the sweetbreads of a seal—simply delicious.

He reverted to the Southern Journey with Wilson and Shackleton. 'We really had great times on that trip. For 95 days I never took off or put on a garment, except to change my foot gear at night. Your flag, my dear, has been to the farthest South!' The worst part of that business, he reflected, was the death of the dogs. 'I don't like to talk or think about them.' The tainted stock fish from Norway probably accounted for that disaster, and he seemed to think that Armitage had some responsibility in that matter. Armitage was 'an excellent chap but *entre nous* a little old for this work. It wants men with the fire and dash of Barne and Skelton', and he was led to consider the characteristics of others in the party.

Do you remember Hodgson?* He has turned out the most solid, sound old person imaginable. He is out and about all day long, winter or summer, and doesn't care a hang what happens next. We delight in him. Bernacchi is an awfully nice little chap too, full of quaint conceits and foibles, but also full of pluck and a hard worker.

Ferrar was a conceited young ass to begin with and it took quite a long time to bring him to his bearings. I sent him on some of the hard spring journeys in which he was worse than useless. This he had to have pointed out to him, so I did it very plainly, finally producing tears. Since that, he is a changed youth and I think would do most things for me. He was objectionable. He is now a nonentity and knows it, therefore in time he will be an acquisition to our little band.

So, my dear, taken altogether you can scarcely imagine a happier or more contented little company than ours. There is very rarely any friction and never a quarrel, and we are all far better friends than when we started even from New Zealand and that is saying a good deal after a polar winter.

CHAPTER EIGHT

THE ADMIRALTY EXPECTS

By 13 March 1903 Scott had 'abandoned all hope of the ice going out'. Facing the likelihood of the *Discovery* being held fast in McMurdo Sound for another year, he pondered in writing: 'I do not think that prospect troubles anyone very much. We are prepared to take things as they come, but one wonders what the future has in store for us.'

On the strength of the cables sent by Colbeck from New Zealand, Markham wrote to the President of the Royal Society: 'Most important scientific results have been attained. Captain

* Marine biologist.

Scott's dash from his last depot in 80° 20′ S. was superb. The zeal of Scott and his companions for science and for the credit of this country deserves admiration; and the Council of the Royal Geographical Society has resolved to record its full approval of Capt. Scott's proceedings and its confidence in his judgment.' Echoes of private satisfaction still ring out strong and clear from that pronouncement by the 'father of the Expedition'.

The reaffirmation of confidence in Scott was important, as there were Fellows of the other Society who questioned the need for him to stay another winter in the Antarctic. *The Times* commented on 27 March: 'It is evident from the report we published yesterday from the National Antarctic Expedition that Captain Scott, following a famous precedent in the Service to which he belongs, has turned a blind eye to his orders.'

An undated draft letter to a member of the Council of the Royal Geographical Society asks 'what justification Scott considers he has for disobeying the positive orders he received from you and Sir C. Markham to return'. The writer of the draft letter notes that Markham 'is highly pleased at what Scott proposes to do', and surmises that Scott's decision 'may be based on some understanding between him and Markham'. The draft letter goes on to state:

'I think possibly also that Scott's further work will be purely geographical discovery and will not make any addition to other scientific knowledge. If he comes home with all the *éclat* of a successful explorer it will be an ideal opportunity for us to endeavour to make him [here the word 'suffer' is crossed out] for disobeying orders. We must wait to hear from Colbeck exactly what are Scott's reasons for disobeying orders.'

Marking his letter 'Quite Private', Sir William Huggins, the astronomer, wrote to a Fellow of the Royal Society on 27 March: 'I suspected all along that Scott had secret instructions from Markham to remain a second year, notwithstanding official instructions to the contrary. Were not our instructions to Scott clear and definite that he was *not* to remain a second year unless unable to extricate himself from the ice?'

The Times pointed out that 'a large margin of discretion must be left to the leader of any expedition, scientific or military. It would mean leaving half the work undone, and

Captain Scott is not that sort of man. By next year we should know all that is worth knowing about this inhospitable region.'

Unaware of the fuss and bother, perhaps suspecting that there might be controversy, Scott recorded in his diary that 'our detention is due to exceptional conditions'. The ice was phenomenally late in breaking up. He asked himself: 'What does our imprisonment mean? ... For us, there must be the gravest possible questions. It is little wonder that I think of these things continually.'

Sir Clements Markham foresaw tragedy if the relief ship arrangement was not renewed. It raised again the awkward business of money and Government aid. Markham to the President of the Royal Society, 2 April 1903: 'Time is of the utmost moment. That the *Morning* should go South with relief in December '03 is a necessity, for the *Discovery* only has a year's provisions, and a terrible disaster might be the consequence. The report that the bulk of the English tinned provisions turned bad is a terrible warning. The culprits will, I believe, be found to be Messrs—'.

His pride in Scott's achievement may have seemed impetuous to some, for he added: 'I did not exaggerate the length of Scott's wonderful journey.' He had given the distance as 835 miles. Scott stated it to be 960 miles.

Markham wrote to the Secretary of the Royal Society on 24 April 1903: '*Discovery* has provisions that will only last till next January and unless the *Morning* brings her supplies there is a great danger of catastrophe.' He wrote to the President of the Royal Society on 28 April: 'If the *Morning* does not go out with relief next December, there will be a dreadful catastrophe.' He wrote to the Secretary again that same day: 'If relief is not sent there will be a terrible catastrophe. It is a matter of life or death.'

Those apprehensions would have seemed excessive to the men of the *Discovery*, who had no sense of impending calamity, while being well aware of the risks if the relief ship did not appear. Bernacchi, the physicist, said that they were 'never in danger'. In some ways, they were better off than in the previous year, for experience had taught them valuable things about food, for instance. They had laid in stores of fresh seal meat, and were fitter men in consequence.

Once more day was merged into night; once more the ship's

thermometers spelt fierce weather, with temperatures falling to 60 below. The boilers were run down again, steam pipes were lagged, ropes coiled away; anti-climax, after all the effort put into getting the *Discovery* ready to sail again, but no detriment to morale, Scott was pleased to record: 'We are entering upon our second winter in the highest spirits' (24 April 1903). Ship and hut were now brightly lit by acetylene lamps brought out by the *Morning*.

Hannah Scott to her son:

> Admiralty House,
> Sheerness.
> May 11th [1903]

My own dear Son,—You will be surprised to see the address on this letter, but Admiral* and Mrs Markham have most kindly asked Monsie† and me to spend a week with them, and as it is entirely for love of you that we get these pleasures I am delighted to begin my monthly letter here.

I have had congratulations on all sides and from all parts of Europe, not only from private friends. All the Polar men are so full of it, they alone understand the difficulties. Sir Clements has written me the most charming letter saying that he thinks it right to let Capt. Scott's mother know that you now take your rank in the very forefront of Polar explorers.

There was a meeting at the Royal Geographical Society and again lots of congratulations of your having changed the maps. I was made much of to my heart's content and all on your account. It is all very delightful to me and I am revelling in the sunshine of your success.

> Ever, dear, your most loving Mother,
> H. SCOTT

Markham wrote to the Secretary of the Royal Society about the need to start a new public fund. 'It is anxious work and it all falls on me, as it has done from the beginning.' He stirred up resounding trouble when, on his own initiative and probably with undiplomatic bluffness, he went to Treasury Chambers, Whitehall, to find out whether or not official help would be

---

* Admiral Sir Albert Markham was a cousin of Sir Clements Markham.
† Captain Scott's sister Grace.

forthcoming again, so as to ensure the continuance of the relief ship operation.

'That duty,' he pointed out in writing, 'has been recognized by all previous Governments and there is no precedent to the contrary. Indeed, it is a duty recognized by the whole civilized world.' In like circumstances, the Germans had granted £20,000, the Swedes £10,000. 'We ask £6,000 this year and £6,000 the next.'

On 14 May 1903 he was notified by the Treasury that nothing could be done. 'They denied the duty, repudiated the responsibility, refused all help.' Answering a question in the House of Commons, Balfour said that 'confidence has been rudely shaken'. The implication was that in their former transaction with the Government, which had led to the grant of £45,000, the two learned Societies had been less than frank about the costs of the Expedition.

It was a smarting rebuke. Blood pressures in those exclusive circles mounted when the next morning there came a *Daily Mail* onslaught on the financial management of the Expedition. The newspaper declared that money given by the Government and the public had been 'administered in such a foolish and unbusinesslike manner that funds have to be begged for in an emergency when these should have been ample for all purposes. More than this, as far as knowledge of what has been done is concerned, the public has really had nothing whatever for its money.' Included in the attack were adverse comments on the provisioning of the Expedition, with its sequel of dangerously deteriorated foodstuffs.

Ironically, Balfour's criticism provided the only opportunity Parliament had so far had of referring to the Expedition. Some thought it deplorable that he spoke no word of praise for Scott and his men wintering in the Antarctic.

Somers Cocks, the London banker who was Treasurer of the Royal Geographical Society, was wryly sensitive to the suggestion of financial inefficiency. 'It is only a misfortune to be a fool,' he wrote to an officer of the Royal Society. 'I have no wish to appear a knave as well. *Quam deus vult perdere,* etc.' Markham's handwriting showed agitation when he wrote on 24 May to the Secretary of the Royal Society: 'I am always made to feel that I am not trusted. I don't know why. Is anyone ready to give the time and trouble that I have done?'

He was the subject of a private comment made by Professor Poulton, F.R.S., the Oxford zoologist, in a letter of 12 June: 'We must all agree in regretting that we ever entered into common action with M', to which the Secretary replied that 'the Antarctic business has been a source of very considerable anxiety'. Referring to the published criticisms, the Lucasian Professor of Mathematics at Cambridge tangentially reported that 'one constantly hears gloomy forebodings as to the scientific work of the Expedition'.

That month the relief ship captain, William Colbeck, cabled for money to be sent to him in New Zealand, saying that he had been obliged to borrow and shortly would have to do so again. The Council of the Royal Geographical Society 'passed a strong resolution against our man having to borrow money out there for current expenses'. Markham considered it 'discreditable to both Societies' and wrote of Colbeck: 'He is young and there is no knowing what trouble he may get us and himself into by going about borrowing.'

Declining to bow the head to what he considered an inhuman decision, Sir Clements at first succeeded in rallying sufficient support behind the scenes to force the Government to think again. The Treasury intimated on 20 June that 'in view of the difficulties in which the Royal Society and the Royal Geographical Society find themselves, the Government would offer to take over the whole responsibility for the further relief expedition that has unfortunately been rendered necessary.' There was an unexpectedly strict proviso. 'The existing relief ship, the *Morning*, shall be handed over absolutely and at once to the Board of Admiralty, who will control the relief operations on behalf of the Government.'

Markham was deeply upset. The Treasury communication recognized the duty of 'providing for the safety of the officers and men of the R.N., but there is no mention of doing so for those who are not naval, including the scientific staff'. He wrote to Scott's mother: 'I shall make a hard fight for the ship single-handed, and for the Expedition, but single-handed, deserted, and beaten down, I must be overpowered at last.' As for the Treasury communication, he considered it 'a cold, heartless letter'.

Hannah Scott, writing to her son, reported that, having refused Markham's request for a grant of £12,000, the Government were going to spend £37,000 on sending out two relief ships. 'No one backs him up, and I am sorry to say he has been hasty and made enemies where he might have made friends. I regret it much on your account, for his loyalty to you and faith in you are beyond anything you can conceive. Were you his son, he could not consider your interests more.'

Putting his signature finally to the documents that transferred the *Morning* to the Admiralty was a painful business for Markham. 'Poor Sir Clements said I had made him sign his death warrant, so I feel rather sad,' the Treasurer of the Royal Geographical Society told the Secretary of the Royal Society. The Expedition secretary, Cyril Longhurst, expressed similarly strong feelings in a letter that reached Scott months later. 'He [Markham] has worked like a slave for the Expedition, and now he gets his ship, the *Morning*, stolen from him. . . .'

On 7 July 1903 the Admiralty addressed a communication to the joint Antarctic committee of the two Societies stating that even if funds permitted the continuance of the Expedition, the officers and men of the Royal Navy serving with it would not be allowed to remain. 'Directions will be sent to Captain Scott that if the *Discovery* cannot be freed from the ice in time to ensure her return to open water she is to be abandoned.'

On holiday in Norway, Sir Clements Markham wrote on 23 July 1903 to the Treasurer of the Royal Geographical Society: 'You must have had a most interesting cruise among the islands. It always makes me sad to think of those wretched French being at Tahiti. There is a narrow-minded, truculent person named Jack Sandars* who is private secretary to Mr Balfour, and has very undue influence. He is an outsider, not a Treasury clerk. He stupidly misunderstood a passage in the letter of application to the Government for help with the relief ship plan and interpreted it as meaning that the Societies always intended to provide a relief ship, and that they kept the fact from Mr Balfour, in order to deceive him as to the whole cost. He succeeded in poisoning Mr Balfour's mind, and hence the refusal. . . . Sandars went about saying "the Societies have behaved abominably". He was full of resentment and spite.'

Markham had provided £800 from his personal resources

*The Rt Hon. J. S. Sandars, P.C., barrister-at-law, is described in the documents as 'confidential secretary' to Balfour, 1892–1905.

to meet certain expenses. 'The Government refuses to pay me back on the ground that the liability was incurred before they took over the relief ship arrangements. I am quite worn out with worry and anxiety.' He declaimed against the 'brutal robbery' by which the Government had acquired the *Morning* without compensation. 'It has nearly driven me mad.'

Hannah Scott to her son:

Chelsea,

11th June [1903]

My own dear Son,—The long looked-for 'Antarctic Night' came off last night at the Royal Geographical Society, and it was most successful. I am quite in love with Sir Clements, for he guards your honour so well, every word of his lecture was to keep back as many matters of interest as possible so that *your* glory should not be shaded. He told us not a word of the wonderful sledge journey but said all should be left to you. Of course it was all of the most intense interest and I thoroughly enjoyed it. Kitty came up from Bath on purpose and we were all there. I felt very proud of my good-looking daughters.

I was much pleased with the high praise of Mr Scott Keltie.* He is a sound man and a word from him means a great deal. 'Are you not a proud woman?' was his greeting. He says what you have done has far and away surpassed anything they had expected, and really, when one sees the maps that Sir Clements has drawn out one realises more what great and enduring work has been accomplished. Sir Clements did not dwell much on the sufferings. He might have made a point or two by saying more about it, but I feel sure it is the work done and not your powers of endurance that *you* would wish to have set before the public.

Dear old Admiral Church called in the afternoon. He anticipates great honours for you, the speediest promotion, a K.C.B., and lots beside. I say I want you safe back, that will be my reward, to see you again and in good health.

The absolute confidence all these clever and learned people have in you is most delightful for me to see and I drink in all the praises with joy and thankfulness.

Mr Shackleton has been to see me and I have met him

* Secretary of the Royal Geographical Society.

several times. He is most interesting and is looking the picture of health. As Miss Dorman [Shackleton's fiancée] says, he looks as if he had gone out of the room and come in again.

I am sorry to say things are not going well. Sir Clements has fairly quarrelled with the Treasury and instead of granting the money required, the answer is that the Admiralty will send out the relief *ships* themselves. They have behaved *most* discourteously to Sir Clements and he, finding they are taking the whole thing into their own hands, has gone to Norway. I think he needs the change and rest badly. I am *so* sorry for him, after all the hard work and worry of years. I am filled with admiration of the way in which both he and Lady Markham have behaved, showing no littleness or meanness. The details of the fuss you will hear from Mr Shackleton, who has behaved like a gentleman all through; not so the Royal Society, who have acted like underbred schoolboys.

God bless you.

Ever your loving Mother,

H. SCOTT

*

Scott was taking daily walks out over the hills, a routine varied only by bad weather. He was keen to maintain his standard of physical well-being in readiness for the coming new sledging season. Usually on his daily outings he had four or five of the more trustworthy dogs with him, keeping them in a constant state of excitement by throwing stones for them to chase 'in a smother of snow'.

He came back from one of the walks feeling 'that there is not much hardship in this sort of life'. The northern horizon was 'dressed in red and gold, and lands about are pink and rosy with the brightness of returning day' (31 July 1903). Within a fortnight everyone was confined to the ship and hut again by the fury of a blizzard. 'Some gusts were so violent that the ship was shaken, notwithstanding that the ice must now be from eighteen to twenty feet thick around us.' Then on 21 August:

'For the first time for many a month the sun's direct rays were gilding our surrounding hills; little warm, pink clouds floated about, growing heavier towards the south, where the deepening shadow was overspread with a rich flush; the smoke of Erebus rose straight in a spreading golden column. It was indeed a goodly scene! One feels that the return of day is beyond all power of description—that splendid view from the hills leaves one with a sense of grandeur and solemnity which no words can paint' (*The Voyage of the 'Discovery'*).

Experience had brought him assurance and given him a steadier view: 'it is now a thing to be counted on,' he wrote on 21 August. He knew what it was like to be tested to the limits of will and strength and not to fail. He added to his diary note for that day: 'Life in these regions has lost any terrors that it ever possessed for us, for we know that, come what may, we can live and live well, for any reasonable number of years to come.' All their thoughts were turned to the work ahead. 'It would be difficult to be blind to the possible extent of its usefulness.' Colbeck, of the *Morning*, said that Scott told him he would 'try raising money in the Colonies' for a third year's work, if necessary.

He gave first place in his plans for the new season's activities to finding out more about the polar ice cap. Various supplementary sledge journeys were to be made, one to the Ferrar Glacier in the West, for geological observations, another to the Emperor penguin colony at Cape Crozier, in which there was biological as well as zoological interest.

Having made his dispositions known, he wrote on 6 September 1903: 'The ship is in a state of bustle, people flying to and fro, packing sledges, weighing loads, and inspecting each detail of equipment. To judge by the laughter and excitement, we might be boys escaping from school.'

The crowning accomplishment of the new season's work was Scott's western journey, started on 12 October. He was prouder of it than of the notable southern journey. Its purpose was to extend knowledge of the polar plateau. He completed it in the company of Petty Officer Edgar Evans, R.N., and Leading Stoker William Lashley, R.N., whose names were to be linked historically with his in the greater polar enterprise of the years ahead. Climbing to 9,000 feet by way of the Ferrar Glacier, they marched, rested, and slept in temperatures varying from minus 25 degrees to minus 44 degrees.

Not only did misfortune compel them to retrace their first ninety miles back to the hut camp for sledge-runner repairs. Nearing the highest altitudes of the mountains along the coast of South Victoria Land, they lost their *Hints to Travellers*, the Royal Geographical Society's invaluable handbook containing logarithmic tables indispensable to navigation. It meant that, as Scott recorded, they were faced with the alternatives of returning to the ship, by then a longer journey than before, or 'the risk of marching away into the unknown without exactly knowing where we were or how to get back'. They held counsel and decided to go forward, giving the leader 'many a bad half hour'.

He wrote on 11 November: 'It is impossible to describe how awful the past week has been; it is a "nightmare" to remember .... Within a hundred yards of the camp we as nearly as possible walked into an enormous chasm; and when we started to ascend the slope we crossed any number of crevasses without waiting to see if the snow bridges would bear. I really believe we were in a state when we none of us really cared much what happened.' Temporarily losing the use of both hands from frostbite, he recorded more privations on 26 November, as they advanced through what he afterwards referred to as the most desolate, barren, and piercingly cold region on earth.

'The wind is the plague of our lives. It has cut us to pieces. We all have deep cracks in our nostrils and cheeks, and our lips are broken and raw; our fingers are also getting in a shocking state; one of Evans's thumbs has a deep cut on either side of the nail which might have been made by a heavy slash with a knife. We try to keep our faces as still as possible; laughing is a really painful process, and so from this point of view jokes are not to be encouraged.'

Evans, long in the arm and with a fine muscular development, had been a Royal Navy gymnastics instructor. 'He weighed 12 st. 10 lb. in hard condition.' Lashly, to Scott, 'the most deceptive man I have ever seen', had one of the largest chest measurements in the Expedition. 'He had been a teetotaller and non-smoker all his life, and was never in anything but the hardest condition.' Aware of his own lesser weight, Scott considered whether he could fairly accept the same food allowance. Appetite supplied the answer.

'With these two men behind me,' he wrote, 'our sledge seemed to become a living thing. We took the rough and smooth alike, working patiently on through the long hours with scarce a word and never a halt between meal and meal.' Evans and Lashly toiled behind their leader in the sledge traces. At night, all three shared the same sleeping-bag.

Scott said that in those weeks he learnt more about lower-deck life in the Royal Navy than in his years as a serving officer. Neither of the other two had his scientific curiosity. It is easy and probably not inaccurate to suppose that there were days when they were silently irritated by his painstaking attention to aneroid readings, rock geology, cloud formations, and geographical problems.

Pushing on up over the lofty polar plateau, they traversed two hundred miles of desolation. 'Before us lay the unknown. What fascination there is in that word!' It drove them forward, 'no matter how comfortless the outlook'. The *sastrugi*, a corrugated surface of frozen snow, made the going very difficult. 'It shakes us up dreadfully; falls are constant, and the harness frequently brings us up with a heavy jerk, exasperating to a tired man.' The rarified air of the 'terrible plateau' reduced their staying power. Often gasping for breath, they marched endlessly on.

The crux came on 30 November 1903 at 77° 59′ S. Knowing only that they were 'a long way to the west', Scott turned back in a far from cheerful frame of mind. 'The scene about us is the same as we have seen for many a day, and shall see for many a day to come—a scene so wildly and awfully desolate that it cannot fail to impress one with gloomy thoughts.'

The *sastrugi* got on his nerves (he said so). Its ridges at their worst were barbed like hooks, and fancy suggested to him that there was a particular menace in them for the returning marchers. The melancholy-mystical mood gripped him so powerfully as he entered up his diary that night that one would not be surprised to find him revising his earlier assertion that life in those regions had lost its terrors.

'We know that beyond the horizon are hundreds and even thousands of miles which can offer no change to the weary eye, while on the vast expanse that one's mind conceives one knows there is neither tree, nor shrub, nor any living thing, nor even inanimate rock—nothing but this terrible limitless expanse of snow. It has been here for countless years, and it will be so for countless more. And we, little human insects, have started to crawl over this awful desert, and are now bent on crawling back again. Could anything be more terrible than this silent, windswept immensity when one thinks such thoughts?'

*

Adversity quickly caught up with them on the return journey, begun on 1 December 1903. The biting winds now blew from behind instead of in their faces, but for that relief there were other penalties to be paid. Their sledge capsized frequently on the rougher surfaces, and the three men 'sprawled in all directions'. They fell so often that Scott feared for their limbs; the prospect of a broken leg or a dislocated shoulder in their circumstances was to be shuddered at. Camping for rest from the repeated stresses of the march, he wrote: 'I don't like the look of things at all.'

As the navigator, he had to tell his companions on 9 December: 'We are in a pretty tight place', travelling by guess and by God. 'The sense of uncertainty is oppressive. One cannot help all sorts of doubts creeping in when the consequences are so serious.'

Three days later they were still in a state of 'horrible uncertainty'. He wrote that 'it is uncanny work, for I haven't any notion where we are'. There was a night when the snow drift was so heavy that at any moment 'we might have been walking over the edge of a precipice'.

What was noted as the most adventurous day of their lives came on 14 December 1903. Travelling due east, they reached a hard surface that was cracked in all directions. There was no clear route by which it could be avoided. Scott asked the other two whether they were ready to take the risk of going forward. 'They answered promptly in the affirmative. I think that after our trying experiences we are all feeling pretty reckless.'

Soon they were moving through a tortuous region of ice hummocks and yawning crevasses. Its angle of incline was steeper than they realized and the loaded sledge outran them. When suddenly, Lashly fell, he skidded forward on his back, struggling unavailingly to regain his balance and dragging Evans and the sledge after him. Scott, in front, tried to intercept them as they hurtled past. He was swept off his feet and followed the other two in their headlong slide before being able to check the velocity of their descent.

'I staggered to my feet in a dazed fashion,' he wrote in his notes of the day, 'wondering what had happened.' Their legs were black with bruises. 'Are you hurt, sir?' the other two had asked, crawling painfully towards him.

Having rested from the severe shaking, they were gladdened

beyond measure by the sight of a distant landmark, and started off briskly in harness again, Scott leading by a few feet ahead of the others. To check the sledge's tendency to skid, he told Lashly to pull wider. A moment later Scott and Evans vanished down a crevasse, with Lashly holding back on his trace with all his might to prevent his weight from being overcome by theirs.

Scott dangled from the end of his trace 'between blue walls on either side and a very horrid-looking gulf below'. Above him, Evans was likewise hanging in space.

Waves of icy air enclosed them, chilling their faces to the bone. Scott did not expect to get to the top. He had to call on his last ounce of energy to reach it. As Lashly pulled him over the edge of the crevasse, he flung himself on the snow, breathing desperately. 'My word, sir, but it was a close call!' Evans exclaimed more than once, reviewing the perils of the day.

*

A demolition party under Armitage had been at work for a fortnight trying to shatter the ice that held the *Discovery* in its grip. Sawing-out, by pulley-and-tackle work with eighteen-foot saws, was supplemented by explosive charges. Neither method was effective. The saw cuts quickly froze over. The explosions produced cracks but not release.

One is perhaps ingenuously amused at this distance in time to find Scott, newly returned to the ship after his exacting journey, apologizing in a letter sent to Armitage at the sawing-out camp, eleven miles over the sea ice, for his inability to lend a hand owing to 'a bad attack of indigestion'.

When on 2 January 1904 he visited the camp he was astonished (his word) at the small result of twelve days' hard labour on ice six feet thick. He called off the operation, which he had himself initiated in written orders issued before he set out westward. He indicated in a diary note that some had recognized it as futile from the start but they loyally carried out his instructions.

On the 'gloriously fine' morning of 5 January, he chanced to be 'gazing dreamily' at a patch of open blue sea beyond the distant ice-edge when a ship came into view. Moments later a second ship appeared in the same frame of vision. The relief ship *Morning* (Captain Colbeck) had arrived in company with the *Terra Nova* (Captain McKay) on Admiralty orders.

Scott had none of the sensations of happy release. His diary note says: 'In spite of the good home news, and in spite of the pleasure of seeing old friends again, I was happier last night than I am tonight.' Such was the dispiriting effect of the Admiralty instructions handed to him that day by Captain McKay, namely, that if the *Discovery* could not at once proceed northward to New Zealand with the two other ships, she was to be abandoned.

'The ties which bound us to the *Discovery*,' he wrote, 'were very far beyond the ordinary; they involved a depth of sentiment which cannot be surprising when it is remembered what we have been through in her.' She was, after all, the finest polar expedition ship that was ever sent to sea. 'It was a little trying to be offered relief to an extent which seemed to suggest that we had been reduced to dire need.'

There was 'stony silence' when the ship's company assembled on the main deck to hear Scott read out the Admiralty decree. He had all the doors locked, to ensure that there would be no intrusion by the relief ships' crews. He then explained the situation to his officers and men, his eyes filling with tears as he spoke of the bond forged between them as members of his Expedition. Armitage said that there was not a man who did not resent the order from London. All felt it unnecessary and humiliating.

The presence of the large whaling ship *Terra Nova* confirmed the official view that the *Morning* might not by herself be a guarantee of the safe return of the naval officers from the *Discovery*'s winter quarters. Bought and refitted at a cost of £20,000, the *Terra Nova* had been hurried out with the help of relays of cruisers that towed her at high speed through the Mediterranean and the Suez Canal *en route* for New Zealand. 'What a "to do" about a handful of men and a small ship, known to be comfortably and safely ensconced in McMurdo Sound!' (Bernacchi)

At home, Sir Clements Markham denounced the enterprise as a waste of public money, 'though it will make some more sailors—fast dying out'. As a serving officer, Scott could only endorse that opinion privately, which he did in a letter to a naval colleague in Cape Town.

Scott to his mother:

My own dearest Mother,— ... The news brought by the relief ships spread some consternation and put me in a difficult position as regards all that has happened at home, the money troubles, etc. Letters received give a good idea of how it came about. I regret the money spent very much, but can't hold myself responsible. From our point of view, however, there was a most annoying circumstance and that was the suggestion that runs through all the official correspondence that our relief was a matter of immediate pressing urgency and our position most grave.

I fear there is no doubt that our dear old friend, Sir C. M., started this. It was he who first adopted the note of 'brave fellows in distress'. Of course the reason is obvious and does him honour, but from our point of view it was extremely annoying.

No one here ever felt or suggested that we were in danger, and as far as I know, all tried to represent the position faithfully.

In face of this, when one is feeling perfectly comfortable and contented, quite prepared to take things as they come, it is not surprising that one feels some chagrin at being suddenly and overwhelmingly 'saved'.

The whole thing has been rather hysterical. Well, never mind, all things considered we have had a good time and I for one shall never regret the second winter. I was really pleased with the spring sledging. From the spirit with which everyone entered on it, it was plain they meant to go, and they went. I don't think better marching has ever been done before.

Goodbye, dearest. We are all in splendid health and, after our necessary repairs, looking forward to starting on the homeward voyage. Of course I won't desert the ship even if it loses me a year's promotion.

Your loving son,
CON

*

Among other documents brought out to Scott by the *Terra Nova* was a long memorandum of commendation and advice from the Royal Geographical Society. It acknowledged, with the Council's 'warm approval', the work that had been done by the Expedition and praised 'the skill and judgement' shown by Scott in his various arrangements. Paragraph 5 dealt with 'the loss of poor George Vince. . . . He had no near relations but his cousin, who has been communicated with. We hope a monument has been erected to his memory. We deeply regret that this sad accident should have cast a gloom on an Expedition which, in all other respects, has been so prosperous.'

Referring to the explorations, the memorandum took note of 'your own memorable journey with your two companions, Shackleton and Wilson, which, when all the special and peculiar obstacles are considered, takes its place in the first rank of polar achievements.' It was pointed out that in all polar expeditions of the previous three decades or more, dogs were the chief means of transport. 'Your gallant fellows have achieved their excellent results mainly without the aid of dogs: by sheer hard work, by a strong sense of duty, and by the indomitable pluck which has ever characterized the British sailor.'

Financial caution was urged on Scott in paragraph 16. 'The balance of the *Discovery* fund is only sufficient to pay the salaries and wages until October 1904. It is necessary, therefore, that you should exercise all possible economy with regard to your further expenditure.' His request that the salaries of Wilson and Hodgson should be increased by £50 a year was granted.

As for the future of the Expedition ship, 'if human forethought, skill, energy, and perseverance can free the *Discovery* from her icy prison, we are convinced that this great object will be achieved. If not, she will remain a monument of a memorable Expedition.' The Council trusted that she would not be left derelict, and that Scott would at least see to it that she was made secure at her mooring place.

There being no sign of the ice yielding, a start was made at sledging instruments, registers, scientific collections, and other records, from the *Discovery* to the two relief vessels. Scott noted at the time that 'not a laugh was heard' among the men. Throughout January 1904 the *Discovery* was shut off from open water by seventeen miles of ice at least six feet thick. He wrote to his cousin, Lieutenant 'Bertie' Scott, R.N. on 30 January:

'It is touch and go whether we get out. The chances are in favour of our *not* doing so. In consequence, I feel extremely bad tempered and impatient with fortune. For if we have to leave the ship it will be damnable luck. We should all be very cheerful if it weren't for this infernal imprisonment.'

Then, in the first week of February 1904, signs of the break-up appeared. Blasting parties were at once formed from all three crews. Their detonations reinforced the 'awful unseen agency' of the ocean swell that, originating in the Ross Sea, was at last 'rending the great ice sheet as though it had been naught but the thinnest paper' (Scott).

A final 67 lb. charge of gun cotton shook the *Discovery* from stem to stern and set her free. The event was celebrated by wave after wave of cheering and subsequent 'wild revelry' of a kind that Scott, the disciplinarian, agreed could 'be excused on such a night'. By 16 February 1904 all three ships were ready to leave the Antarctic.

Ten minutes after getting under way for the first time in two years, the *Discovery* was grounded in three fathoms by a gale that blew up so suddenly as to seem like the deliberate malice of fate. Scott wrote on 17 February: 'We have had a day and no mistake; I hope I may never have such another.' The ship had been spun round like a top and brought crashing on to a shoal that stopped her dead, with masts quivering. 'The hours that followed,' Scott wrote, 'were the most dreadful I have ever spent.' Towering above them, within a stone's throw, was the rocky promontory of Hut Point. Predictably, pensively, he wrote in his diary: 'On its summit and clearly outlined against the sky, stood the cross which we had erected to our shipmate.' *

The force of the storm was such that 'each time the ship descended with a sickening thud into her rocky bed the beams and decks buckled upwards to such an extent that several of our thick glass deadlights were cracked, every timber creaked and groaned, doors flew to and fro, crockery rattled, and every loose article was thrown into some new position. With the heavier blows one could see the whole ship temporarily distorted in shape; through all and directly beneath one's feet could be heard the horrible crunching and grinding of the keel on the stones below.' †

Noting those horrendous details, Scott observed also the effect of the crisis on the men around him. 'Some sat in stony

* Able Seaman G. Vince, R.N. † *The Voyage of the 'Discovery'*.

silence below, some wandered about aimlessly, and some went steadily on with an ordinary task as though nothing had happened.' He was amused by his recollection of a steward 'dusting and sweeping out the wardroom and polishing up the silver'. His own feelings were ravaged by thoughts of disaster. 'I tasted something very near akin to despair.' Dinner on the night of 17 February was 'a dreary meal, the dreariest and most silent I ever remember in the *Discovery*'.

Half-way through it, Mulock burst in with the news that the ship was working astern. Scott said that he never reached the bridge in less time. Wind and sea had dropped in 'the most extraordinary manner'. The current, which had been running strongly to the north, was now running as strongly to the south. He could not 'but regard it as little short of a miracle' that he was able to go to his bunk 'free from anxiety at the end of this horrid day'. Soon the *Discovery* was riding the seas again, sailing proudly homeward with her tidings of one of the greatest polar voyages on which men ever ventured.

Hannah Scott to her son:

> 80 Royal Hospital Road,
> Chelsea, S.W.
>
> [Undated]

My own dear Con,— ... I have had a letter from Mr Royds. He tells me of the dreadful time you had on board when the ship was aground. He says it made you look ten years older.

I am so *proud* that you know our love is so great that I do not need the fact of long letters to tell me so.

We are now full of excitement about next Monday when the Patron's Medal is to be presented and I am to receive it for you. As I have no wish to rival Mrs Baden-Powell, I have asked Willy [her son-in-law, W. Ellison Macartney, M.P.] to go to the platform and bring it to me, which I think is more dignified than going myself.

What an extraordinary conquest you have made of Mr Royds! The high praise he gives you in his letter to me is followed by the same or more to Sir Clements, and Mr Ferrar also is full of good expressions of your power and fitness for the work, saying 'no one could have been so good a leader'. This was in a letter to Sir Clements I read this morning. I really think I am so proud of you that I am almost beside myself. I do feel a very proud woman and I am not ashamed of it.

Just had a postcard from Aunt E. saying you had written to her. How *very* good of you. I am most grateful. She gets so little joy in her life and nothing could have given her greater pleasure.

The girls hope to write to you by this mail but they are very busy—2 Court dresses and lots of other things, though it is really a bad season and no money going.

Dear me, dear me! I cannot write for very happiness and I think I must finish, not being able to remember anything more of interest just now. Dear Mrs McLaughlin expresses her wish to be present at the giving of the Gold Medal on Monday next. She is as pleased as if you were her son. And how proud I am not of that alone but of you, my son, your character, your goodness, and of you, your very own self, apart from your success.

My dearest, God bless you, and thank you a thousand times for your dear letter,

Ever, dear, your most loving Mother,
H. SCOTT

*

They arrived off the Heads of Lyttelton Harbour at daybreak on Good Friday 1904. 'Each of us felt that we were returning to what was very nearly our home' (Scott). First to welcome them, after the port officers, was Dr Wilson's wife, who wrote off at once to Scott's mother: 'It was such a joy to hear that the ships had been sighted. I was asleep when the news came and have never dressed so quickly. My sister and I are staying in a country place and had four miles to walk over the hills before we could get to Lyttelton Harbour, but we were the first ladies there.' She wanted Mrs Scott to know how happy and well Scott appeared to be. 'It is extraordinary how little they have changed. I expected them to look older and thinner and lined, but nearly all of them are decidedly fatter.'

As on the outward voyage, the men of the Expedition were overwhelmed by the local hospitality, for the numerous private manifestations of which Scott was specially grateful, preferring them to the public functions. In effect, he was given the freedom of New Zealand, the extent to which he was fêted making him apprehensive about what might be awaiting him at home. 'I can't look forward with any pleasure to that sort of thing.' He wrote to his mother on 7 June 1904:

'We have had a very good time here, but it is high time we were off, as all our young men are getting engaged. Skelton is actually caught. I believe the young lady is very nice. X has made a fool of himself and is more or less engaged to a very young lady who is not at all desirable. However, there is nothing definite and I hope that getting home will put things straight again. Meanwhile, it is just as well not to mention it to his mother.' He hoped that 'all the squabbles at home' had died away. 'I shall be glad now to be quit of the whole business, which from a financial point of view has been a great worry.'

Edward A. Wilson to Scott's mother:

> Bishopscourt,
> Wellington.

My dear Mrs Scott,— . . . How happily everything has turned out after all! We feel as though the whole thing has been a great success, and I am quite certain that every soul on board agrees that the success is due wholly and solely to the splendid way in which your son has acted towards us all as our leader, from start to finish. Without a doubt he has been the making of the Expedition, and not one of us but will feel more and more grateful to him for the way he has acted throughout.

Notwithstanding that it is a difficult thing, at least I imagine it is, for the Captain to make intimate friends with anyone, I feel as though we were real friends, and I need hardly say I am proud of it.

I am glad indeed for your sake, and for my wife's and parents' sake, and for everybody's, that the thing is so nearly finished. We have had a most interesting experience, but to you it has been a very trying time. May you never be quite so completely cut off from your son again!

> Believe me, Yours very sincerely,
> EDWARD A. WILSON

At sea again, with fifteen hundred miles between them and the next place of call, the Falkland Islands, Scott pondered his chances of promotion to post-captain in the light of his lost sea time as a naval officer. 'My future is dependent on the Admiralty.' The question he put to his mother was: 'How are we going to live when I get back to London?' Unless the rooms at Royal Hospital Road could provide him with a study in which to settle down to the task of writing his book about the Expedition, it might be necessary for them to take another house. 'Is the shoproom I had before vacant? It would suffice.'

He thought they could afford more than the £80 a year they were paying. 'I think we should be justified in going to £120 or £130.' He expected to find 'a good sum' to his credit when he returned, as a result of his long absence. 'I have no intention of saving it.' He asked his mother to 'proceed to look round for the required place and carry on making arrangements to get it'. He knew well, he wrote, what great anxieties she had had on his account. 'I feel that your trials have been infinitely heavier than mine. However, they are pretty well over now, thank goodness, and the future ought to reward you for the past.'

My dear Mrs Scott — . . . How happy everything has turned out after all. We feel as though the whole thing has been a great success, and I am quite certain that every soul on board agrees that the . . . was wholly and solely to the splendid way in which Scott . . . acted towards us all, our leader . . . [? he had] . . . been the making of the Expedition, and not only of

CHAPTER NINE

INTERLUDE AT BALMORAL

THERE was a sense in which Scott, returning home in the early autumn of 1904, reaped some of the goodwill already sown by another British explorer, Colonel (later Sir) Francis Younghusband, whose expedition to Tibet was a news event of the year. When Scott sailed for the Antarctic in 1901, the war in South Africa was disturbing the national conscience, and exploration, however spectacular, was an affair of passing interest.

Now, three years after, with peace honourably secured, there was eager response to any enterprise that renewed the people's self-esteem. Younghusband in the Forbidden City, Scott on the mysterious Polar plateau, were reaffirmations of a spirit that linked them again with their heroic past, compared with which fighting the Boers seemed but a shabby historical interlude.

The *Discovery*'s welcome home began when she entered Stokes Bay, between Southsea and the Isle of Wight, at 11 a.m. on 10 September 1904. In beautiful autumn weather, she was met and surrounded by a host of yachts, naval pinnaces, rowing boats, making a mass of shimmering reflections in the millpond water.

Southsea beach was a grandstand packed with sightseers. As the now famous ship steamed gently through the narrow opening of Portsmouth harbour, the men and boys of Nelson's *Victory*, the signal ship *Hercules*, the Admiralty yacht *Enchantresss*, and H.M. ships *St Vincent*, *Narcissus*, and *Iris*, manned ship, their cheers ringing out over the scene.

In the functions that followed, much was said about perils and privations. Evidence of them was no longer apparent. True, the explorers' faces were like tanned leather, but every man had put on weight. It was noticed that they moved deliberately, as if still encumbered by heavy Polar clothing.

The world was told through the news agencies that Scott had returned to England with more varied and valuable scientific information than had ever before been collected in the Antarctic regions. 'True to his instructions,' said *The Times*, 'he has done what he set out to do, and even more.'

He was hailed as the discoverer of the new domain known as King Edward VII Land, and of the great Victorian mountain range. He was the first man to explore and survey the surface of the Great Ice Barrier and to report the many glaciers descending upon it. He discovered the Polar ice cap. His observations led to the fixing of the South Magnetic Pole. He and his men made twenty-eight organized sledge journeys, all with scientific objectives. They filled in the empty white space of the Antarctic maps with a long and continuous stretch of the coast of the supposed continent. Important researches were carried out in marine biology, glaciology, and terrestrial magnetism.

'Never,' declared old Sir Clements Markham, with pride in his voice, 'has any Polar expedition returned with so great a harvest of results. As a diligent student of Polar voyages, I say this deliberately and with knowledge.' His top-table pronouncement at a Royal Geographical Society banquet received echoing applause.

Newspaper acclaim made Scott a popular hero. The publicity worried him. He had no taste for it and naval tradition discouraged personal aggrandisement. France made him an officer of the Legion of Honour. Gold medals were bestowed on him by the geographical societies of several nations. Presenting him with one of them, the American ambassador in

London, Whitelaw Reid, expressed the wish that Scott would be allowed to continue his Antarctic researches, leaving Commander Peary, the ambassador's compatriot, to conquer the North Pole. 'Thus the two ends of this great world would meet, as it were, in the warm and fraternal embrace of the Anglo-Saxon race.'

Scott was made a Commander of the Victorian Order by the King (a step up from being a Member), and honoured by Cambridge University. The Royal Yacht Squadron elected him honorary member No. 3079. Always, in his public acknowledgements, he divested himself of any claim to conspicuous personal recognition. What the Expedition had achieved, he reiterated often, was to the credit of no one man. Wilson's natural history studies and scenic paintings, Hodgson's work on plankton, Royds's meteorological observation, the geological findings of Ferrar and Koettlitz, Bernacchi's magnetic records, were typical: all had given of their best. Pointedly, and with equal sincerity, he assured the learned Societies that much of the best work was done during the Expedition's controversial second year in the Antarctic.

Submitting his report to the Admiralty, he mentioned that 'some embarrassments' had been caused by the elaborate relief arrangements, 'as our small company were so thoroughly able to take care of themselves'. He proposed to make the services of individual naval members of the Expedition more fully known to Their Lordships. It was a self-affacing document that gained the immediate approval of the First Sea Lord, who circulated it to his colleagues with a personal commendation of Scott's modesty.

His promotion to captain's rank from the day of arrival at Portsmouth was a more solid satisfaction than the formal tributes. It meant a rise in pay to £410 12s. 6d. a year, plus allowances (for example, command money, 18s. a day, when in command of a sea-going battleship).

During his time in the Antarctic, he had been able to save money. His first thought now was to make up his mother's allowance to £200 a year. He also settled her and his two sisters in a rented house, 56 Oakley Street, Chelsea Embankment. As a rare personal indulgence, he went to 'a first-class tailor to be provided with a first-class suit', a gesture of release from the penury that he had so long endured.

A letter from Shackleton (3 September 1904) welcomed him home after the 'long anxious time', and expressed pleasure that 'the whole show was such a complete success'. Shackleton, newly married, had taken the post of secretary to the Royal Scottish Geographical Society, in Edinburgh. 'The pay is only £200 a year, but it is better than going to sea and I had a long time at home to wait before I could get anything.' He told Scott that he had thought of 'trying to go on another expedition some time'. He had given up the idea, 'as there seems to be no money about'. Having settled down, he had to make money. 'It would only break up my life, if I could stand it, which Wilson thinks I could not.' He hoped, he wrote, that Scott would 'do the North West Passage some time'. Though he himself had been 'so long apart from the show', his heart, he assured Scott, 'had ever been turned South'.

*

'I have no wish to advertise myself.' Scott was writing to the First Sea Lord on 21 September 1904 asking for six months' leave 'to undertake a narrative of our voyage, to be published in the spring'. He was also preparing a lecture on the Expedition to be delivered to a distinguished gathering at the Royal Albert Hall in November.

'I should be very sorry to do anything that the Admiralty thought unbecoming to a naval officer. Except in this matter I have mentioned, I am trying to keep as quiet as possible.'

His appeal was phrased in the best tradition of the Service and could hardly have failed of its purpose, though the First Sea Lord hoped for the sake of Scott's naval career that the period would be limited to the six months applied for. Events obliged him to ask for an extension. His Royal Albert Hall lecture on 7 November 1904, given before 7,000 members and guests of the Royal Geographical Society, cost him the previous night's sleep and some concern afterwards when he realized that he had sat down without paying his intended tribute to Armitage, his second-in-command of the Expedition, and other colleagues.

The lecture was extensively reported in the newspapers and brought him invitations from many parts of the country. He went on a hurriedly arranged provincial tour largely as a patriotic duty. As he was on half-pay, expenses had to be considered. Stepping down from a third-class carriage at a Midland railway station and seeing a waiting crowd, he asked a porter who was expected. 'It's the Mayor and Corporation come to meet Captain Scott,' was the reply.

The *Manchester Guardian* suggested that he was the 'fastest speaking' lecturer who had ever addressed an audience in that city; 'but all his words stood out clearly'. He stirred the people with his vivid, unadorned narration of hazards, hardships, and achievements; made them laugh when he ran his hand through his hair in mock despair because lantern slides came up on the screen too early or too late; delighted them with his trick of understatement. Accidents in which men were hauled out of fearful crevasses were 'very unpleasant'. Blizzards that kept him and his companions prisoners in a tent for days on end were 'most annoying'.

Scott to his Mother:

> Tranby Croft,
> Hull.
> November 20th, 1904.

My dearest Mother,—I wrote you last from the Station Hotel, Newcastle. In the afternoon I got across to Middlesbrough, almost luckily in the dark as it is a most distressingly gloomy place. The streets are narrow and the shops wretched. It seems a town of artisan dwellings and there isn't a good hotel in it.

I went to the Grand and set off for the Town Hall after an apology for a dinner. The Hall is a big fine building and the audience excellent. Early yesterday I came over here. My lecture alas! was given to a largely empty hall, the first bad audience I have addressed, and to add to the difficulty the small audience was terribly cold.

I don't know what had gone wrong, but I think one of the reasons was the price of seats—7/6d. It was too high. Anyway, I felt pretty angry and should have cut things very short but for consideration of my own party. Somehow now I know it's not the fault of the lecture. People come up to me again and again to say that it is the most interesting lecture they have heard and so forth. In spite of this, however, I am bound to confess that last night was frigid.

> Your affect. Son,
> ROBT. F. SCOTT

At Edinburgh, his lecture in a hall filled with 2,300 people was followed by 'a really big ovation'. In spite of it, he said that he 'never really felt that they were in sympathy'. He was presented on that occasion with the Livingstone gold medal, 'a really handsome thing', which he sent off to his mother by registered post the next day.

Lecturing made him a social being in a way that was denied to him as a naval officer. It opened doors for him in great houses. It brought him a mass of new acquaintance, giving him a wider view of the lives of his fellow countrymen than was possible through a telescope.

In London, he was meeting writers, publishers, artists, actors, politicians. Conspicuous among his new found friends were J. M. Barrie and A. E. W. Mason, whose fame as men of letters stimulated his wish to win distinction in that *milieu*. He was writing much of his book on the Expedition in railway trains and hotel bedrooms.

The publisher, Reginald Smith, K.C., principal of Smith, Elder & Co., 15 Waterloo Place, London, S.W., and editor of the *Cornhill Magazine*, remembered the day when Scott and Wilson called at his office to discuss illustrations. 'The question of the frontispiece of the first volume came up. It was proposed to give a photograph of the Southern sledge party led by Scott himself. Scott regarded it thoughtfully; then, looking up, said at first tentatively, then with emphasis: "What do you think, Bill? I don't think it ought to be there. The Southern party wasn't any more than any other sledging party. No, we won't have it." And it was thrown out to take a more modest place in the text.'

For Scott, writing the book was 'a treadmill task'. Apparently he was discouraged at finding that it involved a different order of literary labour from keeping the diaries on which it is based. He took each newly finished chapter to the publisher with the gloomiest doubts of its worth.

His despondency at times was such that Reginald Smith felt impelled to write one enheartening note after another: 'I feel no qualms about the book if it goes on telling its story in this clear and simple fashion.' 'I have just been reading your sledging chapters with delight and indeed emotion.' 'I can almost hear you speaking as you write.'

A critical point was reached at which he packed his manuscript and hurriedly went into retreat at The Burlington, Sheringham, Norfolk, determined to finish a task of which he wrote: 'I am very tired of it but I plod along.' He told his mother: 'This place suits me A1. It's really very cheap here, although my sitting-room comes heavy at £2 a week. My board is only £2 a week, which is extraordinarily little for the extreme comfort I enjoy' (3 May 1905). Three days later, he wrote to her: 'I send you a cheque for £60 for Maples and other expenses. I only wish you wouldn't trouble to be "dreadfully sorry", as you say, over matters of this sort.'

The two-volume work, with its 260 illustrations, among them many fine photographs taken by Shackleton and Skelton, with colour reproductions of Wilson's watercolours, was published (price two guineas) in the autumn of 1905, bringing Scott new laurels which for once he could not disclaim. The 'want of literary experience' for which he apologized in the preface was discounted by many fine descriptive passages and by the broad narrative sweep that encompassed the manifold labours of the Expedition and linked it historically with the great endeavours of the past. Looking back to Sir James Ross's formidable nineteenth-century feat of plunging with his two ships into the close-packed floes beyond the Antarctic Circle, he wrote:

'Few things could have looked more hopeless than an attack upon that great ice-bound region; yet out of this desolate prospect Ross wrested an open sea, a vast mountain region, a smoking volcano, and a hundred problems of great interest to the geographer.' Readers were reminded that Ross's 'great Expedition is brought curiously close to our own time when it is remembered that of those who took part in it there is yet one survivor', namely, Sir Joseph Hooker, O.M.

'My dear Sir Joseph Hooker,' he wrote, 'no criticism of my book, public or private, has pleased me so much as your letter. My reviewers have been kind, and in some cases discriminating, but nothing they have said can reward my literary labours so fully as the thought that I have really brought vividly before you those scenes of ice and snow which you knew so well.' (5 November 1905) The dedication of the book 'to Sir Clements Markham, K.C.B., F.R.S.,' named him 'the Father of the Expedition and its Most Constant Friend'.

One who had shared with him the perils of the Antarctic

marches wrote that autumn: 'Dear Sir,—I am very thankful to you for being so good as to let me have your well written book on the voyage of the *Discovery*. It will remind me of being on the veldt [*sic*] again. I am very glad to have the chance of becoming your Cox. Thanking you very much, Sir, for all you have done for me, I remain, Your obedient Servant, CREAN.'

Scott to his mother:

Invereighty,
Forfar.
September '05.

My dearest Mother,—Will you go ahead with the house? You seem to think the whole thing will be a little expensive. If so, it can't be helped. I am prepared to go over the £100 if we get the worth of our money in comfort.

I must tell you of Balmoral. I arrived there on Tuesday. Before dinner I was sent for by the King, who gave me the C.V.O. Dinner 3 round tables. I sat at the King's, Princess of Wales, Duke & Duchess of Connaught, Prince Arthur, Prime Minister and 2 ladies in waiting.

Wednesday, busy all day preparing for lecture. Walked round Estate with equerries for exercise. Dinner, sat at King's table again. Evening, gave lecture—King, Princess of Wales, some of Connaughts, Prime Minister, and many others. Intended an hour, but King asked many questions and ran into 1¾ hours. All sorts of nice things said afterwards, much nicer than by the Prime Minister [Balfour], who said he regarded himself as the *Father of the Expedition*! ! ! ! Don't give this away.

Thursday, went for grouse drive. P. of Wales instructed me in art and had temerity to remain in next butt. Shot 9 myself, less than most, more than some. Evening, dined next but one to King, quiet evening. Everybody awfully nice about lecture. . . .

Friday, walked with H.M. in Park before lunch, sat at his table at lunch, drove out with him in the afternoon.

P.S. I never had to wear knee breeches or a frock coat.

The Voyage of the 'Discovery' was received as a sincere and straightforward account of unparalleled human experience, in which the author communicated the loneliness, wonder and terror of the archaic world of the Far South. 'A masterly work,' was the verdict of *The Times Literary Supplement*. 'The most admirable of all stories of discovery in the South Polar regions,' said *The Bookman* (U.S.A.).

The Athenaeum, then the most influential of literary weeklies, proposed Scott's early return to the Antarctic as a specially gifted explorer. It was generally accepted that he had added more to the knowledge of the Antarctic than all that had been written about it since Ross's time. There was high praise, too, for Wilson's pictures of the wild and strange beauty of the Antarctic scene.

The first edition was sold out before Christmas 1905. Amid the resounding goodwill for the book, the anomaly of its title was generally overlooked. The voyage of the *Discovery*, out and home, occupies 176 pages, while 698 pages are given to the Expedition's activities on shore.

> H.M.S. *Queen*
> 20.5.06

Dear Scott,—I have just read your book, and cannot restrain myself from telling you how interestingly and modestly it is written. I had no idea that you had been through such trials and escapes. I held my breath as you shot down the ice following the sledge and your two companions. I trembled when you were down the crevasse.

Then when I look at the chart and see how yours is the only name not perpetuated on it, I feel that I must ask you to allow me to add my sincerest congratulations. How very lucky they chose you as Captain. The country was just as fortunate.

> Yours sincerely,
> LEWIS BAYLY*

While Scott's book was being featured as a success of the autumn publishing season, the *Discovery* was paid off. Sir Clements Markham had pressed the case for the Admiralty acquiring her as 'a precious asset of the nation, to be lent, thereafter, for scientific explorations'. The Admiralty responded by sending the Royal Geographical Society a bill for naval

---

* In 1918, as Admiral Sir Lewis Bayly, he was Commander-in-Chief, Queenstown.

services rendered to the ship on her homeward voyage. She was sold to the Hudson's Bay Company for £10,000.

At the beginning of the First World War, the French Ministry of Commerce charted her to ferry supplies across the Channel. She was engaged in trading voyages up to 1920, when she went south on whaling research. She made her last appearance as an exploration ship in 1929–30 with the British, Australian and New Zealand Antarctic Research Expedition under Mawson. In 1931, she was laid up in the East India Dock, London, and remained there until 1937.

She was then handed over to the Boy Scouts Association and towed to her present mooring in the Thames. After the Second World War she was taken over by the Admiralty, and for the first time flew the White Ensign, being attached to the Admiral Commanding Reserves and remaining at her Embankment berth, where sightseers continue to crowd her gangways, decks, and cabins.*

Scott had been personally honoured by the monarch. Surprise was expressed at the absence of national recognition of any member of the Expedition. It was the subject of an indignant letter written as late as 1940 by Sir Richard Gregory, F.R.S., editor of *Nature*, and that year's President of the British Association. 'I have no doubt it was the attitude of the Royal Society and Balfour that was the cause. The injustice was an insult to science and to human achievement, and an example of an indifference unworthy of an enlightened people.'†

*

Receiving a second gold medal at the hands of the American ambassador in London, Scott made it known that 'in all probability' his exploring days were over because he was a professionally committed man. He was applauded by a Royal Geographical Society audience whose sensibilities had been touched by his evocation of Antarctic sights and sounds that still had a powerful hold on him.

Currently, he was caught up in a whirl of new social experience, a lion of the London season. His name was on the crested

* On Boxing Day 1965 there were waiting queues of visitors to the *Discovery*.

† Sir R. Gregory to Lieutenant-Commander J. L. Bernacchi, O.B.E., R.N.V.R., 15 January 1940.

invitation lists of the hostesses of Belgravia and Mayfair. He preferred the studios of Chelsea. One of his newly acquired women friends was Aubrey Beardsley's sister Mabel, a young actress who had been on tour with his sister Ettie. She developed a possessive interest in him that became a private joke among those who knew her.

He was more obviously susceptible to the glamour of Pauline Chase, considered the 'most boyish' embodiment of the part of Peter Pan in which she made her name. Scott often took her to supper after the play. They had been introduced by Barrie, who passed messages from or about her when Scott went back to sea.

'I've had enough of notoriety to last me a lifetime,' he wrote to a cousin. 'There has been no peace, no quiet—nothing but one mad rush.' He sighed for the solitudes of New Zealand, 'and the peaceful evenings we used to have there.'

Preparing to take up the post of flag captain to Rear-Admiral G. Le C. Egerton in H.M.S. *Victorious* in August 1906, he wrote to Kathleen O'Reilly, who was in London again, following the death of her father: 'It would be strange indeed if I did not want to see you. Will you tell me when I may come?' He was not sorry, he told her, to be joining his new ship. 'I am tired of London and its rush. I have been doing the season pretty thoroughly for the first time.'

Shortly after he joined the *Victorious* there occurred a momentous repetition of his first meeting with Sir Clements Markham, who was once more a guest of the Royal Navy, this time in Spanish waters. They went on shore trips together on the island of Majorca and it may fairly be deduced that Markham urged him to think patriotically again about returning to the Antarctic, with the South Pole as his prime objective.

Already the twentieth-century spirit was at work on the imagination of specialists in that field of exploration. The use of motor power for sledge pulling was visualized by a well-known geographer. 'If a motor-car ran at the rate of only five miles an hour for a couple of days before it broke down, it would give a sledge party a depot far from their main base and allow of the inspection of a much greater area than could otherwise be examined.' * The same expert thought that 'wireless telegraphy would be useful'.

* Dr H. R. Mill: *The Siege of the Antarctic*.

It was a brave concept. The internal combustion engine and wireless telegraphy (radio) were still in their experimental stages. Broken-down motor-cars were a familiar sight on the roads. The vocabulary of 'the wireless' was restricted as yet to feeble bleep-bleep signals.

That Scott's intentions regarding the Antarctic had been quickened soon after his disavowal of practical interest in it can be inferred from the letter written to him by J. M. Barrie on 8 September 1906: 'I chuckle with joy to hear that all the old hankerings are coming back to you. I feel you have got to go again.' He would keep an eye open, he promised, for a likely millionaire. 'It is one of the few things he can do with his money that *can't* do harm.'

Rumours of new expeditions were in the air. The Antarctic was again to be the arena of contending national ambitions. The names of Charcot, of France, and Arctowski, of Belgium, were heard at meetings of the Royal Geographical Society. Writing from the Atlantic, Scott took soundings of one or two of his *Discovery* colleagues.

Ernest Shackleton, who was obsessively anxious to prove his capacity to a world which he fancied still doubted it, was astonished to be told by Lieutenant G. F. A. Mulock, R.N., who had replaced him in 1903, that he had agreed to go south with Scott again if required. Shackleton had his own dream of Antarctic conquest. He wrote to a friend on 26 December 1906: 'What would I not give to be out there again doing the job, and this time really on the road to the Pole!'

A letter to Lieutenant Michael Barne, R.N., brought the reply that he too was committed to Scott. Barne had himself dreamed of leading a party to the Pole. He had made tentative plans. He now abandoned them in favour of Scott's. On 12 February 1907 newspaper readers learnt that Shackleton would lead a South Pole expedition a year hence, using the old winter quarters of the *Discovery* as its base.

Four days later, Scott had a letter from Dr Edward Wilson, writing from Westal, Cheltenham. 'It was a great joy to me to see your handwriting again, but I wish it had been about something happier.' He was disinclined to believe that Shackleton intended to forestall Scott in any new expedition to the Antarctic. He thought that Shackleton had no idea that Scott contemplated returning there. 'I myself have never heard a hint of your going South again. I have remembered always what you told me once in the South, that it would do you more harm than good with the Admiralty.' He felt that Shackleton had been misled by Scott's silence on the subject.

'It comes to this. If he had any idea of forestalling you, I have nothing more to say, for there can be only one opinion. Knowing how precipitate he is, one can easily imagine him conceiving the idea, getting his supporters together and rushing into print without sufficiently thinking out the possibilities.' Shackleton had written to ask Wilson to go out with him. 'Had I been free I should have gone, but I refused. That led to two more letters and three wires.' Wilson was sure that when Shackleton found that Scott was planning a new expedition, he would throw up his project, leaving the field to Scott. 'Of course the work is yours, was yours to begin with, and is obviously yours to finish.' He could not persuade himself that Shackleton was 'so misguided as to fail in seeing this'. Although they had lived on terms of close propinquity those few years before, Wilson addressed his friend as 'My dear Captain Scott'.

Lieutenant Michael Barne saw Shackleton on 1 March. 'He talked without stopping for half an hour on end,' Barne told Scott in a letter written the next day. Shackleton had been at a Royal Geographical Society dinner at which he heard that the Belgian explorer, Arctowski, was making for the South. 'He also told me that an American expedition is being secretly organized in England.' There was a strong rumour, too, that Charcot, the French explorer, was soon to leave for King Edward VII Land. Worrying about his position *vis-à-vis* Scott, Shackleton told J. Scott Keltie, Secretary of the Royal Geographical Society, that he had not slept for four nights.

*

Defining their respective areas of operation involved Scott and Shackleton in a curious correspondence in those first months of 1907. They were not unlike boxers in the ring, sparring for advantage. Each was obviously concealing more than he told. Each was concerned not to prejudice his position with possible backers.

Scott had staked what he regarded in effect as a *droit-de-seigneur* claim to the old *Discovery* base in McMurdo Sound. Shackleton had already made it known to certain people with money that he would be in a good position to reach the Pole by virtue of his knowledge of the base and the territory around it.

To have to give way in the circumstances was not a comfortable prospect. Shackleton turned for advice to Dr Wilson, whose judgement he deeply respected. Wilson replied that in his opinion Scott had 'a prior claim to the use of the base'.

The correspondence between Scott and Shackleton is remembered by Captain B. M. Peck, R.N. (Retired), a sub-lieutenant when in 1907 he was appointed 'Captain's Clerk', otherwise private secretary, to Scott, who arrived at Chatham on 1 January of that year to take command of the 14,000-ton battleship *Albemarle*. Captain Peck writes: 'There was a certain amount of discussion, amounting almost to friction, about their respective "spheres of influence" in the Antarctic. I got no thanks for my slow and imperfect typing of Captain Scott's letters. He was an ardent and impatient man. I knew him to be kindly at heart. Doubtless for my good, he concealed that part of his nature from me.' *

After much inner wrestling, Shackleton telegraphed to Scott on 6 March 1907: *Will meet your wishes regarding base*. There had been a meeting on 4 March between Wilson and Shackleton. Reporting to Scott, Wilson was confident 'that the whole thing can now be settled amicably'. He assured Scott that Shackleton 'had not the ghost of a suspicion that you had any intention of going South again'. Wilson said that Shackleton had feared that the Belgian expedition would take over the base in McMurdo Sound. Wilson wished that Shackleton had avoided misunderstanding by communicating directly with Scott. 'But he had collected his funds on what he had represented as the best possible chance of the Pole and was met by the disagreeable necessity of explaining to his various supporters that he was going to use their money for a more doubtful chance,' by the change of plans. 'He asked me how far I thought you would consider your right extended, and whether the use of a base in King Edward's land would be open to objection.' For Shackleton, everything was so uncertain, 'except that he starts this year for somewhere. He has even thought of going North instead of South.'

That week, Scott received an application from Lieutenant

* In a letter to the biographer.

'Teddy' Evans, navigating officer of the reilef ship *Morning* in 1903–4, who had agreed to act as navigator to Barne's proposed expedition, and who now asked Scott: 'Will you agree to take me as yours? I promise that you will have no keener officer and no one will work harder than I shall. I am tremendously enthusiastic, Sir, about Antarctic exploration.' (4 March, 1907)

Wilson wrote to Scott on 31 March as another willing volunteer. 'Can you really mean that you would like me to go South again with you? If you do, I may tell you that nothing in the world would please me more, and my wife is entirely with me. Without a doubt, I should like to go with you.'

Acting on Wilson's suggestion, Scott met Shackleton in May that year. Shackleton then drafted a memorandum relinquishing his proposed use of the McMurdo base. It was a formal document, typed on two foolscap sheets. 'My dear Captain Scott,—To make everything clear as regards our arrangement, I am following your suggestion and writing it down. To begin with, as you know, I was unaware that you had any plans for another Expedition, and announced mine on February 12th, which plans were that I was going to make McMurdo Sound my base.' Having since heard of Scott's intentions, and in deference to Scott's wishes, he had changed that part of his plans.

'I am leaving the McMurdo Sound base to you, and will land either at the place known as the Barrier Inlet or at King Edward VII Land, whichever is the most suitable. If I land at either of these places I will not work to the westward of the 170 meridian W. and shall not make any sledge journey going W....' Shackleton went on to state with some precision his future movements, in so far as he could ensure them. He concluded:

'I think this outlines my plan, which I shall rigidly adhere to, and I hope this letter meets you on the points that you desire.—Yours very sincerely, E. H. SHACKLETON.'

Scott sent him a somewhat patronizing acknowledgement. 'Your letter is a very clear statement of the arrangement to which we came. If as you say you will rigidly adhere to it, I do not think our plans will clash....' The undertaking was one which, in the opinion of Shackleton's latest biographers,* 'he

* Margery and James Fisher: *Shackleton* (Barrie, 1957).

should never have made, and which Scott ... should never have demanded'. Shackleton's first biographer, 'never saw the reasonableness of looking upon the McMurdo Sound route as reserved for a possible future expedition which had not even been planned.'* It was undeniably the case that Shackleton's plans were in advance of Scott's.

On the day that he received Shackleton's affirmation, Scott wrote to his mother that, 'after a long talk,' Lord Howard de Walden had entered into an arrangement 'whereby he will undertake to make trial sledges'. Scott hoped that it would be possible to have the first trials in September. 'On the result of them will depend future plans, but of course the whole thing is very hazy and uncertain at present.'

He asked his mother 'not to worry—it is not worth worrying about. If the chance comes it is worth taking. If it does not come I shall not be heartbroken.' Enclosing a cheque for £20, he told her: 'I rely on you to let me know when there is a difficulty in making ends meet.'

Off the west coast of Ireland, he wrote many long letters to his mother about duty and off-duty. 'A horrid accident' had to be related in full. 'In some extraordinary manner a man got mixed up with the wire ropes of the torpedo defence net and in an instant his right arm was taken off close to the shoulder. He fell in the water but swam to a rope, then helped himself up the ship's side and would have walked to the sick bay had he been allowed—an astonishing display of nerve,' rewarded in due course, Scott reported, by a pension of 1s. 3d. a day.

He apologized for keeping his mother waiting for letters during the Fleet's time in Irish waters: 'a press of ship's work has been followed by a press of still more arduous social work,' —a grand ball at Limerick, for which the floor was brought from Dublin; 'we kept it up till 5 a.m. and the Admiral danced every dance'; a big garden party given by Lord and Lady Clarina, 'nice people with a rather overwhelming array of daughters'; and then 'an enormous dinner followed by a dance on board,' and still more dances ashore—'there's a list of gaieties for you'.

He wrote that it would have been 'rather trying' but for the pleasure he had from observing 'the real enjoyment of these Irish girls—they enter into the spirit of things in the most

*H. R. Mill to Mrs Ernest Shackleton, 22 June 1908.

extraordinary fashion. It's delightful to watch them; they are so nice amongst themselves.' He wrote in greater detail about a day spent at Kylemore, as a guest of the Duke of Manchester.

It's an amusing *ménage*. The Duke spends all he can lay hands on when a free agent. The Duchess helps him. She is American, the daughter of a millionaire named Zimmerman. The old man, who was at Kylemore, has paid·debts over and over and says he won't again, so he keeps the Duke here and cuts down expenses. It's an extraordinary family. The Duke is a painful liar, but still he treated us very well so one could put up with that. The place is beautiful, quite beautiful.

Even so, he could not resist giving particulars of a tragic happening that cast a shadow over the ship in those attractive surroundings or, for that matter, reflecting that they had been formed by 'an old glacier valley, like the Norwegian fjords'. Returning to H.M.S. *Albemarle* from Kylemore, 'I heard that one of our young lieutenants, a boy named Pennington, had shot himself. It came with the utmost surprise to everyone and now that I have been into all his affairs the surprise is scarcely lessened, for there was evidently no motive or reason. He did his duty and associated with his messmates to the end without giving a sign . . .' (29 July 1907)

*

That year, 1907, was one of exceptional consequences for Scott, whose cautious attitude to life was no shield against its surprises. During close formation manoeuvres with the Atlantic Fleet off Gibraltar, his ship was in collision with H.M.S. *Commonwealth* —'a sickening sensation', he told his mother in a long letter full of technical information, with diagrams to illustrate precisely what happened. 'It was pitch black but the *Commonwealth*'s lights were close to us, outlining her huge hull, and as she rose and fell with the sea and one saw the twinkling lights and the illuminated figures on her decks, she represented a picture of helplessness and a possibility of catastrophe which is not easily forgotten.' Captain Peck recalls: 'We struck her with terrific force, and nearly went right through her.'

Scott wanted to allay the fears his mother would have on reading newspaper reports. 'There will be a court of enquiry, of course, but I have some doubt if there will be a court martial because it will be difficult to decide who to court martial. I should not wonder if the thing ends with an Admiralty memorandum censuring all round. For this we must wait and see.'

Beneath the exterior calm, he was an anxious man. Published accounts of the collision made it appear that reputations might be at stake. His public prominence would give a court martial more than routine significance. His friends were worried. Barrie: 'I am sure it has been a time of distress for you—just a line of sympathy.' Markham: 'Our confidence in your care and good judgement can never be shaken in the slightest degree.'

A court of inquiry was held. No one was reprimanded. The accident was due to injudicious operation orders from the highest level of command. Scott's friends rejoiced with him in the exonerating verdict without knowing the depth of his satisfaction. Personal prestige had never been more important to him. He was in love. The young woman to whom he had lost his heart was not only wiser than he in the ways of the world. She was in many respects his intellectual superior.

*

Kathleen Bruce, then twenty-nine, was the daughter of the Rev. Lloyd Bruce, rector of Carlton-in-Lindrick, Nottinghamshire, and Canon of York. She was the youngest of the family of eleven, and under that great weight of seniority she developed the masterfully independent spirit that stamped her life. Her maternal grandmother was Greek; her mother the granddaughter of one of Sir Walter Scott's friends, James Skene of Rubislaw. She lost both her parents before she was sixteen and was taken into the Edinburgh home of her grand-uncle, William Forbes Skene, Historiographer of Scotland.

After a sketchy formal education at boarding-schools, she became a pupil at the Slade School of Art, London. When she was twenty-one she went to Paris as an art student, enjoying and despising the life in about equal measure. She had the run of Rodin's studio, where she met and formed a close friendship with the American dancer, Isadora Duncan. She returned to England in 1906, intent on earning her living as a sculptor.

She first saw Scott at a luncheon party given by his eldest sister's friend, Mabel Beardsley, at 32 Westminster Palace Gardens, Artillery Row, S.W. Sitting between Max Beerbohm and J. M. Barrie, she noticed that he was 'not very young, perhaps forty, not very good looking, but healthy and alert'. When they were introduced, 'he wanted to know where I had got my wonderful sunburn. I told him I had been vagabonding in Greece, and he thought it entrancing to vagabond like that.'

Someone who remembers her well has said: 'Two inches taller and she would have been Juno-esque.' She had the rare quality called presence, which men noticed in her more than women, an elemental vitality that was both obvious and elusive. Her blue eyes set the note for the only personal adornment she ever allowed herself, a bright blue stone pendant. Habitually she would say: 'I must have my bit of blue,' however sombre the circumstances. She was as obstinate in disliking the convention of black for mourning as she was in regarding illness as a disgrace. A headache was an occasion for self-criticism. She was a vegetarian who avoided alcohol and stopped short of faddism.

She and Scott did not meet again until near the end of 1907, several months later. That she was regnant in his thoughts was shown by his concern to meet her again as soon as he arrived back at 56 Oakley Street. He asked Mabel Beardsley to invite them both to tea. Kathleen Bruce was living in a three-room flat at 133 Cheyne Walk, along the Chelsea Embankment. She had lost her sun tan in the operating theatre, a victim of civilization's latest penalty, appendicitis. As she approached the waiting surgeon, she had asked: 'Can you promise to leave me enough insides to make a fine baby some day?'

A considerable part of her fantasy life, it appeared, was centred in the desire for a son. She had told one of the girl students with whom she shared lodgings in Paris: 'A son is the only thing I do quite surely and always want.' When her friend remarked: 'Well, you seem to know plenty of eager young men', she ignored 'the touch of mockery' and answered: 'None is worthy to be the father of my son.' In some autobiographical notes she referred to 'the young law student, so teeming with vitality' who had made the declaration: 'With you I can conquer worlds, without you I shall be nothing.' She decided that 'the perfect father for my son is not there. Corn-coloured hair and a crooked smile, maybe, but not the father for my son.'

At Mabel Beardsley's, 'being diverted' by Ernest Thesiger,

actor, and Henry James, novelist, she thought 'what an unexpected setting for a simple, austere naval officer!' Then, 'all
of a sudden, and I did not know how', she was confronted by
'this very well-dressed, rather ugly and celebrated explorer'.
He stood over her as they talked. 'He was of medium height,
with broad shoulders, very small waist, and dull hair beginning
to thin, but with a rare smile, and with eyes of a quite un-
usually dark blue, almost purple. I had never seen their like.'*

They were much together in the next ten days. Then Scott
went back to his naval duties, and Kathleen Bruce was left
wondering whether she could accept him 'as the father of my
son for whom I had been searching'. It seems that she had
instinctively selected him for a eugenics experiment.

CHAPTER TEN

AN ARTIST IN THE FAMILY

'You shorten life, if it is told by the heartbeats.' Waiting to be
posted to his new command, H.M.S. *Essex*, Scott was the restless
slave of love. He called at 133 Cheyne Walk, 'but Somebody
isn't there'. He went to his club, the Naval & Military, in
Piccadilly, 'hoping for a telephone message'. There was no
message. He strode down to Seaford House, Belgrave Square,
the town house of Lord Howard de Walden, who was interested
in a new engineering development that might be of value to
Antarctic explorers. From there he returned to the club; then,
'after some shopping', to Cheyne Walk again. 'The rest lies in
the hands of Somebody.'

Late in the evening, 'uncontrollable footsteps carried me
along the Embankment to find no light—yet I knew you were
there, and it was good to think of. I saw the open window and,
in fancy, a tangled head of hair on the pillow within.... Don't
tell me it's all fancy' (8 November 1907).

Doubting, enraptured, bewildered (his word), he told
Kathleen Bruce in a note the next day: 'What a world you are

* Lady Kennet: *Self-Portrait of an Artist* (John Murray, 1949).

133

opening to me! It's like a dream.' He could not believe that life was laying 'such a treasure' at his feet. 'You seem too good to be true. It will be long before I cease to fear that you are only "such stuff as dreams are made of".'

Bringing him down from the clouds, there came the hint: 'She's at home and going to eat hot pie at 7.30. What'll he do about it?' He would love the hot pie, 'but I've got to dine with my Mother.' The impersonal tone bothered him; he could not sustain it, and begged to know what she would call him. 'What shall I call myself to you?' Diffidently he signed with his initials. Scribbling her always brief answering notes, she as yet gave him no name.

On 12 November he went to Audley End, Saffron Walden, to stay with Howard de Walden. He wrote from there: 'I wanted to write last night but my host kept me talking till two on the sex problem, of all things! I think it must be habit, as I remember the other men walking away and leaving me to bear the brunt.'

Her reply contained the advice: 'Don't discuss the sex problem with Lord Howard if he forms his opinions on his personal and recent experiences. There can be little of interest in them.' She was amused to tell him that at a dinner party she had inwardly laughed at Mabel Beardsley's repeated mention of 'my Captain Scott', and that she had 'peeped to see' if his letter was 'still cosily hidden' in the front of her evening gown. While he was away she had been reading *The Voyage of the 'Discovery'*. 'Do you know, I am enthralled, quite grotesquely wrapped up in it? The countless people who have looked in on me for sympathy on some topic or other during the last few days have met with comforting remarks such as, "Yes, but you've never had a frost-bitten nose!"'

Scott wrote to Barrie for advice on behalf of a cousin who was suffering hideously from cancer. Barrie replied at once to 'the sorrowful tale you have to tell'. There was a hopeful new treatment, based on 'injections of ferment from the cow' (27 November 1907). Scott now had a means of more readily dispelling his sombre preoccupations. 'All serious thought goes when I see that sweet face,' he wrote to Kathleen in the same week. 'Dear, if you know I'm half frightened of you. I'm very humbled before you. I've so little, so very little, to offer you.'

134

On 31 December maternal percipience expressed itself in a letter wishing him 'the very best of good things in the coming year and all happiness and success to you in *all* your undertakings', its underlined words eloquent of his mother's apprehensions. 'I want to say that *whatever* plans you make for the future will be suitable for me and you must never let me be a hindrance to your making a home and a life of your own.' She added a prayer for his happiness and prosperity, and begged that he would 'ever believe in the love of your devoted Mother, H. SCOTT'.

There was a postscript. 'You have carried the burden of the family since 1894. It is time now for you to think of yourself and your future. God bless and keep you.'

Possibly sensing a familiar fixation, Kathleen wrote to Scott on 4 January 1908: 'Don't let's get married. I've been thinking a lot about it and tho' much of it would be beautiful, there is much also that no doubt would be very difficult.' She had wished to marry 'for the *one* reason', namely, that she might have a son. 'Now that very thing seems as though it would only be an encumbrance *we* could scarcely cope with.' She could believe that he would be lonely without her for a time, 'but the relief of knowing that you need not worry or uproot your sweet little mother will soon compensate'.

The fact was, she wrote, 'we're horribly different, you and me. I am not going to tell you to forget me or any nonsense of that sort, but let's abandon the idea of getting married and don't let's look at any more houses. There are things about it I am not sure I can face.' Domesticity was a burden that her artist's temperament could not lightly bear. 'It seems a waste that you should not be married and with all my heart I *quite truly* hope that you will find someone who will fit better—and, dearie, don't be sad.—K.'

By then Scott was committed to the fullest extent of his emotional resources. He had poured out his heart in letters written to Kathleen sometimes twice a day, telling her that the thought of her meant 'a catch of the breath', that she was his heart's 'daintiest treasure', that her 'dear, sweet, blue eyes' haunted him, that she was 'altogether precious' to him. He was none the less capable of steadying his feelings.

'I want to marry you very badly, but it is absurd to pretend

I can do so without facing great difficulty and risking a great deal for others as well as for myself. If I was very young I should probably take all risks and win through. In facing poverty we should be living and believing in a better future. The old can only live in the present. My mother is 67, only a strand of life remains. She has had a hard life in many respects. I set myself to make her last years free from anxiety. I can't lightheartedly think of events that may disturb that decision.' He had often told the family, he said, 'half in joke, that if I married I should look out that the young lady had lots of money'.

As for their being 'horribly different', did she mean that she would not act with caution as he did? 'Little girl, if you care, be patient, and we'll pull things straight—have that faith in me. But you must work with me, dearest, not against me. Dearest heart, I love you very much. So much that it is making me un-happy now to think how little it can mean to you' (5 January 1908).

The advent of Kathleen Bruce was a more disturbing element in his family life than he had foreseen. Misunderstandings arose, causing him private distress, the more because he knew the 'sordid motive' (his phrase) that led to them. His allusion to marrying for money was not so jocular as he pretended. He was expected to 'marry well', in the crude middle-class sense. Kathleen Bruce had the approved social qualifications— there was a baronetcy in her family—but she had no money.

*

News that Shackleton was back in the Antarctic gave uneasy urgency to Scott's dream of reaching the South Pole with the aid of motor traction. An engineer named Hamilton, who had a workshop at Finchley, was building a motor-propelled sledge with the distinctive feature of a threaded steel band running over wheels that enabled it to surmount obstacles, caterpillar fashion. Financial support for the project was being given by Lord Howard de Walden, who subsequently took out patents.

The house in Oakley Street was given up and arrangements were made for Scott's mother to live with his sister, Mrs Brownlow, at Holcombe, St Mark's Avenue, Henley-on-Thames. Believing that 'things will gradually work straight, and that we have *got* to make them come right', he told

Kathleen Bruce that he had been collecting figures of house-keeping costs.

He set them out under the heading: *Estimate for 2 persons living in a small house in London in this year of grace*: Rent £65, rates & taxes £27, e. light or gas £12, coals etc., £15, servants' wages £45, house repairs & cleaning £20, laundress £25, papers, stationery & small incidentals £6, food for 4 persons at 10s. per head per week £104, renewals of linen etc., £10. Total £329.

He gave his mother £200 a year; he had mess bills and other shipboard expenses, all coming out of his captain's pay, plus command money, amounting to £740 a year. 'It isn't quite cheerful. I had a real despondent mood last night, but slept like a log. All's well with this world indeed if you and I really mean it to be' (8 January 1908). Typically, he did not look into his pay position on taking command of the *Essex*. Months afterwards he found that he had dropped £100 a year. 'Was there ever such a casual idiot as I?'

Kathleen went to a 'fabulous Greek wedding' with one of her aunts. 'She plied me with questions about you (always ignorant of who you are). Said she gathered you were "cooling off" (her expression, not mine). Are you, are you? Said she was sure you were. Poor little humiliated me. I bear up wonderfully. Bless you, bless you, bless you. The sun is shining. I'm as happy as can be.' She had been down to Seaford in Sussex, walking alone by the shore. 'It was perfectly wonderful, full of delight for me. The sun was shining gaily and it was all beautiful. The whole day was splendid. I climbed on the Downs. I lay on the breakwaters in the sun. I was happy.—Yrs, K.'

He read her letter, he confessed in his next, 'with a rather dreadful sense of fear'. That she could so easily, so self-sufficingly, find happiness without him evidently disturbed his thoughts. 'Oh, little girl, I do think of you very often and wonder what you are doing. Write again, dear, and tell me if I am to see you. I long for you very much.' He told her jauntily: 'Do you know, I'm next senior to the Admiral in our Fleet? So that I take charge not only of my ship but of a division of our small Fleet. Isn't it amusing?' Long forgotten manoeuvres come to life again in his letters.

'Swanage.—Dearest, such a rush for the last few days. Night attacks by destroyers, a weird scene, then a dash to the Isle of

Wight, 20 knots with three cruisers to catch the *Adriatic*. Caught her in mid-Channel, rushed for Cherbourg with my three cruisers, much to the pleasure of my Admiral, back to Torbay, more cruiser tactics, then another night attack last night. I have scarcely left the bridge. But now is peace. Close by stands a sweet little town under chalk cliffs. Why are you not there on shore at the hotel or in a lodging? Why cannot you come? Oh, dearest, can't you? Be my guest on shore, sweetheart. We know each other well enough, don't we?' (15 February 1908)

Wanting her 'to see the ship, and to catch a glimpse of this life of mine,' he followed up his plea with the suggestion that she could 'bring a girl friend as chaperone'. The reply came: 'I'd *love* to come, love to, love to, but I mustn't. It would be too unwise. It wouldn't look serious for you to be seen with little ladies on shore. What a pity! For indeed it would be fun.' She added: 'Chasing the *Adriatic* at 20 knots appeals to me immensely.'

Her delight in life appears in nearly every letter she wrote to him, contrasting with his caution, mistrust, and melancholy. 'I've got my bed right across the window now and the sun is pouring in. It will surely be counted to me for great virtue that I do not come, for the idea of the sun, and the sea, and you, is very, very enticing.' She wrote in the same week: 'I do find your love for me so precious, so very precious. The flat is full of flowers today, flowers and sunshine.'

His answering letter announced that he was the victim of 'a stupefying cold, never more snuffy and tearful. You must immediately, as a preventative, take some cinnamon or ammoniated quinine. Enjoyment of life is non-existent at the moment.' Lines of tender sentiment were followed by the stark aside: 'I'm afraid the man who was injured at coaling will die. He is in a very bad way.'

Having told her on 5 March: 'You give me strength and courage', he wrote from H.M.S. *Essex* next day: 'Dearest, I've been looking at poverty here as represented by those who live on pay alone. I don't find it attractive to them. I don't believe it would be attractive to you or me', and confessed himself 'a little despondent'.

He received the reply: 'Your letter makes me rather sad.' She had called on Mabel Beardsley the previous day. 'For about

138

an hour she nobly forbore mentioning you, but then she told me she's asked you and Max [Beerbohm] to tea and I told her you had gone away, and then, my dear, began a woeful cross-questioning.'

She had asked Kathleen whether Scott wanted to marry her. 'I said no, I don't suppose you could marry, you are too poor. She pumped, and pumped, and pumped, all kindly and nicely. Then she told my fortune by cards, and said that I was going to have trouble with a fairish man because of a woman's treachery, but that all would be made happy for me with a very dark man with much wealth and good fortune. *What* rot!'

Remarking that the gay life was 'very bad' for her work as an artist, she concluded abruptly: 'I won't marry you, Con, anyhow. Goodbye, dearest. I love you very, very much.—Yrs, K.'

*

On leave again in March 1908, Scott went to Lautaret, in the High Alps, near Grenoble, to watch tests of the motor sledge that had been built at Finchley. Engineer-Lieutenant Skelton, R.N., who had been with him in the Antarctic and whom Scott had privately decided should be his second-in-command of a new expedition, accompanied him. The third observer was Lord Howard de Walden. Passing through Paris, Scott read in the *Daily Mail* that Shackleton had been baulked by the ice-pack in carrying out his original plan and was falling back on McMurdo Sound, where he had promised not to go.

Scott wrote to his mother from H.M.S. *Essex*: 'I have been getting some copies made of Shackleton's letter to me and send you one. The breach of faith is so emphatic that I propose to let certain persons see the letter' (26 March 1908). If at this distance Scott's severity of temper seems to have been hard on Shackleton, we must see it as part of a code that for Scott was inflexible.

'Did I tell you about his agreement with me?' he asked Kathleen Bruce, writing from the Hotel Continental, Paris. 'It was a perfectly plain distinct statement absolutely binding him in an honourable sense. He definitely agreed not to approach my old quarters. I am bound to confess, in spite of his past behaviour, I thought he meant to abide by this, but, as you can see, he hasn't.' He referred to the 'far consequences' of Shackleton's action. 'You can guess something of my thoughts,' which no doubt were much exercised by the possibility of Shackleton forestalling him in attaining the grand final objective. He intended persevering 'to get this sledge business as nearly right as can be'. After that, 'I really don't know.'

Nor had he the means of knowing that Shackleton had stated in a long impassioned letter to his wife, written five weeks previously (26 January 1908), his reason for the dramatic change of decision and the mental discomfort it caused him. 'If I had not promised Scott that I would not use "his" place, I would have gone on to McMurdo Sound with a light heart, but I had promised and I felt that each mile I went to the West was a horror to me.'

He protested that his word of honour had been given under pressure. He had been compelled to break it by circumstances beyond his control: acute shortage of fuel, and confrontation with exceptionally severe conditions in the ice-pack, exposing his little ship *Nimrod* and all in her to 'the overwhelming forces of Nature'. He had been through 'a sort of Hell', he wrote, trying to reconcile his promise to Scott with the physical problems that had to be solved.

That it was indeed a testing time for Shackleton cannot fairly be doubted. 'All the anxiety I have been feeling,' he went on to say in the letter to his wife, 'coupled with the desire to really do the right thing, has made me older than I can ever say. I never knew what it was to make such a decision as the one I was forced to make last night,' whether to go on to McMurdo Sound or to stand by his promise, remembering his responsibility for 'the lives and families of the 40 odd men on board', not to speak of his duty to those who were his financial mainstay at home.

Pressing heavily on him also was the fear of disapproval in influential quarters; for example, the Royal Geographical Society, and the enmity of what he called 'the Scott faction'. His stress of mind would have been still greater could he have foreseen that the decision he took would cost him a friendship he valued more than most, that of Edward Wilson. He might properly have asked what Wilson and Scott, those men of strict behaviour, would have done in his circumstances. Their solution of a classic moral dilemma might have been both inspiring and disastrous. Wilson wrote to J. Scott Keltie, Secretary of the

Royal Geographical Society: 'I am sorry for Mrs Shackleton. I fear she will feel this unhappy decision in going to McMurdo Sound more than anyone else' (14 June 1908).

Sending Kathleen Bruce snapshots of the sledge trials at Lautaret, Scott enclosed a copy of the letter of agreement that Shackleton had signed. 'Don't trouble to return it, as I have many copies. You will see that by wintering in McMurdo Sound he has just gone bang through it, with unanswerable breach of faith. I had a suspicion he might, and find others had the same, also bit by bit I get evidence of similar actions in his history during the past few years. He seems to have almost deliberately adopted the part of plausible rogue and to have thrown scruples to the winds.' Wondering whether 'such tactics can succeed', Scott said that he was 'more shocked at the terrible vulgarizing which Shackleton has introduced into the Southern field of enterprise, hitherto so clean and whole-some'.

Kathleen thought Shackleton's letter 'extraordinary, or rather his action after it'. She asked: 'May I show it to people?' She felt that Scott need not worry too much about him, 'tho' of course you know and I don't. Have you seen about his fight with his captain?' Newspapers had exaggerated a dispute between Shackleton and England, captain of his exploring ship *Nimrod*, into a rough-and-tumble on the bridge.

For the moment, Kathleen's attention was more exhilaratingly engaged. 'Tenterden.—I'm staying with Ellen Terry. She says she's met you and she'd like to marry you very much. She's the biggest, greatest, largest, loveliest person to be with, with a magnetism and affection positively overwhelming. It does one good to meet such people.' Then, dutifully: 'You have had bad luck. Why *can't* I help you?' It was like a *cri de coeur*, the first glimmering of a doubt, later expressed as an intuitive belief that success was not in his stars.

Within a few days she was at Cranmore Hall, Shepton Mallet, the guest of another new friend, Lady Muriel Paget. 'There are seven or eight men staying here and I'm desperately in love with several, of course! But I'm being very good in spite of all the coercion! It *is* fun! Balfour and George Wyndham, and Speyer', the City man whom she set out to impress as a potential supporter of Scott's second expedition.

After comparing motor sledge capabilities at Lautaret with

Jean Charcot, the French explorer, an admiring rival in the Antarctic arena, Scott rejoined his ship, from which he reported in his next letter to Kathleen 'a very shocking accident'. They were steaming for Portland, 'without lights in single line at 10 tonight with destroyers attacking us out of the darkness, when one unfortunate destroyer, the *Tiger*, ran foul of our sister ship, the *Berwick*. We were brought up in a heap, inky blackness about and searchlights, suddenly flaring out, on a pitiable central object, the sinking destroyer.' She vanished before boats could reach her. 'I'm afraid several lives were lost' (2 April 1908).

His recital of tragedy inspired the heartening reassurance: 'Con, dearest, I'm afraid I'm getting very, very fond of you. That accident made me imagine for just one short moment what it would be like to lose you. Silly, of course, but there it is.'

In the same letter she mentioned an incident involving an elderly literary celebrity who, having been invited to tea with her, attempted familiarities that caused her 'to run from the house'. Scott was suitably indignant. 'I feel inclined to punch the egregious Mallock's head. What a senile ruffian—and I had a sort of failing for him. How dare he. It's because you are the sweetest, dearest girl in the whole world. My girl, I love you, I love you. It's just ridiculous! I'm too lonely for words without you' (7 April 1908).

He was paying the rent of the Oakley Street House, which his mother had left to live at Henley. There was the prospect of someone, 'Lady White's father', taking over the lease. 'I feel much better about this,' he wrote. 'You know how it has worried me. I think they will pay the premium [£115]. I hope so, as that will then really put things in order at Henley.'

Hearing that there was a hitch in the letting, he wrote to his mother: 'I expect it is useless for me to tell you not to worry. Really, dear, don't take all this too seriously. I'm afraid we're all of us prone to allow small reverses to weigh too heavily' (11 April). Within a day or two, the prospect brightened.

'Con, how glad I am to see the house is let', Kathleen wrote. 'I do hope it *is*. It's a most *enormous* weight off my mind. I used to hate passing that way on account of those horrid boards.'

She had been to Kew and had basked in the sun. 'It's these lovely spring days that make you love me so much. Aren't they

142

wonderful?' But he was in the grip of his fatalistic mood and darkened her day by telling of the sudden death of the ship's engineer lieutenant, 'an aneurism case'.

She was preparing to leave for Italy on a month's tramping holiday. Troubled about it, he adopted the lovesick gallant's stance, hinting that if she changed her mind about him she would find him a model of sympathetic understanding and seemly behaviour. 'I shall have only a silent memory of what has been. I am to be trusted altogether in such a case', an assurance that she may not have required.

He wrote three days after: 'Kathleen, there is no one like you—never a girl who looked life so boldly in the face. I love your splendid independence and the unswerving directness of you. Words are cheap, dear heart, yet right down in the innermost cells I feel that I love you for this.'

Pleading that his 'hereditary instincts of caution' made it impossible for him to face the future with an easy heart, he asserted that the struggle for existence had been 'specially hard' for him, and he appealed for her understanding of his fear of yet further struggle. 'I'm a coward to write like this' (11 May 1908), as if he foresaw her response to his moody prosing.

'You really must not be so afraid,' she wrote chidingly, '—afraid of yourself, and me, and the future, and all sorts of things.' From Italy, shortly after, she was revelling in 'the freedom and irresponsibility that are so precious to me'. She adored the vagabond life. 'I'm crammed full of sun and intoxicated by it.'

She walked through pine woods, slept in olive groves, talked to strangers, practised the language. When Scott sent her a somewhat laborious account of his recent duties at sea, she glancingly replied: 'What is light calibre gunnery?'

Hoping to convince her that he was more flexible than perhaps she knew, he declared: 'By nature I think I must be a freelance. I love the open air, the trees, the fields, the seas, the open spaces of life and thought. Darling, you are the spirit of all this to me, though we have loved each other in crowded places' (22 May 1908).

He sent her the satisfactory news of his having been 'offered H.M.S. *Bulwark* this very instant', and of his acceptance. 'She is flagship to the Nore Division, Home Fleet. From a Service point of view, this is a very good appointment. I shall be the most junior captain in separate command of a battleship.' The extra £100 a year, he was glad to say, 'will really come this time' (25 May 1908).

Isadora Duncan had arrived in London. Scott wrote to Kathleen: 'I see the great heart of you going out to her. I see you half worshipful, wholly and beautifully alive—and I love you for it.' He saw that the famous dancer and her art were 'the antithesis of all that's worldly and conventional', and protested his impatience with the rigidity of Service life, 'a mechanical existence'. He confessed to being still half fearful of their future together. 'Shall I satisfy you, girl of my heart? The thought of you is wonderful to me.'

Momentarily uplifted, he who had dared and endured so much thought it necessary to affirm: 'I'll just do something with my life yet because there's a little lady supremely interested' (3 June 1908).

Scott to his mother:

H.M.S. *Bulwark*
[Undated]

My dearest Mother,—It has been a great annoyance to me not to be able to see you because I had a most especial thing to talk of. Dear Mother, you know I spoke to you some little time ago about Miss Bruce. It is so hard for an undemonstrative person like myself to break through reserve, but I think you must have guessed that I had learnt to care much for her.

Now, dear, I must tell you I want to marry Kathleen Bruce—but she and I are agreed that under no circumstances must your comfort suffer. Now all I ask of you is to get to know the girl I love and to break up this horrid condition of strain in which we have been living.

Oh, I know, I know that all this is against your hopes, but don't judge till you know all the facts. I do so want to make for a happier state of affairs all round.

So, dear, will you please ask Kathleen Bruce to come and see you as my future wife? Will you be kind to her. She will be perfectly frank with you. You know of course that she is a lady by birth, breeding and association. But now, oh let there be no misunderstanding. I have written to her to say that you will get this letter on Monday, that in it I have asked you to send for her. The rest is for you and her.

We go to sea on Monday at noon and shall be off Deal on Tuesday night. Will you send me a wire on Monday morning to Sheerness before we sail?

Goodnight, dear Mother. I do not want to be selfish, indeed, indeed, and I know she does not.

Your loving son,

CON

*

He paid a hurried visit to Belstead, Ipswich, to confer on Antarctic matters with Michael Barne, who was watching the motor sledge developments on his behalf; then wrote to Kathleen Bruce 'from miles off the sandbanks of the Thames', deploring again that it was his fate to 'dwell in the machine'. The reverberating mystery-of-life chord was struck in his letter of 4 June. 'Have you had first-hand knowledge of the occult?' He reported a curious happening in the ship.

The second doctor on board H.M.S. *Bulwark* went to sleep in an armchair after lunch on the previous Thursday. He woke to recount 'an extraordinary dream'. In it, he was at the Derby and saw 'quite plainly, the colours of a jockey, blue-and-white, passing the winning post, and heard people shouting "Sinetta! Sinetta!"' It was certain, on the clearest evidence, Scott went on to relate, 'that this young man knew nothing of racing matters, nothing of the horses likely to start for the Derby'. When the list of runners was consulted, it was seen that among them was 'a rank outsider named Signorinetta, colours white and blue hoops'.

The coincidence was too strong to be ignored. The dream became common talk, 'half in jest, half in earnest, and the majority (not betting men) sent one or two pounds, according to their means, to be placed on the "dream" horse. Today we learn that Signorinetta has won the Derby at 100 to 1, and our wardroom officers are jointly richer by about £2,000.'

While he could not agree that it was 'a manifestation of the prophetic spirit', he considered that 'as a chain of circumstance' it was remarkable. 'Can one wonder that superstition exists?' he asked. Like many who are tormented by the confusions and emergencies of this world, he was hopefully receptive of the idea of another in which a more benevolent reality prevailed.

To his mother at Henley he sent a *précis* of the account he had received of an experience that befell a former shipmate,

Commander Crawford Maclachan,* of H.M.S. *Scylla* in West Indian waters. Known in the Navy as 'the pocket Hercules', the Commander went for a sail by himself in a skiff. He was picked up after fifty-six hours adrift, through most of which time he was up to his neck in water. The skiff was several times overturned by the heavy seas. Once a shark swam into the boat and 'made a grab' at him. He was attacked by hordes of screaming seabirds, fending them off with a board torn from the skiff's bottom. Five times during darkness a search party in a steam launch came within hailing distance, once as close as a hundred yards, without seeing or hearing him. 'It was the merest fluke that he was seen at all.'

Scott wrote: 'Isn't this a very remarkable adventure? I know Mac very well—he's just the man for it—dogged, persistent, full of health and courage—with an *exceedingly* bald head. A novelist would scarcely dare to make the climax of rescue come and go five times without loss of reason.' It was a marvellous demonstration of human fortitude. For Scott, the dauntless nerve of the bald-headed commander, 'under the burning tropic sun, with no hat on', ranked him with the saga heroes. 'KEEP THIS' he wrote in bold capitals at the top of the descriptive letter, as if it had been refreshment for his soul and might be again.

Scott to his mother:

H.M.S. *Bulwark*,
23.6.'08.

My dearest Mother,—Thank you very much for the cheque (£50). You are not to dream of paying back more till everything is settled up.

Dearest Mother, of course Kathleen loved you. I felt that she would. She came back full of her visit to you. She told me again and again how sweet you had been to her and Rose also—her whole mind has been centred on the hope that *you* liked *her*—and she has been longing to hear either directly or through me that you did.

Did you? Dear, you said something to Kathleen about your love not interfering with hers. She was touched and

* Commander Maclachan was appointed to the command of the cruiser *Scylla* on 14 May 1907. He was promoted Captain on 31 December 1908. *The Times* stated that he was 'very ill' after the experience recorded above.

puzzled, puzzled because the thought that she would come between you and I had not entered her head and even your suggestion of it did not make it real.

Indeed, I fear you don't understand her. Long before she knew you her thought was of you and her most often expressed hope was that she would be able to help you and care for you. My dear, she may not be all you wish, but there isn't an ounce of jealousy in her frank nature.

Oh, don't you see she came to you feeling very, very humble and hoping, hoping you would like her and trust her? Since then she has been full of anxiety as to the result of her visit. Have you written to her? She hoped so much you would.

I fear it is difficult to understand one another in this world, but, my dear, do believe that you and your opinion count very highly with us both—so highly that we would not be happy without your blessing and your love.

Try to be kind to Kathleen. She has lots of friends and people who love her, but she has never had a home.

Goodnight, dear. But I must tell you of our gay doings first. The Princess Louise spent Monday on board. She was very, very charming to me, saying all sorts of nice things. I took her over the ship. She got her frock covered with paint but didn't seem to mind and went away in high feather.

Goodnight really this time.

Your loving son,

CON

CHAPTER ELEVEN

'WEDDING PRESENTS ARE NEEDED'

THE scientists gave Scott more bad moments when, after four years of collating and editing, the observations of his first Antarctic expedition began to appear in volume form. The President of the Physical Society, Dr Charles Chree, F.R.S., proposed in a speech that the leadership of any future expedition to the Antarctic should be entrusted to 'a physicist of resource and ripe experience', who would not be 'overshadowed by the doers of exploits which appeal to the popular imagination'. In a reference to the 'unpropitious start' of the National Antarctic Expedition of 1901–4, he suggested 'something equivalent to a scientific court-martial', by which the results of nationally organized expeditions would be thoroughly investigated.

It was embarrassing for Scott to have such things said at a time when he was preparing a new expedition and hoping to secure public support for it. Still more galling criticism was to come. For the present, his change of command was all-absorbing. 'I am very, very busy from 6.30 when I rise to 11.30 when I seek my bed. You can imagine how much is to be done—new ship, new officers, new men, and such quantities of all', the *Bulwark*'s complement numbering 750.

He was fully enmeshed in the machine that had impelled him to repeated protest; and seemed to be not uncongenially so. 'We have been very hard at work. For me, learning and teaching. I find it a great fact, this enormous fleet with its wonderful collective organization and underneath its myriad individual interests.'

His long working day with its manifold activities was a serial theme of his letters. 'You can't think what a lot there is to do. There are things that please, and others that displease me, it's a mix-up.' The phrase was highly suggestive of his personal situation. He professed disdain of 'this regulated life' in a letter to Jean Charcot, the French polar explorer, and could not suppress his satisfaction in letting Kathleen Bruce know that 'the Admiral tells me all the secrets'. He was preparing himself for the anchored stability of the married state and no less earnestly making ready to sever himself from it with what could be disastrous finality.

They were to marry in September 1908, three months away. Scott was still worrying about their future together. 'What's making us half unhappy?' he wrote to Kathleen on 25 June from H.M.S. *Bulwark*. 'It's just simply lack of money. I see it all. My people's attitude, delighted with you personally, ready to love you, yet vaguely disappointed because their minds have nursed a thought of worldly things and in me lay their women's hopes. Don't blame them. Why, oh, why, can't things be beautiful without sadness?'

Kathleen bade him believe that 'all's sure to come right and if it *doesn't*, why then it's probably far better that it shouldn't. *I shall be happy whatever things happen and that is true!*' In that reply of hers he detected 'a little note of discouragement', and was despondent again. 'Oh, my dear heart, we must pull through now.'

His mother wrote also on 25 June: 'My own dear, dear son, I am anxious to know how your dear Kathleen takes us.... We shall all make her as welcome as you would wish, if she does not mind entering a family who are and always have been so very fond of each other.' His happiness, she said, was of the greatest concern to her. 'I am quite ready to take your dear one to my heart and to love her as much as I admire her. God bless and keep you. Ever your most loving Mother, H. SCOTT.'

Scott told Kathleen: 'I never doubted they'd all love you when they know you but I didn't think they'd all get over the money difficulty so easily.' He countered her doubt whether the newspapers should be told of their impending marriage by remarking: 'It will remind people that wedding presents are needed.'

She had found a little Georgian terrace house, with a garden studio, 174 Buckingham Palace Road; in the excitement of giving him news of it she addressed her letter to 'Capt. R. Scott, Esq.' It was offered at £50 a year, '8 rooms and a studio. Oh, dearie, don't marry me if you'd sooner not. But if we go on loving each other as we have done, I think it'll be all right.'

He wrote 'very solemnly' to say that the permission he had given her to seize her freedom at the last moment was withdrawn. 'I can't lose you now. Dear heart, you mean that to me which it would go hard with me to go without. I feel tonight I couldn't face it.' Six months before he thought he knew much of the world. 'You have taught me something which I did not dream of. Whence comes your unerring sense of values? Why now, at this age, should I realize ideals? Oh, it's perilously near the impossible. Shall I shake myself and wake to find you only a dear little girl with a pretty face?' (29 June 1908)

She prayed—'how reverently I pray'—that they might be able to read that letter of his in three years' time without either laughing or crying. 'Surely two people who so much

149

want to be fine and good and splendid ought to be able to keep from the ordinary disgustingness that makes the beautiful world ugly. We will try very hard. Only if you are absent-minded, I shall be irritable. Mind you wear your hat as little as possible in the sunshine. I *will* not have a bald husband. Don't send more than the £200 to my bank. If I can't make that house habitable on £200, then I'm no good.'

The states of abstraction in Scott that disconcerted Kathleen Bruce were a subject of comment by Sir James Barrie, who wrote that Scott was 'a strange mixture of the dreamy and the practical, and never more practical than after he had been dreamy'. Barrie gave a dinner party. 'He dressed to come out and then fell into one of his reveries. He forgot all about our engagement, dined by himself, and went to bed. As he was falling asleep he remembered where he should have been. He rose and joined us as speedily as possible.'

Arriving for another evening occasion in polite company, and being helped out of his overcoat by a manservant, he stood in his shirtsleeves, having forgotten to put on his dinner jacket. Mrs Philip Dumas, who knew Scott well through her father, Rear-Admiral Sir George Egerton, remembers 'those queer blank phases when he seemed to be far away, although standing there before you. He always came back with a most engaging smile.'

Such eclipsing forgetfulness could be construed as misanthropic, a sign of a lack of interest in others. Scott's daydreaming was by no means egocentric. It seems to have been a kind of self-hypnosis serving no significant inner purpose.

*

Off the Kent coast, he wrote on 3 July 1908: 'Hurrah, the house is ours! Will you be a perfect angel and get me two wedding presents? No. 1 for Captain C. Greatorex, R.N., 11 King Edward Road, Rochester, No. 2 for Captain A. Glyn, 27 Grosvenor Place, S.W. Dear heart, I enclose cheque for £5 for this. We are too poor to spend the whole sum on those presents, so get two little old silver boxes or something of the sort and put the balance into our furnishing account.'

The request drew a provocative reply. 'The man I told you of wrote to me many sheets this morning, telling me his income, prospects, etc. I wish he hadn't. Don't ever again give me anything so fearful to do as to buy wedding presents for you. I *really* don't know how to do things like that.'

A. E. W. Mason had not kept his lips closed, as requested, on the subject of their engagement. Barrie was upset because they had not directly told him of it. 'We must not hurt so sensitive and dear a person', Kathleen wrote. 'Please write *quite* by return of post. He's at Blacklake Cottage, Farnham. As nice a letter as ever you can think of.' At the Savoy, 'I saw your little Pauline Chase supping with three of the stupidest-looking youths. However, she was sweet and charming in her way.'

Doing as he was told, Scott wrote from Queen's Ferry that he was 'in trouble elsewhere', over the same matter. 'I don't believe you appreciate for a moment how busy I am. Allow me to give you an instance. Tomorrow I shall have to rise at 3.30. I shall be on deck most of the day. I have at least 2 hours paper work to wedge in at night. We shall anchor late, and the next day be off early again. (It's a huge business, the paper work of the fleet) . . . On top of all this, forsooth, you wonder why I don't make arrangements and write letters.'

Probably, like most families of their class and kind, the Scotts were suspicious of artists, and Kathleen Bruce at first did not find it easy to go among them. Having dutifully been to see Hannah Scott at Henley, she told Scott that she had a sort of 'hotted-up feeling', and could not repeat the visit. Aware of 'a little difficulty', he begged her to 'make allowance, and understand the courage and fortitude with which my Mother faces things'. When Kathleen tactfully settled a difference between Scott and his eldest sister Ettie, he wrote from a full heart:

'God in heaven, what a *gem* you are. Little wonderful girl, do you really and truly belong to me? I can scarcely believe it possible! Dearest, we'll only have nice-hearted people within our circle, won't we?' (11 July 1908)

Receiving a letter from Kathleen's solicitor, with reference to settlements, life insurance, and other provisions, he wrote that he was 'extremely frightened', reminding her that she knew his financial situation. 'My will leaves what I've got to my Mother. I couldn't change that, could I? I told you I hadn't a life insurance. And you know also there's a pension of £70 or £90, I've forgotten which, for you.'

He hated not being able to give her all that she ought to have. 'It's so strong sometimes that I'm irritable and wretched about it—and that lawyer, with his "settlements" and "insurances" just went straight to the centre of my most sensitive spot. Be sparing to my meanness when it peeps out' (17 July 1908).

She had soothing words for him. 'Oh, my dear, how lovely we are going to make everything. You and me. You and me. You and me. I've always been just *me* before. Now it's you and me and it's *good*.' Sir Clements Markham had been talking to her about the new polar expedition. 'How magnificently exciting it all is! You shall go to the South Pole. Oh, dear, what's the use of having energy and enterprise if a little thing like that can't be done. It's got to be done, so hurry up and leave no stone unturned.'

*

Because an aunt of Kathleen's was the widow of Archbishop Thomson of York, and lived in grace-and-favour accommodation at Hampton Court, it was suggested that the wedding should take place in the Chapel Royal there. Scott thought it a desirable preliminary to give the venerable lady some information about his financial prospects.

'They are not good, but of course Kathleen knows everything. My Mother is dependent on me and that is a trust never to be interfered with. My life is not insured and my money will remain willed to my Mother. Kathleen stands thus: during my life she'll always be poor.'

He pointed out that she was acquainted with poverty, 'and finds no terrors in it'. He trusted that they would keep their heads above water. When he went to the Lord Chamberlain's office, to seek advice on obtaining the King's permission for the wedding to be celebrated at Hampton Court, he found 'the various officials away *shooting*' (it being the second week of August).

'What fun! Our home—oh, I'm longing, longing, for the day when we shall just go inside and know there's nothing but our two selves. . . . Most important—whatever happens you must have a surveyor to report on the drains. Mind you remember that,' he wrote commandingly (26 July 1908). Kathleen replied: 'Oh, dearie me, I'm beginning to have awful misgivings. It's all right about the drains. I've had that seen to', and then went on to say that she had been 'extraordinarily happy' in the last few days. 'I haven't spoken to a soul since the day before yesterday. I find myself curiously good company.'

She had been reading *Dorian Gray*. 'It's the most inspiring book and people are rank, staring, raving mad who call it immoral.' She considered it 'an awe-inspiring tract'. When she showed impatience with 'this silly ceremony, and banns—banns —how absurd', Scott rebounded with new doubts. 'Girl, I'm a little frightened, vaguely. You're so uncommon and I so conventionalized.' Once again he asked his haunting question: 'What does it all mean?' and confessed himself 'stupidly anxious'.

Aware of her impatience 'with the great mass that lives by rule', expressing all over again his admiration for her 'glowing independence of thought', he wondered 'how it will sort with the disciplined, precedent-seeking education of a naval officer?' He begged her: 'Try to be long-suffering with me. With all your might keep before you the conditions that have made me what I am, and be merciful in expectation.' He was convincing himself that he lacked the ingredients of a magnetic personality, though, as she undoubtedly knew, behind the pre-cast *persona* of the naval officer were elements of boldness and timidity, languor and vitality, confidence and anxiety, weakness and strength, that gave him unsuspected depths.

She had sent him a photograph of her great friend Isadora Duncan,* dancing. He thought fit to return it. 'I see the beauty of it, yet it is for you, not me. Will many things,' he asked in a tone that may not have been so plaintive as it sounds, 'be for one and not for the other?' It gave him 'the feeling of growing old' (with an exclamation mark), he wrote, when he reflected that he, too, had been 'something of the dreamer, the enthusiast, the idealist'. The 'dreaming part' of him, he conceded, 'was and is a failure. All has been so suppressed in me.'

He feared that she might be impatient with his limitations,

* Isadora Duncan, b. 1878, was the daughter of a San Francisco theatre manager. Her classical dancing in Grecian costume to the music of the masters brought her acclaim on the Continent, though her love affairs, as much as her art, made her a public figure. When Kathleen Scott first met her in Rodin's studio her name was intimately linked with Gordon Craig, the theatre designer. Tragedy followed her through life. Her two children were drowned, her Russian poet husband committed suicide, she herself was killed in a bizarre accident on the Riviera in 1927.

or tolerate them with indifference. 'I'm afraid of what I shall be to you. Will you grow to think me only fitted for the outer courtyard of your heart? I pause to wonder if I have a soul that such a freethinking creature as you could ever find companionable. The distrust is all for myself, remember. I never distrust you' (27 July 1908).

'Don't forget,' he warned her in his next letter, 'that at forty the reserve of a lifetime is not easily broken. It has been built up to protect the most sensitive spots.' Another down-phase ensued. 'Oh, darling, it's such a tremendous enterprise, ours. The beginning's all right, but where's the end? I'm in low spirits.'

He wished to say 'an important thing' for which he anticipated she would think him stupid. 'I want you to consider your trousseau. I want you to consider it from my point of view because you will otherwise be denying yourself lots of things for poverty's sake. When we are married you mustn't only look nice (which you can't help) but you must look as though there wasn't any poverty. Am I dreadfully sensitive to appearances?'

She would get some clothes, she told him, 'but they will always be little simple ones. I can't bear myself dressed up.' On the money question, she was firmly determined, she said, never to ask for help from her family. 'We would never hear the last of it.'

When he assured her gravely in writing that he would try to be worthy of her, she begged him not to. 'My sense of humour can't do with it.' To his declaration, 'I do love you,' he added the proviso: 'But I wonder how it is all going to work out.' She retorted: 'Bless you, frightened one. I don't believe you love me a bit, or you wouldn't have all those qualms about the ridiculous myth of "the future".'

Discussing the wedding arrangements, she supposed that the occasion would attract 'all sorts of relations who mean nothing to us'. It was important 'to find means to do this awful deed without personal discomfort'. Max Beerbohm wrote on 26 August: 'I shall be sending you some hideous presents in a day or two.' A goodly array had already been received. Scott informed his bride-to-be a week before the appointed day: 'I haven't any fresh loot to report, except a pair of gold sleeve links.' To Dr Wilson's letter of good wishes, 'the nicest I have ever had', he replied that he valued them particularly because

Wilson and his wife were 'a glaring example of how happiness may be achieved without a large share of worldly gear'.

By the King's permission, the marriage took place at the Chapel Royal, Hampton Court, on 2 September 1908. The 'happy couple' were saluted by a clap of thunder as they walked up the aisle. Seeing 'the splendid figure' of Captain Campbell, R.N., their best man, the bride whispered to her husband-to-be: 'Could I marry him instead?'

After the service, 'they left the chapel by the grand staircase, passing through the haunted gallery and the State rooms to the armoury and the oak room, where a reception was held for 100 guests' (*The Times*). Among those present were many of Scott's naval colleagues and some of his old companions of the *Discovery* voyage. The bride's artistic affinities were notably represented by Rodin, the sculptor. Blue wings were conspicuous in her going-away hat. The honeymoon was spent at the Hôtel de la Plage, Etretat.

To its report of the wedding *The Times* added the announcement: 'We are asked to state that the marriage will make no difference to Capt. Scott's future plans with regard to Antarctic exploration.'

*

Scott to Sir Archibald Geikie, Secretary of the Royal Society, 1908–13: 'I have spent the interval getting married! On this account only I am late in writing a strong protest. My indignation is shared by other members of the Expedition.' He was angered by the published remarks of Napier Shaw, Director of the Meteorological office, after examining the results of the Expeditions' observations on Antarctic weather. Scott complained that Shaw's comments implied 'a wholly unwarrantable measure of default on the part of those responsible for the instruments and their use', and asked: 'What of the feelings of Lieut. Royds and Mr Bernacchi?' who made the observations. According to Scott, Shaw made nonsense of some of their calculations, to the extent of suggesting 'that frostbites they remember on the right cheek were really on the left, and *vice versa*' (September 1908).

He expressed his resentment in a number of letters written at sea. 'I hate quarrelling,' he told Geikie, 'but this has been forced on me.' Geikie counselled moderation. Scott agreed that 'indignation is liable to superfluous expression. I am grateful to you for this curb' (22 October 1908). He continued to press the issue.

H.M.S. *Bulwark* putting in at Plymouth that month, he took the chance of a brief shore leave to call at the old family home, Outlands, where he was hospitably received by the tenant, Mr Love, the draper. 'He met me with many smiles and a conscious satisfaction with his own care as custodian of the property.' Scott was persuaded to cut his name in the bark of a birch tree in the garden. That souvenir of his visit is still locally cherished.

From their little terrace house, 174 Buckingham Palace Road,* Kathleen, addressing him quaintly as 'Dearest friend...' wrote to express 'wonderous content' in her new state. 'Isn't it lovely to be alive? There's an electric light bill come which shows that we spend 2s. a week. That's not much, is it? I wish we could be quite the nicest people in the world. It *is* lovely to be alive. I emit little shrieks from time to time, now there's no one to hear.' And again, a day later: 'Life's so thrilling just at present. I wish you were here to share it. May circles of blessing play around you, dear, to keep off the black blight,' induced by his feud with Napier Shaw. 'I'm preparing some more thunderbolts for him,' Scott wrote.

He had been dicussing Napier Shaw 'and his sins' with Hodgson, the marine biologist of the Expedition. 'Then a good deal of interesting talk on the sex discussion at the British Association. He says much was highly technical, hingeing on chromosomes. There was much to prove the absence of influence of the embryo by the physical or mental condition of the mother. Hereditary tendencies were considered to play a very large part, and then (this is much supported by stockbreeders) the dates with reference to the periodical tribulations of the female. All this,' he concluded, perhaps meaningfully, 'would have interested you greatly.'

In the same letter, he gave 'a glimpse of the life of a sailor', apparently by way of helping his wife better to comprehend it. H.M.S. *Bulwark* was in the Irish Sea. 'As the day wore on, the elements of risk crept into our position, and soon after five the wind shifted and came with terrific force from the open sea ... the ship straining heavily at her cable, the sea dashing

* The terrace was demolished in 1928 to make way for Victoria Coach Station.

past and breaking in mountains of foam on the rocks a few
hundred yards behind ... the wind roaring through the rigging.

'Steam ordered on the instant, but an hour and a half to
wait. As darkness fell, steam was reported ready and with infinite care we slipped our cable and clawed her clear of the
mooring buoys. Five minutes later we breathed a sigh of relief
as we plunged headlong to seaward. In an hour we came
abreast of Berehaven, turned in at the entrance and as we
quietly anchored in smooth water the clouds broke, the moon
shone forth and the last of the storm swept by.

'Now as I write, all is so calm and placid on board that it is
impossible to realize the trouble of four hours ago, yet with
glass I can see the forlorn outline of a collier ashore on the reef,
and the seas breaking high over her funnel. "They that go
down to the sea in ships." How curious it all is—to live on the
verge of mischance,' as if for him, who had braved the terrors
of the Antarctic, it was still a novel experience.

*

His wife thinks she would like to be known as Mrs R. Falcon
Scott, not Mrs Robert F. Scott. 'What say you?' Expressing no
opinion, he tells her: 'I'm very lonely tonight and I want you
so badly. Why can't I look up and see you? I'm impatient. It's
being caged here; breakfast, lunch and dinner, all alone in this
palatial prison. I get up and walk about, then dash out on to
the stern walk, and then return to sit and wonder about you
again. Pity me' (9 October 1908).

When she enthuses over *The Sway Boat*, a 'sex problem'
play at the Haymarket Theatre, he reminds her: 'Don't think
a play can't live without a sex problem. The mind of man
grows heartily sick of too great a stress on this subject. It's the
women, I believe, who keep it in so foremost a place. Granting
the play's realistic excellence, educational and otherwise, leave
room for the million other interests with which the world
teems. I can't see a few modern playwrights held up as philosophers of the ages. Don't be narrowly enthusiastic' (28
October 1908).

She protests, 'absolutely and entirely, against this onslaught.
Who's holding up a few modern playwrights as philosophers of
the ages? Who—who? Of course it's the women who keep up

the interest in the sex problem—it's their *life*, whether they will or no. They can't get rid of it, however intellectual or well educated they are.' His letter, she says, depressed her. 'I never thought I should become just exactly like all the other women and be dependent on one man's moods and comments, especially when they are so utterly illogical.'

He affects delight in her 'outburst—I rather love it. Burst out always,' he proposes, 'upbraid me, argue with me. Between us let there grow the best and surest understanding. You're the dearest darling of a wife as well as the most intelligent that man ever had. If you stop loving me—well, there'll be a bad smash. We picked up a boat at sea today—bottom up, hinting at a tale of disaster, I'm afraid a real one' (30 October 1908).

Agreeing that her enthusiasms 'are unduly enthusiastic', she reminds him that they are more catholic than he thinks. 'I am just as capable of overdoing it about Haldane, Beethoven, Socrates, Euripides, Anatole France, Muriel Paget, Mahomet, or Leonardo da Vinci. So don't call me *narrowly* anything.' The next day she is telling him: 'There is something terribly real about you. I never used to know anything about loneliness. Have you robbed me of my self-sufficiency?'

Scott, with the Channel Fleet, goes ashore on the Dorset coast for a few hours' exercise and walks over the downs. The landscape sets him brooding, as the great Antarctic vistas did, on the panorama of life in this world.

'A hill close by was carved and moulded by prehistoric marauders. The Romans completed and occupied the camp, and there it is and must be till countless generations have passed, a grimly rectilinear figure amidst rolling contours. What a monument!' (31 October 1908)

After another day's evolutions at sea, 'ships are arriving tonight, one after the other, creeping out of the fog and into the harbour in the glare of lights. The harbour is very like a small town', and he is part of the implacable machine again. 'I've had to report a midshipman for lying. It worries me' (4 November 1908).

Scott to Dr E. A. Wilson:

H.M.S. *Bulwark*,
Nov. 14, '08.

Dear old Bill,—You are just you—there never was anybody so absolutely straight and honest. In a world of grinding axes it's pure refreshment to me to see you or hear from you. *Imprimis,* will you drop my title—I understand perfectly, but I liked one letter written 'dear old chap' immensely. Next, *do* make use of our funny semi-occupied house in London. My wife has written, I know—but what I want you to understand is the *real pleasure* you'd give us both by staying there.

Yours ever,

R. SCOTT

Scott's displeasure with Napier Shaw, of the Meteorological Office, was unappeased. Shaw thought Scott's attitude 'not very generous', and suggested that such 'resentment of *bona fide* criticism would put an end to all scientific progress'. He claimed that he and his department deserved 'something better than a letter of angry rebuke'.

Earnestly advising Scott to 'let the matter drop' the Secretary of the Royal Geographical Society, J. Scott Keltie, pointed out that 'when Dr Shaw came to discuss the details of the work he found them to be below the standard of precision and accuracy to which he is accustomed in the most advanced modern meteorological research'. It would be disastrous, the Secretary urged, to prolong the controversy, 'and especially to allow it to become public. It could not fail to furnish material for caustic remarks on the part of our foreign rivals in Arctic and Antarctic exploration. I appeal to you in the interests of Antarctic research, and of harmony among men of science, to take the magnanimous course I have suggested' (November 1908).

That view was strongly endorsed by Admiral Field, of the Hydrographic Department of the Admiralty. 'Captain Scott appears to me to be ill-advised in resenting legitimate criticism. I have the highest admiration for the way he conducted the Expedition, and as a leader of men he showed that no officer could be better qualified for carrying out what he undertook.' The Admiral regarded it as unfortunate that Scott's staff was imperfectly trained on the scientific side of the Expedition. 'The hypersensitiveness that refuses to accept criticism is very unfortunate. In my judgement, by pressing for an inquiry he will do himself and the reputation of the Expedition much harm....'

Napier Shaw had used the words 'incompetence' and 'inexperience' in assessing the value of the Expedition's meteorological work. To Scott, they were irritants not easily dislodged. 'It is preposterous to allow such enormities of misstatement to go unchallenged, promulgated as they have been in the whole scientific world. Such loose statements would have been libellous if the Expedition had been a commercial undertaking' (23 November 1908).

To his friend George Simpson,* at the Indian Weather Bureau, Simla, he wrote that he was 'engaged in a serious quarrel with the Director of the Meteorological Office in London, concerning the volume which contains the meteorological results of our Expedition. It is full of inaccuracies and insupportable theories ... and I anticipate the necessity of publishing some startling errata. It's a pity that some of your Indian efficiency cannot be imported into the London office.'

There was balm for Scott in the review in *Nature* which stated that 'in zoology, it cannot be doubted that *Discovery* was true to her name'. In those same authoritative columns Professor Gregory, F.R.S., spoke of 'imprecisions' in the Expedition's physical observations. He also considered it doubtful that the *Discovery* was 'a complete success' as an expedition ship. 'Her engines required a large consumption of fuel. It meant that she could not be employed while the boss was on land.'

*

Not in genuflection to the scientists, Scott denounced himself as 'a clod, a clown, a blockhead'. He was overwhelmed by 'the absolute conviction' of his unworthiness *vis-à-vis* his wife. 'I'm privileged beyond all men. You're so exalted, I somehow can't reach up.' Writing his letter, he was interrupted 'by having to dash out to dinner with our vice-admiral,† a snob of snobs.' He returned to finish what he had begun: 'Oh, darling wife, be just what you have been—there never was, there never could be, anything more beautiful, such a treasure as you.' He cannot but have been delighted by her answer: 'Of

* Later Sir George Simpson, F.R.S., Director of the Meteorological Office, London, and a member of the British Antarctic Expedition, 1910–13.

† Vice-Admiral Sir Berkeley Milne, K.C.V.O. (1855–1938), then C-in-C 2nd Division, Home Fleet.

CAPTAIN IN THE ROYAL NAVY

Scott received his promotion to that rank on the day of his return to
England from his first Antarctic voyage, 10 September 1904

John Scott, father of Captain Scott, was a Devonshire brewer who inherited a family business that brought him more worry than profit

Hannah Scott, Captain Scott's mother. After her son's death she was granted grace-and-favour apartments at Hampton Court

Ancestral Home: Outlands, Milehouse, Devonport, where Captain Scott was born (From a water colour sketch made in the 1880s)

Scott, then Commander, R.N., on the deck of the *Discovery* at Cowes just after he had been invested with the Royal Victorian Order by King Edward VII

Sub-Lieutenant Ernest Shackleton, R.N.R., aged twenty-seven. A Norwood doctor's son, he served in the Mercantile Marine before being appointed third lieutenant in the *Discovery*

Lieutenant Albert A. Armitage, R.N.R., a Scarborough doctor's son and Scott's navigator and second-in-command of the National Antarctic Expedition 1901–4

Lieutenant Charles W. R. Royds, R.N., of Rochdale, Lancashire, first lieutenant in the *Discovery*. He became a seasoned sledge hand in the Antarctic

Dr Edward Wilson, of Cheltenham, at the time of his appointment as assistant surgeon with Scott's first expedition

Lieutenant Michael Barne, R.N., of Sotterley, Suffolk. One of Scott's messmates in H.M.S. *Majestic*, he was second officer in the *Discovery*

Lieutenant Reginald Skelton, R.N., of Norwich, engineer officer of the *Discovery*. He was described by Sir Clements Markham as 'a general favourite and best of the sledgers'

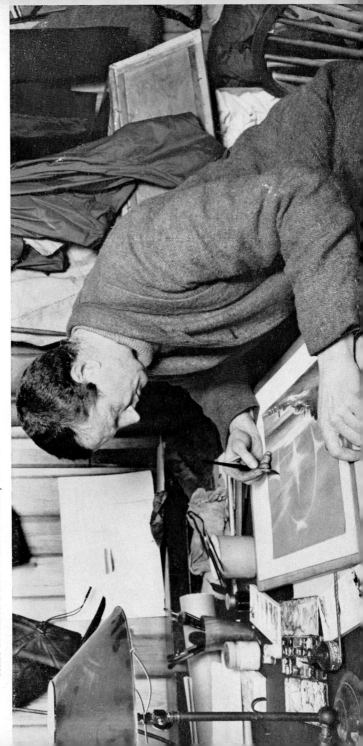

Above Ice sixteen feet thick immobilized the *Discovery* at her mooring in McMurdo Sound. Not knowing that a relief ship was on the way, Scott wrote in his diary: 'One wonders what the future has in store for us'

Below Edward Wilson, in the winter hut at Cape Evans, working on one of his water colour drawings. His colour sense revealed a new world of beauty in the Antarctic

The Scotts in Cape Town, awaiting the arrival of the *Terra Nova* on her way south

Peter Scott, aged two,
with his mother at 174
Buckingham Palace
Road, London, S.W.

Terra Nova, on her outward voyage, 1910. Scott relaxing on deck
with some of the members of the scientific staff

Scott, the leader. The pouch
over his left-hand pocket
contained the notebooks in
which he kept his
subsequently famous journal

Petty Officer Edgar Evans,
R.N., who marched with
Scott to the South Pole

In the pack, a photograp
taken by Ponting on 1
December 191

Mount Erebus, a familiar landmark of both Scott's expeditions. It was so named after one of Sir James Ross's ships that went to the Antarctic in the 1840s

Making camp near the polar plateau, December 1911

On the Polar Plateau. Petty Officer Evans with Captain Oates, Dr Wilson, and Captain Scott

Sastrugi, the ridges and furrows of frozen ice that often slowed down the polar march to little more than a mile an hour

Winter quarters with Erebus, the volcano, in the background

Glacier face, north of Cape Evans, which also gives an approximate idea of the edge of the Great Ice Barrier (now called the Ice Shelf), extending for about 400 miles across the open sea

course I'm not any of the beautiful things you say I am, but you make me want to be.'

The Commander-in-Chief, Lord Charles Beresford, was reported ill, shaken by recent criticisms of the Navy in and out of Parliament. 'Already I miss in the Fleet,' Scott wrote, 'the consciousness that high authority is interested in detail. That's bad for efficiency. In point of fact, the C-in-C can never know half that goes on in a great Fleet, but the art of a great commander is to create and preserve the impression of this all-pervading scrutiny' (13 November 1908).

He was uplifted by a sunset—'how you would have loved it. Never in England have I seen a finer. To the west, all red gold shading to lavender, to the east a glorious rose flush; oh, but much more, my stupid pen! ... Isn't this the pith—to you, it's you and I and a friendly world; to me, it's you and I and the rest inimical?'

He wrote describing preparations for battle practice. 'I wonder how we shall do? I don't mind much. I do mind about you. What does it all mean?' She flicked him with reproach. 'How dare you say you don't mind? You *do* mind. You must and shall mind.' There was a chance of his being given an appointment at the Admiralty. Considering it, his wife wrote that 'one would be rather less lonely, perhaps less appreciative, who knows? Perhaps more.'

She sent him a statuette she had modelled, not disclosing until afterwards that it was of a young friend of hers, the novelist Gilbert Cannan. Scott wrote that he was 'delightfully proud' of her. 'You really are a wonder. My dear, dear heart, there's something so astonishing fine about your work, such truth and vigour, that you must go on.' Of that there could be no question. Her creativity was central in her life.

In the same presumptuous vein, he urged her not to think too much of money getting. Their circumstances, and his forebodings, he suggested, had turned her thoughts in that direction. 'Really, we are all right. I can go on earning enough. Your art is too good to be spoilt by notions of gain' (8 December 1908).

She replied with the reminder: 'I couldn't do things I don't like doing. But I love making money—not because I don't want to spend yours. It's because I want us not to think about it. It's rather like the Big Navy policy.'

161

A Miss Madeline Morrison had told Scott's fortune at a tea party ashore, reciting his characteristics with 'such candour' that he was quietly impressed. She remarked his indolence, his untidiness, his quickness to take offence, his tendency to 'look on the dark side of things'. Receiving this information, Kathleen Scott answered that 'one would think she had been married to you for years instead of only reading your palm.' (3 January, 1909)

She seldom dated her letters. Suddenly, dates had a meaning. '*4th January, '09.*—My very, very dear love, I'm getting so excited and so frightened. I'm just going out to post a letter to my doctor. I feel as tho' that will clinch matters.' She had received the first intimations of motherhood. Recalling years later her feelings then, she wrote that 'not for a moment did I fear that the gods would interfere with this *gloria in excelsis*. It would be safely born and it would be a boy.' *

She evidently forgot that her ardour to be the mother of a son had been curiously transposed in those first days of 1909. She wrote to Scott: 'I am making all sorts of plans. I have christened her, given her godparents, estimated her wardrobe, designed her tiny trousseau, educated her and soon shall have married her. Oh, dear, oh, dear, it's too wonderful. But I suppose something will happen to prevent it,' as if she had picked up a characteristic thought wave from Scott.

Doubt was banished quickly. 'Con, darling, everything is so intensely interesting, enthralling.' She was fancying herself the mother of a daughter who would be called Griselda.

She bade Scott in her next letter (undated): 'Throw up your cap and shout triumphantly. Don't begin to think of all the worrying things it will mean. We're agreed that it's not wise to make life into hell by anticipating things that may never happen, not, for that matter, by anticipating those that most surely will happen.... I'm going nowhere. Too busy blowing the spark into a flame. Once I'm sure that the fire's ablaze, I shall have time, and the inclination, to go out again.'

He had not flung up his cap, he told her. 'A growing sedateness of demeanour prevented me.' Neither had he shouted nor sung, 'but not from want of inclination'. He had not been above joining in jubilant horse-play. 'I confess that after the receipt of

* Lady Kennet: *Self-Portrait of an Artist.*

your letter, I rolled Everett [a bearded fellow officer] on the floor of my cabin.'

He had dined that night with the Admiral, 'very dull except for a rather pretty American wife of the Captain of the *Queen* —David Beatty.* I remember him as a lieutenant on his pay, with mediocre prospects and intelligence. He slipped into two wars and will be an admiral at thirty-eight, the record for a century. His wife was a Marshall Field, inherited a million and a half, and went to America to fight for more and, I believe, got it. Oh, my dear heart, I'm very delightfully infatuated with you and somehow I feel the infatuation is getting dreadfully permanent.'

CHAPTER TWELVE

BRITISH ANTARCTIC EXPEDITION 1910

PLANS for the new Antarctic expedition matured slowly. Scott's absences at sea were a hindrance. He asked his friend of the *Majestic* and *Discovery* days, Michael Barne, to act as his agent and to report in particular on progress at the Finchley engineering shop. The motor sledge tests in the Alps had been unsatisfactory. Barne travelled down to Portland to see Scott in the last weeks of 1908. 'Alas, poor chap, there was little to tell him.'

In January 1909, Shackleton with three companions, Adams, Wild and Marshall, completed a tremendous march that took them to within 113 miles of the South Pole, 'the remotest men from their kind in all the world' (Mill). Not for two months would the cables spell out the news. Scott could have been in no doubt of Shackleton's ambition to stand before the public as a great twentieth-century explorer. Scott showed no sign of being an agitated rival.

The Admiralty post for which he had been recommended† was that of Naval Assistant to the newly appointed Second Sea

* The future Admiral of the Fleet Earl Beatty, P.C., G.C.B., O.M., G.C.V.O., D.S.O.

† By Admiral Mark Kerr, C.B. (1864–1944), later a founding father of the Royal Air Force.

Lord.* He thought it prudent to accept. 'From a naval point of view the thing would be good enough, and from a private one eminently desirable!' He would be able to live at home during the coming critical months in his domestic life, and he would be in a far more favourable position to promote his expedition plans.

The more settled prospect did not insulate him from a new attack of depression in which he seemed to lose his mental bearings. 'I can't describe what overcomes me. I'm obsessed with the view of life as a struggle for existence, and then forced to see how little past efforts have done to give me a place in the struggle. I seem to hold in reserve something that makes for success and yet to see no worthy field for it and so there is this consciousness of a truly deep unrest.'

He complained that his thoughts and sensations disturbed the current of his daily life. 'The outward signs are the black moods that come and go with such apparent disregard for the feelings of those dear to me. I long to be up and achieving things for your dear sake' (17 January 1909).

His wife answered that she understood how powerless he was against 'the dread thundercloud', that it would pass, as thunderclouds do. 'I wish you would write another book. I can't imagine what on, but I do wish you would write another one. My dear, I love you much, even when the moods come, because I know they are making you unhappier than me.' Would he think it 'wildly extravagant' that she was ordering a piano? 'A beautiful Broadwood for 16/– or £1 a month. Oh, my dear one, be merry, for life holds very much for us if only we would hold out our hands for it.'

Her dislike of affectation was stirred to protest again when he professed unconcern for some of his routine duties. 'I was rather shocked by your suggesting what I'm sure you didn't mean, that when there are such big things going on in the world what did it matter whether one little captain inspected boats, etc. What a wicked and fallacious saying. Good-bye, and make the *Bulwark* as fine as you can before you leave her.'

Their 'blessed event' reaffirmed by medical prognosis, she was going out and about again, as she had said she would. In March 1909 she was in Paris, revelling in 'the old feeling of freedom'. Whatever happened, she wrote to say, 'all will be

* Admiral Sir Francis Bridgeman, formerly C-in-C Home Fleet.

well. There's colour in my cheeks and joy in my heart.' She wished that she could give him some of her gaiety. 'It's so selfish of me, but it seems as tho' everything is in tune.'

He chose to see in 'that glimpse of old-time freedom' a reaction from the restraint imposed by her marriage to him. 'I am to you the representative of convention.' He quoted a phrase from one of her last letters: 'I *will* love you.' To him it suggested that she was 'determined to make the best of things'. He threw out the seemingly uncalled-for hint that in their new circumstances the thought of parting was impossible.

Kathleen had no time just then for the petty emotions. 'It's 12.30 and Isadora has danced. I'm *mad, mad* with it. She's more wonderful by far than ever before. I wonder if you have any notion what this means to me. She met me at the station yesterday. She has grown thin and dresses quite conventionally. She is so, so lovely. I wish that you could see her. And yet I'm afraid to let you. It would be awful if you couldn't see how great she is' (16 March 1909).

They had hurt each other; and she wrote to him at Lough Swilly to deplore it. He would not agree that she hurt him purposely; only that he struck back, 'meanly, with a vague intention to hurt'. When he had spoken of parting, she thought he implied that she could not fend for herself. 'The thought is too crude,' and he besought her: 'Oh, sweetheart, try to understand. I want someone to anchor to, someone sweet and sound and sure, like yourself. Part of me is wanting this with heart and soul, part is bitterly critical and sceptical of the possible realization of such a dream. There are times when I seem to read your detachment and ask myself, "*cui bono?*"'

He was pleased about the piano. 'Wise woman. It'll make everything nice. We'll get friend Holbrooke* to perform when he returns. I like the man because I can tell him how his counter point is too abstruse without him suspecting me of idiocy,' and in a postscript: 'Be candid about me. Tell me if I thwart your spirit' (17 March 1909).

He wrote from the Irish Sea about 'the big responsibility' of commanding a ship like H.M.S. *Bulwark*, a flourish of power

---

* Josef Holbrooke (1878–1958), born at Croydon, was a dedicated musician who composed opera, ballet music, chamber music, and pieces for military bands, with about equal facility. He introduced British music into many countries.

that may not have impressed her whose respect he wished to win and hold. 'We left Portland on Wednesday—manoeuvred in a half fog in the afternoon and continued down Channel before a furious easterly gale, a newly commissioned ship in front, another behind, and my own officers rather rusty in their work, created a trying position, so I stuck to the bridge throughout the night and there wasn't much comfort in it.' He hoped for 'some intermittent sleep' during the coming night but felt there was little chance of it: he had to be 'up at 2, again at 4, and then at 6'.

Working out a scheme whereby 'a very large fleet' could form a battle line four miles long was 'not a simple problem'. It was 'a cumbrous body' to handle. 'The fact that the masses moved are so costly, ponderous and filled with human life, and the risks taken consequently so important, makes the game more absorbing and fascinating than probably any that times of peace can produce' (20 March 1909).

He wrote his last letter from the Channel Fleet a week later, a week in which he had scarcely known rest—'all day on deck and five or six calls a night with ten minutes on deck on each occasion. I wish I had someone intelligent to discuss matters with.' Reverting to domestic affairs, 'this side of life makes me more anxious than all the manoeuvres that were ever performed'.

He had received a letter, noted as an afterthought, written from 2,000 miles up the Amazon. 'It has fired my wandering spirit' (29 March 1909).

*

His Admiralty appointment was dated 24 March 1909. In place of 'command money', it gave him 'maintenance pay' (now called 'London allowance'), based on the cost of living in the metropolis. Doing the simple arithmetic of his income, he made it £950 a year.

The post had always been filled by a Civil Servant. Scott was the first naval officer to hold it. The work involved interviewing candidates for specialized appointments within the Service; a 10 till 5 desk job. His free time was given to expedition business. Soon Kathleen Scott was telling their friends: 'Con begrudges even half an hour's absence from his room.'

One of the friends was with them in the small first-floor drawing-room of 174 Buckingham Palace Road when the news

166

of Shackleton's success was being shouted in the streets. Kathleen Scott, in her brown holland overall, was sitting on the floor, leaning against Scott's knees on which was spread a large map of the south polar regions. The guest was touched by that glimpse of a felicity that both knew might be brief.

'Scott was enthusiastic, in his quiet way, over what his one-time lieutenant had done.' Tracing the stages of Shackleton's journey, he spoke of the awesome nature of it, so that the visitor looked at him in fresh wonder at what Scott himself had endured. At the same time, 'there was that in his voice and eyes which declared unmistakably his resolve to endure it all again'.

He had kept in touch with Edward Wilson, making it clear to him: 'If I go South, there is no question you would be wanted more than anyone else in the world. I can scarcely hope that you will be free if the time comes. If you are, why it's worth it—it really is worth it. I'm going to try to get South again if circumstances permit you to come too. That is all that need be said for the present....'

Wilson told his wife: 'I should not feel it right to desert Scott if he goes again', a tribute that influenced the decision of others to return to the Antarctic under his leadership when the time came. Scott was in correspondence with naval officers and men whose services he hoped to secure. Lashly and Edgar Evans, his valiant companions in 1903, were ready to go South with him again. For general consultation, there was Sir Clements Markham, whose house in Eccleston Square was five minutes' walk from the Scotts' in Buckingham Palace Road. And Markham's faith in Scott was resolutely undimmed.

The widespread publicity given to Shackleton's use of an Arrol-Johnston motor-car as part of his expedition equipment reinforced Scott's determination to press on with his more original experiment in polar transport. Work was renewed with zest on the motorized sledge at Finchley. Its tortoise-crawl in the by-ways of that north-western suburb confirmed Scott in his belief that it could be the means of his reaching the South Pole well ahead of any other man.

*

News of Shackleton's great exploit made huge headlines in those last days of March 1909, with appended descriptions of the

167

tremendous welcome he received in New Zealand and Australia. Scott at once let it be known to the President of the Royal Geographical Society that he did not intend to let 'past incidents' prejudice his opinion of Shackleton's achievement. Shackleton arrived in London on 14 June. Out of the clamour a new image of him appeared.

That day, Scott was at the offices of the Royal Geographical Society, 1 Savile Row, W. He could not make up his mind about meeting Shackleton. Dr H. R. Mill, who was with him, said that 'he did not wish to go, and had to be persuaded to do so. Always a slave to duty, he went with us to Charing Cross Station, and took first place at the reception.'

What the handshakes of the two explorers told each other was not apparent to those gathered about them. There was surface geniality. Scott's congratulations were sincere enough. It was Shackleton's hour. 'No one who was present is ever likely to forget the roar of cheering from the crowd which filled the Strand and Trafalgar Square as the open carriage, with Shackleton, his wife and children, made its way slowly along the streets.'* Pushing through the throng in the station forecourt, Scott went unrecognized.

Triumph for Shackleton was followed by scrutineering doubts of his claim to have been within 113 miles of the South Pole. Markham candidly stated his disbelief. Shackleton's latest biographers say that there was another critic 'who accused him of deliberate falsification' and that 'the doubt seems to have persisted, and echoes of it sound down to the present day'.†

Evidence in favour of Shackleton's calculations was as strong as its counter assumptions. Standing apart from the controversy, Scott presided at a Savage Club dinner to Shackleton, and broke the unwritten rule of the club forbidding speeches from the chair. He made it an occasion for declaring that 'the Pole must be discovered by an Englishman', and that Great Britain should organize an Antarctic expedition 'before another country steps in' (19 June 1909).

*

From then on, it was a topic of printed gossip that both men

* H. R. Mill: *The Life of Sir Ernest Shackleton*.
† Margery and James Fisher: *Shackleton*.

were planning rival attempts to reach the South Pole. The Vice-President of the Royal Geographical Society (Admiral Sir Lewis Beaumont) wrote to the President (Major Leonard Darwin): 'I have thought carefully over what you told me of the Scott-Shackleton difficulty and I cannot think of any better way for the Geographical Society to deal with it ... than to reply as you said you thought of doing, that is, that the Society could not encourage or support an expedition merely intended to reach the Pole, but as individuals the members of the Council could not help hoping that it would be reached by an Englishman!'

The Vice-President thought that little real importance could be attached to 'standing at the point of the Pole itself', while recognizing that it would mean 'a remarkable success' to the public. He spoke of Shackleton's recent exploit as being 'still shrouded in mystery'. Whatever Shackleton might intend, the Vice-President was 'quite clear' that Scott should not be encouraged to join in a race for the Pole.

'Let him lead another Antarctic expedition if he will. Let it be a scientific expedition primarily, with exploration and the Pole as secondary objects—and so add to the fine reputation which he already has. All this long story is to incline you to put Scott off from making what I think will be a great mistake', that is, competing with Shackleton (19 June 1909).

The explorers addressed each other stiffly on the subject of their respective planning spheres. 'Dear Shackleton, I propose to organize the Expedition to the Ross Sea, which as you know, I have had so long in preparation so as to start next year ... I am sure you will wish me success; but of course I should be glad to have your assurance that I am not disconcerting any plan of your own' (1 July 1909). 'Dear Captain Scott, I understand that you have already your expedition in preparation, and it will not interfere with any plans of mine ...' (6 July 1909).

The humiliations of 1903 no longer plagued Shackleton. Vindicating his powers of endurance, he had uplifted the hearts of his fellow countrymen at a time when the theme of national decline was being debated at home and abroad. He had already proclaimed in a letter to his wife: 'I am representing 400 million British subjects.'

Jean Charcot, the French explorer, was about to sail South

again. The voice of Dr Cook, the controversial American explorer of the Arctic, was grating on English ears with his insistence that the conquest of the South Pole must be high on the agenda of United States policy. Germany, Japan and Belgium aspired to the same hollow glory. *The Times* was saying: 'Great Britain now holds the leading place in South polar expeditionary enterprise; but that position cannot be held without continuity of effort.' Young Lieutenant 'Teddy' Evans, of the Navigation School, Portsmouth, formerly second-in-command of the relief ship *Morning*, was fancying himself the hero of a new Polar exploit. He submitted to Sir Clements Markham an outline plan to take a party to King Edward VII Land, 'establish winter quarters, and push forward to a high Southern latitude' (7 July 1909).

Scott's plans were suddenly accelerated in the late summer of 1909. He told Admiral Sir Arthur Moore, Commander-in-Chief, Portsmouth, in a letter: 'I hear, on reliable authority, that the Americans are going.' It was a possibility that, fatefully for Scott, also disturbed the thought of the Norwegian explorer, Roald Amundsen, who had been frustrated in his hope of being first at the North Pole (though Peary's claim was being sceptically reviewed by geographers).

*

An office for what was formally styled the 'British Antarctic Expedition 1910' was opened at forty-eight hours' notice on 13 September 1909: address, 36–38 Victoria Street, S.W. (Telephone: Gerrard 1840. Telegrams: Onwardness, London). Cheerfully abandoning his own dream of Antarctic leadership, 'Teddy' Evans agreed to serve as Scott's second-in-command. An Expedition secretary, Assistant Paymaster Francis Drake, R.N., was put in charge of the office at £4 a week.

The next morning Scott's expedition plans were published in full. 'The main object of this Expedition is to reach the South Pole, and to secure for the British Empire the honour of this achievement.' The chief geographical purpose was to explore King Edward's Land, 'to throw further light on the nature and extent of the great Barrier ice formation, and to continue the survey of the high mountainous region of Victoria Land'. Extensive provision for scientific work under the headings of geology, meteorology, and terrestrial magnetism, endowed the Expedition with a scope and responsibilities far beyond those of any previous venture of the kind.

Those particulars prefaced an appeal for financial help to cover 'a total estimated expenditure of £40,000'. *The Times* hoped 'that the expedition will not be hampered by lack of funds. The work of Antarctic exploration,' that newspaper noted, 'which was begun by Captain Cook in the 18th century, and has been continuously carried forward by British explorers, in the face of desperate difficulties, should not be dropped now that the goal seems attainable.'

The following day, 14 September 1909, a son was born to the Scotts. 'And then a strange thing happened to me', Kathleen Scott wrote. 'I fell for the first time gloriously, passionately, wildly in love with my husband.' Until then, she could say, 'he had been a probationer, a means to an end. Now my aim, my desire, had been abundantly accomplished. I worshipped the two of them.' The boy was named Peter Markham.

For Scott, a memorable week. On 15 September a Reuter message stated that 'apparently there is to be a race to the South Pole between England, represented by Captain Scott, and America, represented by Commander Peary. On arrival at St John's of the Labrador mailboat, it was stated on what is described as absolutely authentic information that Commander Peary has decided on an expedition to the South Pole.'

Scott to the President of the Royal Geographical Society:

> 174 Buckingham Palace Road,
> S.W.
> [Undated]

My dear Major Darwin,—At this juncture in the history of Polar Exploration I think it is absolutely necessary to continue those efforts which have given to this country the foremost place in Antarctic Research. I have undertaken the task of organising an expedition and submit to you in brief the programme which I propose to adopt.

I believe that the main object, that of reaching the South Pole, will appeal to all our countrymen as the one rightly to be pursued at this moment, but the plan which I present provides also for the scientific exploration of a considerable extent of the Antarctic continent and will therefore I hope commend itself to the Royal Geographical Society.

I should be glad to receive an expression of your approval and trust that I may have the benefit of your advice and assistance in preparing the Expedition.

Believe me,

Your sincerely,

R. SCOTT

That same day, Scott telegraphed to Wilson, asking him to organize and lead the scientific staff of the British Antarctic Expedition 1910. Accepting the invitation Wilson wrote immediately to tell his father that he had done so. 'Scott is worth working for as a man.' Meeting Scott in London that year, Sir Aurel Stein (1862–1943), learned authority on the geography of India and Central Asia, had a firm impression of 'the classic greatness of his character'.

Like Shackleton's before him, Scott's new expedition was a personal venture. Like Shackleton, too, he was nagged by the past, in his case, by the criticisms of the scientific inadequacies of his first expedition.

From the beginning, he bore the burden. He had no official sponsors as before. He could not be sure of Government aid. There was no munificent private donor this time to provide £25,000. Scott put in most of his savings from his book and lecturing (thought to have been under £3,000) and counted on patriotism and persuasion to yield the rest.

Going cap-in-hand round the country was an errand for which he had no stomach, none at all. Evans thought it 'a trifle hard' that he should have to do so, saying that it was harder to ask than to give. Scott resigned his congenial post at the Admiralty in December 1909, went on half pay at considerable financial discomfort to himself and his wife, and set forth on a mission that was often dispiriting, occasionally humiliating, and more rewarding in goodwill than in cash.

His personal feelings apart, it meant breasting a tide of public sentiment that was still running strongly in favour of Shackleton, who, before the end of the year, received the crowning honour of a knighthood, which some thought Scott had earned long before. Shackleton's book, *The Heart of the Antarctic*, just published, survived critical comparisons with Scott's book, *The Voyage of the 'Discovery'*. It was discreetly silent on the McMurdo Sound controversy. Shackleton's ship, the *Nimrod*, came up the Thames to a mooring off Temple Pier on 30 September. She was 'inspected by a constant flow of visitors' (*Daily Mail*).

J. M. Barrie to Scott:

Lausanne,
23 September '09.

I shall be delighted to be godfather to the boy and am very glad you asked me. May he be a great source of happiness to you both and, let me say, please, to all three of us. Also I am very glad the expedition is to come off and it will be a real pleasure to me to subscribe.

*

The campaign for funds opened on 13 October 1909, at a meeting at the Mansion House, London, the Lord Mayor presiding. The attendance was representative rather than large. Scott had to listen to the recital of a number of telegrams from prominent men who were 'otherwise engaged'. The President and Council of the Royal Geographical Society, 'while giving Captain Scott their full approval and support,' were unable to contribute more than £500, 'in view of the pressing claims made by other expeditions on the funds of the Society this year.' Instead, they circularized 3,250 Fellows with an appeal for £2 10s. each, 'or any multiple of that sum.' The President of the Royal Society telegraphed good wishes.

Sir Edgar Speyer, the City financier who was introduced as a founder of the Whitechapel Art Gallery, agreed to act as treasurer to the fund and put his name down for a personal subscription of £1,000. ('Hear, hear.'—*The Times*.) Sir Arthur Conan Doyle, the creator of Sherlock Holmes, claiming to speak 'for that humble individual, the man in the street', warmly endorsed the aims of the Expedition, and subscribed an initial £10. Viscount Goschen, a former member of the Government, reminded the meeting that 'Captain Scott and those who are going with him are willing to give their knowledge, abilities, and courage, even their lives, for the sake of getting to the South Pole.'

Scott gave the meeting his word that his supporters 'need never fear that the dignity of the country will suffer from anything which may be done by our Expedition. We may fail, but they shall have no reason for doubting the story which we tell.'

It may or may not have been a double-edged allusion. An unseemly wrangle had been conducted in public over the rival claims of Dr Cook and Commander Peary to have been the first at the North Pole in April 1909. Cook, an American medical man, provoked scornful mirth by his account of himself 'striding across the boreal nadir'. Peary, of the United States Navy, solemnly annexed a floating icefield 'in the name of the President'. Behind the doors of the Royal Geographical Society argument was still heard about the worth of Shackleton's claim to have put a little over a hundred miles between himself and the Pole.

Addressing members of the Baltic Mercantile and Shipping Exchange in the City on 21 October 1909, Scott explained that as a naval officer he was 'not used to raising money'. He had to get it, he said, 'by hook or by crook', and he 'looked confidently to the wealthiest city in the world to give in accordance with its importance'. While the Baltic men were making up their minds what to do, the Stock Exchange set an example by contributing £500.

Scott was by then committed to the purchase of the *Terra Nova*, one of the two ships that had gone out to relieve the *Discovery* in 1903-4. He had hoped to secure the use of his old exploring ship again. Her new owners, the Hudson Bay Company, decided that she could not then be spared from their service. He thereupon settled to buy the *Terra Nova* from Bowring Brothers, of St John's, Newfoundland, making an agreement to pay £5,000 down and a balance of £7,500 when it could be found. The first payment was due on 8 December 1909. He told his wife in a letter: 'I don't know how I shall manage it.'

Scott to J. J. Kinsey: *

> 174 Buckingham Palace Road,
> London, S.W.
> 26.10.09.

Dear Mr Kinsey,—I am writing to ask boldly if you will act as agent to the British Antarctic Expedition 1910. Your kindness to the *Discovery* expedition is still very fresh in

* J. J. Kinsey (1852–1936) was head of Kinsey & Co., shipping agents, of Christchurch, New Zealand, and Belgian consul for New Zealand. Born in Kent, he was for some years a master at Dulwich College. He was knighted in 1918 for his services to British Exploration in the Antarctic.

my memory and I cannot think that your interest in the subject is exhausted.

I haven't much doubt that the money for the Expedition can be raised in this country; in fact, it must be done for the *Terra Nova* is already on her way to the Thames and will duly sail out of it again in August next.

We must on this occasion get to the South Pole, if not at the first attempt, then at the second, but the enterprise must not be relinquished till the work is done.

If you will kindly undertake to pilot the *Terra Nova* through her difficulties at Lyttelton when she comes and goes you will, I hope, have the satisfaction of an active share in the final stages of a campaign to which you have already rendered constant and invaluable service.

Yours very sincerely,
R. SCOTT

Travelling 'countless miles by motor' on his fund-raising crusade, Scott wrote letters to his wife that often indicated impatience and seldom expressed satisfaction. 'This place won't do—wasting my time. I don't think there's a great deal of money in the neighbourhood.' At Redcar, Yorkshire, he dined with a man of wealth named Cochrane, who said 'he would give something, but not very much, and when he asked others to join his party, hinting broadly at the object, there was a mighty poor attendance!' Receiving an offer of £30 a year for four years, he hailed it as 'a really fine subscription'. At Harrogate, 'Captain R. F. Scott, C.V.O., R.N., addressed a meeting at the Majestic Hotel, explaining the preparations he is making for his dash to the Pole. There was only a small attendance' (*Yorkshire Herald*).

After visiting Wolverhampton, where the response amounted to 'between £20 and £30, *c'est tout*,' he reported 'another very poor day yesterday, nearly everyone out'. He had started from London with a pocket full of introductions 'but the— great difficulty is to find people in'. He had rosy hopes of Manchester, and looked forward to 'some good business' at Middlesbrough, Darlington and York.

At a preliminary meeting in Liverpool, he was called on to speak 'in a room that was beastly'. There was more encouragement for him at an assembly of business men at the Town Hall, from which local optimists thought 'that £1,000 would result'. The seventeenth Earl of Derby, presiding, said that the hope of being first at the South Pole, and of beating the German and American expeditions, 'appeals to all Englishmen'. Applause from all parts of the hall stirred his lordship to Chauvinistic conceit. 'I am not unduly insular, but I have a feeling, which is shared by a good many of our fellow countrymen, that every uninhabited part of this globe belongs of right to England.'

A *Liverpool Post* reporter, calling on Scott 'at the residence of his host, Mr F. C. Bowring, of Croxteth Drive, Sefton Park', described him as 'not of the type of American explorer who announces that he will "reach the Pole or bust"'. His lack of self-emphasis was commended. 'There is nothing of the braggart or blusterer in his appearance. The first person singular was only occasionally invoked during the interview.'

Manchester provided £2,000, against the expectation of its Lord Mayor, who, mindful of local unemployment, 'feared that there would be a good deal of difficulty in finding that sum'. Bristol found £740, Newcastle £1,000, Cardiff £1,387.

Too often for his liking, Scott was challenged after his speeches to explain 'what is the good of going to the South Pole'. Standing before his audiences, smiling with faint tolerance, he embodied the spirit of the eighteenth-century venturers who had sailed out of his home port of Plymouth, a man of nerve and courage who was prepared to face extremities of danger and privation in what he held to be a worthy cause. He carried more conviction when he struck the patriotic chord than when he answered that his Expedition might discover new sources of pitchblende. 'Englishmen cannot be slow to support this enterprise, for undoubtedly its objects will be attempted by other nations if we hang back', and so on.

Of the 'other nations', the United States was the most serious contender, so he then believed. The leader of a German Antarctic Expedition, Lieutenant Wilhelm Filchner, let it be known that he would recast his plans in order not to interfere with Scott's.

Unknown to Scott, Commander Robert Peary, the American explorer of the Arctic, had written a 'private and confidential' letter to a New York news agency manager concerning published reports of his intention to try to reach the South Pole.

He understood that the reports were causing 'a certain feeling as a possible trenching on the rights of Scott and Shackleton. There are reasons why I should like to head off at once any unpleasant feelings of this nature.' Outlining a plan 'to attack the problem by way of the Weddell Sea, along the coast of Victoria Land', he asked the news agency man to 'find out quietly' whether Scott would 'have any feeling whatever if attempts were made to materialize such an American expedition' (29 November 1909).

An appeal for Government aid was lodged with the Chancellor of the Exchequer on 14 December 1909. 'It is anticipated that the accomplishment of very important scientific work will be fulfilled, but perhaps above all in that of Geology, where the possibilities of discovery in an enormous uncovered area are almost limitless. The steps which are being taken will ensure the Expedition being better equipped to deal with scientific problems than any other Polar expedition that has ever left these shores. . . .'

Scott was relieved to hear from New Zealand that he could count on Kinsey's 'important help'. He wrote Kinsey a long and informative letter in the course of which he indicated the part that commercial advertising had in his arrangements. 'The advertisement to be derived from the supply of stores to an Expedition such as this is thought very highly of in this country, and thanks to this and to a patriotic wish for our success, we are getting goods on extraordinarily favourable terms.' They would be 'handsomely paid' to take a wide range of branded articles, from woollen garments to chocolate, carbide to boots, jam to petrol. 'I find it possible to persuade people who come to see me that it is an honour to have their goods taken on the Expedition, and that the advertisement is well worth the cost.' Profiting from the experience of the *Discovery* expedition, he was taking 'relatively small' supplies of tinned meat.

Touching on 'the general plans', he reckoned that a party of about 22 men would be landed in McMurdo Sound, and 6 or 7 in the region of King Edward's Land. 'Besides the shore party, the ship will have a crew of about 25 officers and men. I hope to get naval people in the main.' Expressing great pleasure that Kinsey would be acting on behalf of the Expedition in

New Zealand, he had no doubt that 'it ensures all difficulties being removed from our path' (22 January 1910).

*

In the first weeks of 1910, Peary and Scott exchanged letters. Writing from The Oakland, Washington, D.C., Peary thanked Scott, for his 'big, manly characteristic attitude' (21 January). Writing, on 9 February, from Ayton Hall, Great Ayton, Yorkshire, Scott thanked Peary for his 'generous letter' and looked forward to meeting him in May. The *Daily Mail*, in a 'special interview', quoted Peary as saying: 'You may take my word for it, the race for the South Pole between the Americans and the British, which is to start in seven months, will be the most exciting and nerve-racking the world has ever known' (12 February).

Scott wrote to Kinsey: 'I am devoting all my energies this month to completing the funds for the Expedition. . . .' and in a postscript: 'My small boy has had whooping cough, but is now much better' (29 January 1910). The fund gathered pace in the New Year with the announcement that the Government would make a grant of £20,000. The total at the end of January was still well short of the £40,000 needed. The Royal Geographical Society gave £500, the Royal Society £250. A Fellow of the Royal Society wrote from the Athenaeum to Sir Archibald Geikie, Secretary of the Royal Society: 'We are by no means as confident as you are that Scott will find all the money he requires.'

The news of the Government grant was coldly received north of the Tweed. Long letters of grievance appeared in the press about official neglect of the Scottish Antarctic Expedition, under Dr W. S. Bruce, who was preparing to extend his already considerable explorations of the Weddell Sea. Letters in the local papers raised awkward questions about the good sense of supporting the Expedition when there was dire need at home. Typical of them was the comment quoted from *Sussex News*: 'I call it scientific cheek to come along and ask for £40,000 for such a purpose when so many thousands are out of work' (19 February 1910). *Vanity Fair* could not 'rouse any enthusiasm over the discovery of the Pole. The search for it is profitless.' As for the Government grant, 'we see no objection to it, but there is no need to associate it with rubbish about human progress and the advance of civilization'.

While Scott was in the Midlands and the North, his boyishly exuberant second-in-command, Lieutenant 'Teddy' Evans, had gone to take financial soundings in South Wales. The Cardiff shipping magnates were less attentive to his constantly re-iterated assertion of Welsh antecedents than to his artfully deployed hints of wealth waiting to be won in the Antarctic. 'I'm telling you what only a few of us know. There is commercial value in the Antarctic and the Norwegians are already on to it. They have started a colony in Graham's Land for their whaling industry. They are making profits—big profits.'

Unlike Scott, Evans discovered 'excitement in raising funds'. After his speech at a Cardiff luncheon, he was handed cheques and cash to the amount of £222 17s. 'It's no good talking to business men about magnetism, geology, meteorology, or any of that scientific stuff.'

Scott missed few opportunities of stressing the 'scientific stuff' in his appeal speeches. He preferred the unexpressed goodwill of the nation's best brains to convivial handshakes in mayors' parlours where there was too much uninformed chatter about 'the race to the Pole'. He emphasized the value to navigators of more information about magnetic conditions, and the worth of studying the effect of climatic changes in the polar regions on the weather of the temperate zones. There was also 'the fauna of the sea'. Who could say that there would be no beneficial results from a more proficient study of it?

Battling with public listlessness, he was beset, too, by private problems arising out of his reduced income. Continuing his allowance to his mother and one of his sisters, he was left for a time with less than £50 a month. When he formally assumed the leadership of the Expedition in the autumn of 1909, he went on the payroll at £20 a week.

Fearing that their recent straitened circumstances had produced tensions, he apologized to his wife. 'I was lying abed thinking last night, and all you'd done and are doing for me spread itself out.... When things look bad, when I'm tiresome or petulant, don't think your care is wasted. When I'm away in the snows it will be bad to remember that I've grieved you, but it would be infinitely worse if I thought you didn't know that

I understood your sacrifices. My dear, my dear, my heart is very full of you ...' (14 February 1910).

His mother, at Henley, was following every line printed about him and the Expedition. She wrote to a friend of the family that, greatly admiring his determination to complete the work he had begun in the Antarctic nearly ten years before, she none the less 'had a dread of his going'.

CHAPTER THIRTEEN

SOUTHWARD IN THE *TERRA NOVA*

'COMPLETING the funds of the Expedition is arduous work'— Scott to Kinsey (19 February 1910). He hoped that by March he would be free to settle personally all the details of the preparations.

He went to Lillehammer and Fefor in Norway with his wife early in March to supervise trials of a remodelled motor sledge-hauler in the mountain valleys of Fefor, north of Christiania (now Oslo). The new prototype, built on lines suggested by Scott and Skelton, had come from the works of the Wolseley Tool and Motor Company (a Vickers–Maxim subsidiary), of Adderley Road, Birmingham. It was driven by a four-cylinder, air-cooled, 12 horse-power, two-speed engine, capable of pulling heavy loads at $3\frac{1}{2}$ m.p.h. The tractor laid its own track, and the 'feet' of the endless chain anchored themselves in the snow, while the body of the sledge moved forward on rollers. At Fefor, it hauled 3,000 lb. up a snow slope of 1 in $4\frac{1}{2}$. New alloys, combining lightness and strength, were used in its construction. Photographs prove its kinship, as an engineering development, with the Sno-cats used by Fuchs and Hillary on the Commonwealth Trans-Antarctic Expedition 1955–8.

In Norway, as before, Scott sought the advice of Fridtjof Nansen, who believed that dogs and skis provided the most reliable form of polar transport. Meeting Kathleen Scott, the famous Norwegian was attracted by her quick enlivening intelligence as an artist to whom he could talk as to few women he had known. The outcome was a friendship that on Nansen's side touched admiring devotion. His letters to her were those of a majestically lonely man.

Through Nansen, Scott met young Tryggve Gran, of the Norwegian naval reserve. Aged twenty-one, good looking, well off, and splendidly fit, Gran was an accomplished skier, whose services Scott thought would be valuable in the Antarctic, both as an explorer and as an instructor. He invited Gran to join the Expedition. On Nansen's advice, Gran did so. He was entered in the *Terra Nova*'s register as a midshipman at a shilling a month.

Letters of request to take part in the Expedition were arriving in great numbers at the London office. 'Dear Sir,—I have heard that you are contemplating another Expedition to the South. I am wondering if there is any truth in it at all, dear Sir, I hope when the time comes for the selection of your crew you will not omit me. I feel convinced in myself that I can do much more for you than I did before for the simple reason that I know myself better now than then or in plainer words I am getting older but wiser. Trusting you will favour me with a line and let me know if there is any chance of my serving under you again, I am, Sir, Yours obediently, T. WILLIAMSON.' Petty Officer Williamson, R.N., served with Scott in both expeditions.

Many applicants called in person, hoping to see the leader, some on the strength of old naval association, and 'awfully hard to turn down', he found. Those who had known him in other years saw that at forty-one he was thicker-set than they remembered, that his hair line had receded, that his cheekbones seemed higher, that his inherent modesty had withstood the battering of modern publicity, and that his personal force was as quietly dominant as before.

Doctors, railwaymen, Civil Servants, clerks, surveyors, students, factory workers, sailors, soldiers: the call of the Antarctic was like a bugle blast rallying men to inspiring duty. Officers of the Royal Navy and the Army offered their services as grooms, stewards, deck-hands, rather than be left out. There were those who unashamedly avowed patriotic feelings. The motives of others were undisclosed. When Scott first went to the Antarctic in 1901, few civilians were willing to go with him. Since then, what was being diagnosed in consulting room and pulpit as 'the strain of modern life' had been intensified. In 1910, Scott could man his ship and choose his shore parties from 8,000 volunteers.

Admiral of the Fleet Sir Edward Seymour, G.C.B., to Scott:

Hedsor View,
Maidenhead.
2.6.10.

Dear Captain Scott,—I was so interested in my visit to the *Terra Nova*. I should, for certain reasons—if asked—have advised you not to go. But Nicholson [an old shipmate of Scott's] said you want only to show an example of enterprise, and of facing risks and hardships, much needed in these days when money and pleasure are the things most desired and worshipped. These things will as surely ruin us as they ruined the Roman Empire.

No one can visit the ship, or talk to her people, without feeling greatly impressed with the zeal and enthusiasm existing, without any hope of pecuniary reward and the certainty of much peril and discomfort. I hope to greet you on your successful return.

Yours v. sincerely,
E. H. SEYMOUR

With the exception of Evans, his second-in-command (£10 a week), and Wilson, head of the scientific staff (£10 a week), Scott held firmly to his policy of not making any appointments until the Expedition fund justified them. He was in touch with members of the *Discovery* company, and was giving heed to the recommendations of naval colleagues and trusted advisers of the Royal Geographical Society.

The appointment of Lieutenant Evans was a painful shock to Engineer Lieutenant Reginald Skelton, R.N., who, as a successful and popular member of Scott's earlier expedition, had been keenly awaiting an invitation to join the new venture. Acting for Scott, he had supervised the design and construction of the latest model motor sledges. Scott had told him in a letter: 'I have cherished the idea that if ever I went South again you would join.' The summons had not come. The letter he wrote to Scott on 7 April 1910 appealed for an explanation. He was the victim, he thought, of malice on the part of Evans. 'I'm told that he has put in a special plea that I should not go.' He besought Scott: 'Hang it all, judge the case fairly,' which, at this remove, it is not possible for a biographer to do in the absence of other records.

*

Choosing the scientists who were to work with him, Wilson agreed with Scott that there should be some recruitment from the Dominions, making the Expedition more broadly representative of its British origins, and thereby commending it favourably to overseas governments. Presumably with that in mind, Scott told Douglas Mawson, a young Australian physicist, that if he joined he could be sure of a place in the party selected to go to the Pole. Mawson's interest was in 'pure scientific discovery'. He was flattered by Scott's offer but declined it.

Two of the young Commonwealth scientists engaged for the Expedition, T. Griffith Taylor (Australia) and Charles Wright (Canada), saw in the London office Petty Officer Edgar Evans, R.N., packing sledges. Impressed by his fine physique and manifest strength, they resolved to show Scott that scientists, too, were capable of standing up to rigorous physical tests. A few days afterwards they did the standard London-to-Brighton walk of fifty miles in twenty-four hours.

Published explanations of Shackleton's inability to serve with Scott again, 'owing to his forthcoming American and Canadian lecture tour, and business interests', were beside the mark. He was thinking of leading an expedition 'to operate along the coast of Antarctica commencing in 1911'. The quotation is from the letter in which he submitted his plan to the Royal Society, the Royal Geographical Society, and to Scott. He had no intention, he wrote, of attempting to reach the Pole. Nor would he prejudice Scott's fund by appealing for public support.

Mawson, it appeared, wanted to explore the same coastal region and discussed with Scott the possibility of forming a subsidiary expedition, working under Scott's supervision. Scott could see no place for it in his programme. Shackleton approached Mawson and, after studying his expedition idea, somewhat arbitrarily adopted it as his own and proposed himself as leader.

The notion of two expeditions colliding in that immeasurable vastness seems far-fetched to the lay mind. Scott was taking no risks. His letter to the President of the Royal Geographical Society had an undertone of peevishness. 'I think Shackleton wants the coast from Cape North to Gaussberg left alone till 1911—I have no objection to his going there but I don't want any objection from him to my going there. He has not answered my last letter but I want it settled before I leave that I am free to go where I please without the reproach that I am trespassing on his ground' (29 March 1910).

Unlike Scott, Shackleton lacked the stand-by of a professional career with its regular if inadequate income. His financial harassments, acute in 1910, were not eased on the personal plane by a Treasury grant of £20,000 towards his recent expedition costs. The modified new expedition that he proposed to lead became the Australian Antarctic Expedition 1911–14, under Mawson. Shackleton was obliged to put his plan into abeyance while he fulfilled his contractual obligations as a lecturer.

Addressing a meeting at Southwark, London, S.E., Scott spoke of the menacing situation that was growing in Europe. His recent work at the Admiralty, he said, caused him to think that there might soon come a crisis in which the nation would have to defend itself.

Looking to his future, he took the opportunity of a visit to the *Daily Mail* offices at Carmelite House, London, E.C., to ask the editor, Thomas Marlowe, whether Fleet Street considered that war was likely. The editor told him that there was a strong expectation that Germany would be 'ready to strike in the summer of 1914'. After a moment's reflection, Scott answered: 'By then I shall be entitled to command a battle cruiser of the *Invincible* class. The summer of nineteen-fourteen will suit me very well.'

*

Enough money had come in to enable him to sail in August 1910. To guarantee the payment of full salaries throughout the term of the Expedition he needed another £8,000. That would bring the fund up to the £40,000 asked for. By May, he was having to revise his estimate. He wrote to Kinsey: 'I do not think £40,000 will see us through, but I hope that our fund will eventually exceed that figure and I anticipate we shall not require many thousands more.'

184

Small sums from individual well-wishers accounted for a great part of the moneys received. Fear of the Americans forestalling the British to the Pole was a spur to many of the donors. Over 100 public, secondary and private schools contributed to the cost of purchasing dogs (£3 3s. each), sledges (£5 12s. 6d.), sleeping bags (£2), and ponies. 'Please convey my personal thanks to the boys and girls, and tell them the dog will be called "Steyne", as they wish.' Scott's acknowledgement of a cash gift from Steyne School, Worthing, was typical. He made a point of signing all the letters himself.

There were offers of money from men eager to secure a place in the Expedition. Whether Captain Lawrence E. G. Oates, 6th Inniskilling Dragoons, and Apsley Cherry-Garrard, just down from Oxford, enlisted on that conditional basis is not noted in the records. Each contributed £1,000. Neither was paid a salary.

Lieutenant V. L. A. Campbell, R.N. (Retd.), served on an honorary footing. Lieutenant H. L. L. Pennell, R.N., was enrolled at £5 a week, Lieutenant H. E. de P. Rennick, R.N., at £2 a week, Lieutenant H. R. Bowers, Royal Indian Marine, at £4 4s. a week. The two naval doctors, Surgeon Lieutenant G. Murray Levick and Surgeon Lieutenant E. L. Atkinson, received £2 a week each. Lieutenant Wilfrid M. Bruce, R.N.R., Scott's brother-in-law, was content with a token shilling a month.

Petty officers and leading seamen, picked men from the naval depots of Chatham and Portsmouth, were paid 15s. and 13s. 6d. a week, respectively. For the scientific staff under Wilson there was a flat rate of £4 a week. H. G. Ponting, the photographer, was engaged at £5 a week.

The ship's crew were signed on with no surety of being paid beyond the duration of the outward voyage. Fitting out the *Terra Nova*, Lieutenant Evans's responsibility, was subject to the same financial duress. 'We never knew whether the most trivial alteration would be permitted owing to the continual heavy drawings on the Fund.' The ship was largely re-rigged by voluntary labour. Petty officers of the Royal Naval Volunteer Reserve gave up their week-ends to help make her ready.

Built in 1884 as the biggest whaling ship afloat, 749 tons and 187 feet long, the *Terra Nova* was a wooden three-masted barque that had later been equipped with auxiliary steam power. Her iron-sheathed bow and square stern were sufficiently tested during her Antarctic relief voyage of 1903–4. She had proved herself in the two extremes of the navigable waters of the globe, from the Ross Sea to the North polar pack. Now she was being prepared for one of the last true voyages of discovery that men would ever make.

After 1913, she was bought back by her former owners, Bowring Brothers, Ltd., and returned to St John's, Newfoundland, where she was square-rigged, her boiler and funnel being replaced by those from the naval vessel *Lobelia*. Between 1914–1942, she was engaged in the Newfoundland seal fisheries, and used also for coastal trading. In the latter year she was chartered to carry supplies to United States war stations in Greenland. She sprang a leak and sank off south-west Greenland on 13 September 1943.

Opposite her in West India Docks in 1910 lay the *Discovery*, that dull sailer and not much of a steamer that remained fondly harboured in the memory of Scott and those who sailed with him on her great voyage of ten years ago. She was being loaded for a North America port by her new owners, the Hudson Bay Company. The *Birmingham Post* stated that 'she looks very unkempt and forlorn'.

*

The offer of a Zodiac monoplane by the British & Colonial Aeroplane Company, of Bristol, was an exciting gesture but not one that could be seriously considered—'too experimental', Scott said. 'Wireless Telegraphy At The South Pole' was a headline in several newspapers. His hope of being the first Antarctic explorer to use it was frustrated. The necessary equipment was 'too cumbersome'. Mawson was able to claim that pioneering distinction a few years after. Scott's motor sledges had done well in Norway. There was no guarantee that they would do equally well on the Barrier. A gift of telephonic apparatus from the National Telephone Company supplied a means of communication up to fifteen miles from the shore base in McMurdo Sound.

A greater technological triumph, and one that looked more impressive in print, was implied by the announcement that 'two cinematographs are being taken. One of these is the most wonderful moving picture machine ever devised. It places in the hands of the operator a power hitherto unknown in this work. In addition, a large stock of photographic plates is being taken for securing the effects of the Antarctic in true natural colours' (Reuter, 28 May 1910).

For Scott, it was gratifying to command the services of a body of men whose work was unlikely to involve him in controversy, as that of some of their untrained predecessors had after his first expedition. The scientific staff recruited for his new venture was the best qualified and the most competent that ever went to the Antarctic. It consisted of G. C. Simpson, D.Sc., meteorologist; three geologists, Frank Debenham, B.A., B.Sc. (Australia); Charles S. Wright, B.A., physicist (Canada); Edward W. Nelson, and D. G. Lillie, M.A., biologists. As well as being head of the scientific staff, E. A. Wilson, B.A., M.B. (Cantab.) was the Expedition's zoologist. Apsley Cherry-Garrard, B.A., was his assistant.

Nominally attached to the scientific staff were Bernard C. Day, motor engineer, Cecil H. Meares, 'in charge of dogs', H. G. Ponting, F.R.G.S., photographer (who preferred to be called 'Camera Artist'), and Tryggve Gran, ski expert. The average age was twenty-six. Scott's seniority tended to confirm him in the isolation that he had known as a captain in the Royal Navy.

Forestalling further criticism of the merits of the Expedition, he wrote an article for the *Strand Magazine* (May 1910), recapitulating his aims as leader, and making it plain that 'when the *Terra Nova* leaves England's shores it will be for scientific purposes'. He proposed to explore 'the entirely unknown region of King Edward's Land', to investigate 'the nature and extent of the Great Ice Barrier formation', and to survey the higher regions of Victoria Land. There would be an intensive study of marine biology. The geologists would search for radium-bearing pitchblende, 'just as gold was found in Alaska'. More knowledge of the magnetic pole would be sought. Meteorology would figure prominently in their researches.

'I admit that the main object of the Expedition is to reach the South Pole, but this is largely a matter of sentiment. If we drop our Antarctic work, in which England leads the world, the Americans will take it up and the Stars & Stripes will fly there instead of the Union Jack. Every Englishman would be glad to know that it was a British subject who was the first to get to the Pole.'

⁕

''Ware open hatchways!' The shout was heard frequently on the *Terra Nova* in the last few days before she left London Docks. It was a warning to those thronging her deck who had come to bid farewell to the ship and all who were sailing in her. Blazing sunshine made the visitors in their mourning clothes for King Edward VII, who had died a fortnight ago, seem like performers in a charade. They were escorted through a maze of piled-up stores by Scott's lieutenants in their white-topped caps and gold lace. Stevedores were swinging pig-iron ballast into the ship's thick-ribbed hold. Spick and span on her bow, boats, and lifebelts, was the new inscription: *Terra Nova*, R.Y.S.

Scott had been made an honorary member of the Royal Yacht Squadron after his return from the *Discovery* voyage in 1904. He was now elected to full membership, involving an entrance fee of £100, charged to the Expedition funds, 'which we could ill-afford' (Evans). Besides raising the *Terra Nova* above the common order of shipping, the privilege had practical advantages; registered as a yacht, she was immune from Board of Trade regulations that she might not have been able to meet. 'Having avoided the scrutiny of the efficient and official, we painted out our Plimsoll mark with tongue in cheek and eyelid dropped, and, this done, took our stores aboard and packed them pretty tight,' Evans recorded.

The shouting and hammering, the rumble from the holds, the exclamatory social chatter, the rusty seagull cries of dockland, were to echo through many a long vigil in the polar solitudes to come. By sailing two months earlier, Scott hoped to penetrate the sea ice sooner than previous expeditions, which meant that, all being well, the *Terra Nova* would anchor in McMurdo Sound again by Christmas.

He spoke one evening in that last week of May 1910 at the Royal Institution, in London, to 'a crowded and distinguished audience' (*Morning Post*, 28 May). He did not wish it to be supposed, he said, that he had failed to contemplate the possibility of circumstances that might upset some, if not all, of his calculations and cause the results of his expedition to be very different from those which he was attempting to foreshadow.

'There is a sharp difference of opinion as to the value of Polar expeditions. People whose knowledge is derived from the sensational Press count success in degrees of latitude. Others have a contempt for all results except those arising from advanced scientific studies in the regions visited.' Between those extremes, there were many shades of opinion. 'I submit that efforts to reach a spot on the surface of the globe which has hitherto been untrodden by human feet and unseen by human eyes is in itself laudable.' The pronouncement, according to the *Morning Post*, was received with cheers.

Soon after the sun was over the yard-arm of the *Terra Nova* on 30 May, the bo'sun gave the order: 'All hands aft!' Officers, men, scientists, trooped to the captain's cabin to sign articles for the coming voyage. The following day, at the Royal Geographical Society's send-off luncheon at the Holborn Restaurant, London, Scott spoke of the relief he would feel at having 'no more bills to come, and not having to know the value of a pound or a shilling—one will be as good as the other where we are going' (Laughter).

The financial incubus still lay heavily on him. He was unable, at that late hour, to guarantee full salaries throughout the period of the Expedition. He intended to work right up to sailing time to get the money that was needed. If he did not succeed, 'it shall be done when I return', a vow that he was to grieve over in the last hours of his life. The President's speech of farewell ended with the words: 'They mean to do or die— that is the spirit in which they are going to the Antarctic.'

By the intervention of Scott's former Admiralty chief, Admiral Sir Francis Bridgeman, the *Terra Nova* was allowed to fly the White Ensign. It was formally broken from the mainmast by Lady Bridgeman at a final sailing ceremony on 1 June. The privilege was acknowledged by loud cheers from the entire ship's company, taken up by the crowd that had assembled at the dockside to see the departure. Punctually at 5 p.m., the *Terra Nova* was towed through the lines of docked merchantmen, most of them dressed with flags and streamers, their shore crews waving and cheering as she passed. Every vessel with sufficient steam in her boilers shrieked a whistle or gave a syren groan in farewell; others dipped their ensigns.

'If this is your send-off,' Ponting, the photographer, remarked to Scott, as the cheers died on the wind, 'what will your homecoming be like?' Scott replied: 'I don't much care for this sort of thing. All I want is to finish the work we began in the *Discovery*. Then I'll get back to my job in the Navy.'

The *Morning Post* noted approvingly that 'it was a modest setting-out. In such quiet spirit should all great work be undertaken.' The *Evening Standard* recorded the departure as 'a solemn moment', postulating the thought: 'We may never see them again.'

*

Rowed ashore at Greenhithe, Scott returned to his desk in the office in Victoria Street, S.W., where there were more letters of appeal waiting to be signed and news agency and film business to be completed. He had also to stand by for an audience with the new king, George V, and to receive from the hands of Queen Alexandra, consort of the late monarch, a Union Jack to be hoisted at the South Pole.

Terra Nova had sailed to Cardiff, to fill her bunkers with free coal and to show herself, after cleaning down, to the Lord Mayor, burgesses, and citizens, who produced a further £1,000 for the funds. In recognition, Scott was moved to announce that Cardiff would be their first port of call in the United Kingdom when the Expedition came home.

A farewell banquet at the Royal Hotel, Cardiff, on 13 June was more memorable for the splendid singing of the Royal Welsh Ladies' Choir than for the speeches that filled columns of the local press next day. 'I have never seen anything approaching the enthusiasm at last night's dinner. Even the meanest of us was stirred, and felt like asking whether there was not a spare berth in the ship. The sight of the officers and crew was an inspiration. Such seamen, with faces of bronze and necks that Roman gladiators would have given the world for, were never gathered before in any ship that ever sailed from a British port' (*Western Mail* correspondent, 14 June 1910).

Not all was harmony behind the scenes. Tensions had arisen between Lieutenant Evans and Petty Officer Evans, who, as a Swansea man, was seated at the top table at the banquet between Scott and the Lord Mayor. There had been close concord between Scott and Edgar Evans, the petty officer, since their *Discovery* days, when they had slogged, suffered and endured together on the polar plateau.

Edgar Evans had upset his namesake by pointing out directly to Scott a defect in the skis that had been delivered from Norway. As a result, Petty Officer Evans was put in charge of the equipment, which up to then had been Lieutenant Evans's responsibility. Thereafter, the two men were not at ease with each other.

The situation was worsened by Petty Officer Evans's conduct after the banquet. Late night revelry resulted in his becoming fighting drunk. Six men were required to get him back to the ship. A splendid figure of a man, he drank only because, as Kipling put it, other men were thirsty. His behaviour that night finally alienated him from the regard of 'Teddy' Evans, who abhorred drunkenness or any other practice that he thought derogatory to personal efficiency. 'Our departure from Cardiff did not do some of us credit', Lieutenant 'Birdie' Bowers wrote to Scott's wife months later in apologetic reminiscence.

The *Terra Nova*—'she is not much to look at' (*Cardiff Evening Express*)—sailed for the Cape on 15 June. Long before she moved away from her berth in the Bute Docks the quayside was packed with sightseers whose 'joyous shouts' rang out over the scene when the Red Dragon flag presented by the Corporation of Cardiff was run up to the masthead and unfurled. The docks were 'magnificently decorated' for the day, which was loud with whistles and syrens as the steam tugs *Falcon* and *Bantam Cock* towed the ship seaward. Her progress down the Bristol Channel was watched by spectators at many points along the coast. In a talk with local reporters, Scott spoke of the chance of 'the venture not meeting with success'.

Dr Edward A. Wilson to Scott:

S.Y. *Terra Nova*, Madeira.
June 25, 1910.

My dear Captain Scott,—You have got a crew of pirates that would be exceedingly difficult to beat—or equal. I have never been with such a persistently cheery lot before. As for your N. Os [naval officers], they are without exception the most charming lot of men I have ever struck—and this is my deliberate opinion, the result so far of a week of very dirty and more or less heavy labour finding things, shaking down.

restowing here and there, and generally settling in and getting clean for Madeira at the same time.

Evans is simply splendid, so are Campbell, Rennick, Pennell, and Atkinson—indeed, all of them—but these five are more than first-class. Neither would I have a single one of our staff altered. Nelson is a perfect treasure. He works like a navvy all day in the holds and turns up at every meal immaculate in a clean collar. Lillie is all right, though very quiet—Nelson's brilliance puts him in the background, but he is all right, I feel sure.

Simpson and Wright are everlastingly at work with complex instruments when they aren't cleaning paint work. Cherry-Garrard is a general favourite and leaves nothing untried. He was the first of the new lot up the rigging, and beams genially when three people want him for odd jobs at once as though he at last found life worth living. Oates (or Titus, I need hardly add) is just beginning to come out now, and, as one began to suspect, there is far more than meets the eye—or the ear either, for that matter—in his rather amused taciturnity. I began to suspect him of being the author of *Round the Horn before the Mast* when I saw him double up the ratlines and handle the sails as though he had been at it all his days. There's a delightful suppressed geniality in him which bubbles over now and again. When it comes to hard and heavy work, he will be a great standby.

I pick out Atkinson, too, as a real worker in a quiet way, but in a way which wouldn't stick at anything or make a song about comfort or discomfort. Of the naval men, I am sure Campbell will be a splendid leader of the Eastern Party, with Pennell for brains and Rennick for hard manual labour, the harder the better. I imagine them all in a sleeping bag and turning out to pack up traps at 40 below. Pity we can't have Pennell as well as Rennick on shore.

What strikes me more than anything else in the mess is that there is a complete absence of mutual antipathies. Of course they may come—but the way everyone in two days treated everyone else in two days, as though they had been tent mates for a season, was really remarkable.

Yours ever,

BILL

The spectre of failure reappeared in the letter that Scott wrote to Admiral Sir Lewis Beaumont, K.C.B., Director of Naval Intelligence, on 11 July 1910. 'If nothing is heard of the ship by the middle of January 1912, it would be well to consider the organization of a relief Expedition, but no active steps (save possibly to obtain an option on a ship) should be taken until the close of the open season of 1911–12. At the end of March 1912, failing news, a relief Expedition should be organized.'

Prudence suggested those tentative proposals; none the less, Scott was visualizing calamity rather than predicating triumph. 'In McMurdo Sound there exists an ample supply of seals and penguins from which food, fuel and clothing can be drawn for an indefinite number of years. The fate of those who remain in the *Terra Nova* would be more problematical. . . .'

*

'A last message?' Scott was repeating the question asked him by a *Morning Post* man who called while he was packing his trunks. He was leaving for South Africa in the mail steamer *Saxon* the following day, 16 July. An answer was all too readily supplied by the perpetual problem of money. 'There is still a deficiency in the amount required to maintain the Expedition on full pay and to provide for the dependents of the crew.' A letter to *The Times* from the London Devonian Society made an urgent final appeal to the public to relieve Scott of his remaining anxieties.

After much heart searching as the mother of a nine-months-old son—'would he know me when I came back: would he be looking to someone else by then?'—Kathleen Scott took the decision to accompany her husband to the last outpost of the civilization that, but for them, he seemed glad to put behind him. Travelling with them were Mrs Wilson and Mrs Evans, wife of the commander of the *Terra Nova*. They were seen off at Waterloo station by a surprisingly small company of well-wishers, among them Sir Ernest Shackleton and officers of the Royal Geographical Society. Public interest was limited to that of other travellers and members of the station staff. Raising his bowler hat on high as the train began to move, Shackleton drew a somewhat self-conscious cheer from those around him.

The party reached Cape Town on 2 August 1910. 'My poor

Con was very dejected,' Kathleen Scott wrote in her diary on 22 August. The *Terra Nova* had been nearly a fortnight overdue. 'He talked over all the possible things that could have happened,' letting his anxiety take such a grip on him that he began to 'wonder whether one could equip another ship in time!' She referred in the same entry to his 'horrid nightmares'. The *Terra Nova*'s showing as an auxiliary steamer was not impressive. Lieutenant Evans explained also that her large four-bladed propeller hampered her sailing performance. Her best day's run was 201 miles.

During Scott's previous visit to South Africa, in 1901, the country was at war. Now, nine years after, it was distracted by a general election, equally unfavourable to his hope of engaging government and public sympathy for his cause. Outside the United Kingdom, his only financial support thus far had come from the Government of New Zealand, which made a grant of £1,000. He had great expectations from South Africa, where there was so much new wealth.

An official gift of £500 was forthcoming after he had travelled to Pretoria to see the Finance Minister and other members of the Government, among them Smuts and Botha. It was a disappointment that he kept to himself. He gave a short series of lectures. It yielded £180. Mr James G. Davidson, now of Upper Mill Street Gardens, Cape Town, was present at the first lecture, in the City Hall, His clearest memory of the occasion is of Scott's 'fine head and features and his magnificent chest'.

Letters appealing for money went to the mayors of most towns in the Union. A subscription list was opened by the Governor-General, Lord Gladstone. Those who could not afford pounds were urged to make it shillings. A nationalist newspaper, criticizing the Government grant on the ground that the nation had only lately emerged from a trade depression, pointed out that there were Rand mining millionaires who could easily see Scott through his difficulties. 'They have recently exported gold and diamonds to the value of £25,000,000.'

South Africa's total response to the Expedition fund was considerably less than Cardiff's.* Scott seemed pleased to tell

* As lately as 1960, South Africa honoured the memory of Scott and his companions by erecting a new monument to them at Cape Town.

his mother in a letter: 'We leave with a large addition to our list of friends. Kathleen is popular everywhere' (2 September 1910).

*

'It will be interesting to see how they turn out.' Kathleen Scott was making diary notes about some of the officers and scientists who had arrived in the *Terra Nova*, remarking that 'everybody was charmingly enthusiastic about everybody else'. She noted that 'only two were not regarded as perfect marvels', naming no names. 'One I didn't think anything of when he came to dine in London.' She mentioned Simpson, the meteorologist,* who had so soon acquired a nickname, 'Sunny Jim'. He was 'very keen and eager'. One day, while dressing, he stood in the doorway of his cabin 'in a complete state of nudity, haranguing Mr Lillie and announcing: "When I marry I shall marry a really intellectual woman!"'

Lillie, the young biologist, was down with measles, 'which coincides with his childish appearance. He is full of theories,' Kathleen Scott wrote, 'and has mad eyes.' She found his personality amusing. 'I could walk and talk much with him.' Edward Nelson, who came from the Plymouth Marine Laboratory, 'spends all his time on shore being a man about town, which makes him look exceedingly tired'. She had 'a very ridiculous feeling' that Lieutenant Victor Campbell 'may fare hardly somehow'. She thought him 'an exceedingly charming person', and supposed that it was 'the reason for feeling that he will meet with ill luck'.

Personal complications arose when Scott decided to sail to Australia in the *Terra Nova* instead of going on ahead by mail steamer, as he had intended. 'Teddy' Evans, acting as captain of the Expedition ship, took it as a reflection on his capability. 'Evans was much upset at Con's decision.' Kathleen Scott thought it 'petty of him', adding: 'Mrs Evans is scared to death of her fellow humans.' She was an attractive New Zealand girl, Hilda Russell, from Christchurch, whom Evans had met and married during the *Discovery* voyage.

Evans's published version of Scott's change of mind contained no word of discord. 'Our leader was without doubt delighted to make the longer voyage with us in the *Terra Nova*

* Later, Sir George Simpson, F.R.S., Director of the Meteorological Office.

to get away from the hum of commerce and the small talk of the many people who were pleased to meet him, until the hat was handed round—that awful fund collecting.' *

The voyage served another purpose, as Scott showed in a letter to his mother. 'It gave me a chance of selecting the members of the Shore Party, of studying the characters of those on board, and of appreciating the splendid qualities of the men who have been chosen for our enterprise.' His remarks on the disparate personalities around him fill many pages of his diary for September 1910. They have remained unquoted until now. He begins: 'My companions are delightful. There seem to be only two weak spots in the organization and these might have been worse.'

Lieutenant 'Teddy' Evans was emphatically 'the right man in the right place'. Scott made much of him in his notes. 'I could not have selected a fitter man as my *alter ego* or to command the ship.' To be sure, Evans was not clever, and there was a touch of the primitive man about him, but 'his energy and vitality are enormous'. He compared Evans's lively temperament with that of the *Terra Nova*'s first lieutenant, Victor Campbell, visualizing both men entering a room full of strangers. Evans would bounce in, 'wanting to tell everybody everything'. Campbell, 'a refined gentleman', would be subdued by the dominant English reluctance to talk of himself.

Aged thirty-five, born at Brighton, the son of a naval captain, educated at Eton, Victor Campbell joined the Merchant Service when he was sixteen, serving in the Shaw Savill barques. He became a naval sub-lieutenant in 1895, and retired as a lieutenant seven years later. Having considerable private means, he chose to live in Norway. His experience of snow, mountains, glaciers, gave him a special status with Scott, who had already marked him out as leader of one of the sledge parties.

The strongest man in the wardroom, Lieutenant H. de P. Rennick, R.N., aged twenty-nine, was a disappointment to Scott, who could not feel that Rennick's heart was 'in this work. He sometimes appears *distrait* and blank.' According to Scott, the strongest impression he made was of being colourless. 'Neither his brain nor his energy seems equal to his appearance.'

*Evans: *South With Scott* (Collins, 1921).

196

Bowers (twenty-seven) was 'a treasure.' The phrase recurs again and again in Scott's references to that 'tough little square block of a man,' as Oates called him. Born in Renfrewshire, Bowers went to Sidcup College, Kent, and then became a *Worcester* cadet. He served in merchant ships and received a master's certificate. Scott sketched him in words: 'A very plain pink face carrying an immense beak-like nose (which has of course gained him the name of "Birdie"), surmounted by close-cropped red hair.' Scott's eulogy of Bowers fills two of the quarto pages of his diary of the outward voyage. 'His ardour is inspiring.'

Lieutenant H. L. L. Pennell, R.N., twenty-eight, the navigator of the *Terra Nova*, was destined to go far, in Scott's opinion. 'He possesses a very high order of intelligence.' As for Lawrence E. G. Oates, 'a better fellow never stepped'. Oates, aged thirty, was an old Etonian who 'had little in common with the popular conception of the cavalry officer' (Inniskilling Dragoons). His mahogany face was pock-marked, his black bristly hair exceedingly close cropped. He tended to slouch and his worn and ancient clothes were 'of uncertain fit'. His slight limp, from an old war wound, was accentuated by the nautical gait acquired in those first few weeks at sea. 'He has all his heart in this project, no transcendant abilities, but a shrewd insight into most of the affairs of our enterprise.'

Apsley Cherry-Garrard, always called Cherry, was twenty-four, educated at Winchester and Oxford, and a student of the Middle Temple. 'Very quiet and not very clever, but a hard, keen worker, with all the best instincts of a gentleman.' Next to him on the page came Tryggve Gran, twenty-two, from Bergen, Norway, 'strong, good-natured, generous'. Scott wondered in writing whether 'he has heart enough for the final stages of this journey'. Gran was 'temporarily waning in popularity' because of his reluctance 'to go under the hose. He says it is not the custom of his country. He continues weeks on end in the same clothes without washing.'

Surveying the scientific staff, Scott dwelt at considerable length on the role of George (later Sir George) Simpson, D.Sc., aged thirty-two, from Owens College, Manchester University, the Expedition's meteorologist, who had been lent by the Government of India. 'It is a joy to me to have a man whose position in the scientific world is so well assured.' Simpson's presence set the stamp of authority on the Expedition's work for science. It was a guarantee that there would be no repetition of the embarrassing criticisms that were a sequel to the *Discovery* voyage. ' "Sunny Jim" Simpson is decidedly popular,' Scott wrote, 'the most unselfish, cheerful companion and messmate.'

Toronto-born Charles (later Sir Charles) S. Wright, twenty-three, and not long down from Caius College, Cambridge, was to be the Expedition's glaciologist. 'A charmingly simple, straightforward young man with intelligence of a high order.' Recording also that Wright was 'decidedly anaemic' on joining, Scott observed that 'the trip is doing much for his physique,' and added the tribute: 'I like him very much.'

Edward W. Nelson, aged twenty-seven, born in London and educated at Clifton, Tonbridge, and Cambridge University, joined the Expedition from the biology department of Plymouth Museum. 'A man of the world,' in Scott's view; 'eminently practical and full of resource, with a remarkable head for mechanical detail.' His popularity on board was established from the first, 'as his many nicknames prove', Scott wrote. One of them was 'Bronte'. He made himself as useful in the engine-room as in the laboratory.

'In contradistinction' (Scott), Dennis G. Lillie, twenty-six, was 'shy and quiet, his head in the clouds'. He was educated at United Services College, Westward Ho, Birmingham University, St John's College, Cambridge. Like Nelson, he joined from the marine laboratory at Plymouth. 'Thoughtful and imaginative,' Scott could believe that 'he might do great things some day,' with the proviso that 'it might lead to crankiness, for he has odd beliefs,' in reincarnation, for example. 'In all seriousness, he holds that in former existences he has been a Persian and a Roman.'

Noting Lillie's physical improvement—'he was rather a weakling when he first came on board'—Scott recorded that the development of the younger men in that respect was 'very noticeable'. It led to the reflection that 'one cannot but think that there is a similar robust, healthful development of character'.

Then, finally, came his private evaluation of the two naval doctors, G. Murray Levick, L.R.C.P., and Edward L. Atkinson, M.R.C.S., Levick, thirty-four, St Paul's School and St

Bartholomew's Hospital; Atkinson, twenty-eight, Harrow and St Thomas's Hospital. Levick was a physical training expert and athlete whose muscularity Scott seemed to think might prove to be his chief asset in the Antarctic. 'I am told that he has some knowledge of his profession, but there it ends. He seems quite incapable of learning anything fresh. Left alone, I verily believe he would do nothing from sheer lack of initiative.' Noting his persistent amiability and 'vacant smile', Scott appeared to be trying to find some positive qualities to record, without result, save that 'he cheerfully accepts any amount of chaff'. He was liked by all on board, where he was familiarly known as 'Toffarino'. Scott's summary verdict: 'I am afraid there is little to be expected from him,' has to be considered rigidly in its context. He would doubtless have modified it in the light of Dr Levick's later career. Before Melbourne was reached, he was observing that 'Levick has a really charming nature'.

Atkinson was set down as being 'of a very different calibre', 'one of the cleverest men in the Expedition'. His excellent physique, short sturdy figure, and strong limbs 'point him out as a certain splendid sledger'. He did 'practically all the doctoring on board,' and had already inspired 'remarkable confidence'. His laboratory work, as the scientist dealing with bacteriology and helminthology, involved 'the most delicate investigations to be made by anyone in the party. If anything is to be made of this work, he is the man to make it.' Scott was 'delighted with Atkinson. He combines in the rarest degree those qualities of mind, body, and spirit which we require.'

The sharpest note of criticism was reserved for the ship's engineer, Edgar G. Riley, from Dublin. 'At present I do not like Riley,' Scott wrote after three weeks at sea. The engineer, who was thirty-four, and technically well qualified, insisted on a place in the order of precedence at the mess table to which it was felt that he was not entitled. 'He put himself next to Evans, displacing Wilson,' which brought him close to Scott's appointed place—'for my sins!' Finding it amusing 'that this man should get on my nerves so much', Scott had already decided that 'he cannot be included in the landing party'. Before they reached Australia, he had resolved that 'Riley must go'.

*

199

Wilson and his wife, with Kathleen Scott and Mrs 'Teddy' Evans, took separate passage in the S.S. *Corinthic* to Australia. At Melbourne, they waited for the *Terra Nova*. From Kathleen Scott's diary, it is evident that she found herself at a disadvantage with 'Bill' Wilson. 'It is rather dreary being treated as an outsider as regards Expedition affairs.' Presuming that he was 'judging from his long experience', which had apparently taught him 'that women aren't much use', she wrote that she 'bore him no malice for his funny mistrust'.

A rare absence of wind in the famous Forties delayed the *Terra Nova* four days. Scott had lapsed into a mood in which he could believe that 'fortune seems to be treating us with exceptional disfavour'. Cherry-Garrard wrote: 'Scott was impatient; there was much to be done and the time for doing it not too long.'

On 10 October, when they were down to 75 tons of coal, the ship was struck by the first big squall of the voyage. It was expected that the topgallant mast would go. Nothing could be done while the full fury of the wind lasted. The watch was grouped round the ratlines ready to go aloft. It was touch and go with the mast, by Cherry-Garrard's account. The squall was followed by the biggest hailstorm they had ever known: 'hail inches in circumference', that hurt them through their oilskins.

When word came on 12 October that the *Terra Nova* was approaching Melbourne harbour, Kathleen Scott immediately declared her intention of going out to meet the ship. Wilson, at first, would not hear of it. She answered that she could not bring herself 'to do such an unsporting thing' as remain ashore, waiting. 'Bill was furious and protested that the other women were cold and hungry.' It was late evening, very dark and raining, and blowing hard.

'Humours were questionable, but I knew my man would expect me,' and Kathleen Scott's will prevailed. She and Wilson, with his wife and Hilda Evans, were taken out to the incoming ship by a Shell Petroleum launch. 'It pitched and heaved horribly, but I was far too excited to be seasick and it didn't occur to me to be frightened.'

On the weather side of the *Terra Nova*, 'our little launch got into a bad swell, and the ladies thought it was capsizing and wanted to return without going aboard, but I had heard my good man's voice and was sure there was no danger, and so insisted, getting more unpopular.' Wilson objected that 'it would be very dangerous' to go alongside in such a sea. 'But the launch men said they thought it would be all right, so after much to-ing and fro-ing we at last got close to the beautiful *Terra Nova* with our beautiful husbands on board. They came and looked down into our faces with lanterns.' The others stayed in the launch. 'But I went on board and Mr Campbell and Mr Rennick were so nice. The relief at getting back to sane folk who understood me was more than can be written about' (12 October 1910).

Scott's briefly renewed felicity was disrupted by the cablegram that was handed to him when the ship berthed in Melbourne harbour late that night. It had been sent from Funchal, Madeira, and it read: *Am going south Amundsen.*

CHAPTER FOURTEEN

'BETTER STILL—NO WIVES'

How Scott took Amundsen's message, what feelings he showed, or whether he showed none, was not specifically noted by his colleagues. Yet it can hardly have been other than disturbing to him, whose long, elaborate, and costly preparations largely rested on the assumption that, as a pathfinder of ten years earlier, he had acquired a certain exclusive right to complete the work he had then begun. Many people thought Amundsen's peremptoriness as offensive as his proposed trespass. They also disliked being reminded that he was in the Antarctic before Scott (as a member of the Belgica Expedition, 1897).

Amundsen himself had recently experienced the perversity of fortune. Having been given the use of Nansen's famous exploring ship *Fram,* he made all the arrangements necessary for an attempt to reach the North Pole. Everything was ready for his start when the news came that Peary had hoisted the American flag there in April 1909. 'This was a blow indeed! If I was to maintain my prestige as an explorer, I must quickly achieve a success of some sort. I resolved upon a coup.'*

* Roald Amundsen: *My Life as an Explorer* (Heinemann, 1927).

He had collected money for his northern venture, and his financial commitments had an important bearing on his seemingly ruthless change of mind. He was said to have feared that a distraint might be levied on the *Fram* if he stayed in northern waters. On the other hand, he could hardly have organized his South Pole expedition in a few days, for which reason it was assumed by some of his critics that he had known all along what his objective was going to be.

Shackleton publicly expressed his surprise that Amundsen had 'so considerably altered his plans without giving a more explicit explanation'. Shackleton did not believe that the little *Fram* was capable of riding out 'the enormous seas' of the Far South, or that Amundsen would reach the Pole unless he had 'a large number of ponies on board'. He might have dogs, Shackleton conceded, 'but they are not very reliable' (*Daily Express*, 4 October 1910). Amundsen had no use for ponies; and it was dogs that gave him the victory.

*

Scott in Melborne wrote to Kinsey at Christchurch, New Zealand, on 17 October: 'The ship left today, and should be with you in about 11 days. You will find aboard her the finest collection of people you ever saw, and all inspired with a spirit which I have never seen equalled.' He had warned them: 'It will be hard work from start to finish at Lyttelton—no holidays. I want the whole ship unstowed, the huts erected, everything put back again.' The purpose was three-fold; an overhaul in dry dock; to find space for additional stores; and to provide practice for the coming landing at the Antarctic base.

Scott's letter to Kinsey informed him: 'We have had a struggle with the Government here. The campaign was started badly, but in the end I think all will be well. The Labour Ministers are now our personal friends. We found them very good fellows when we got to know them.'

He had stayed on in Melbourne, awaiting the result of overtures to the Federal Government that encouraged him to expect a grant of £5,000, the amount voted for Shackleton's expedition three years before. Scott's most helpful sponsors in Australia were the Warden of Trinity College, Melbourne University, Dr Alexander Leeper; Professor Baldwin Spencer, 'whose great influence' opened official doors to him; and Pro-

fessor T. Edgeworth David, 'really the most charming character we have met on our travels' (Scott). When it became clear
that Government generosity would be limited to £2,500, the
Melbourne press wrote of it as 'niggardly treatment'.

The protests were infused with prejudice. A Japanese
Antarctic Expedition, under Lieutenant Choku Shirase, was
fitting out to explore King Edward VII Land. Australians
could not comfortably contemplate a Japanese success in the
Antarctic.

The same newspapers were impressed by Scott's quiet bearing. 'He knows the Antarctic too well to boast about what
he will do with it.' They observed that he did not show himself
to be 'overweighted by the magnitude of what is in front of
him'. He appeared to approach it 'in the cheerful style of a man
going to keep a pleasant tryst'. When the reporters asked him
about his prospects of getting to the Pole, he answered: 'We
may get through, we may not. We may lose our lives. We may
be wiped out. It is all a matter of providence and luck.'

Scott to Professor Baldwin Spencer:

The Australia Hotel,
Sydney.
[Undated]

Dear Professor Spencer,—There was a great dinner last night
at which a young man called Hordern got up and said that
if the Government didn't give the remaining £2,500, he
would! Isn't it fine of him?

Of course we have to be very silent about this until we
know what the Government intends. We would like to tell
the young man we need his £2,500 anyhow, but we don't
like to do that.

It is indeed fine to find a rich young man with such high
ideals. He is looking for absolutely nothing from it. It's
really very splendid, isn't it?

I thought I must impart our good news to you.

Professor David is being beyond words splendid. What a
delightful character he is, isn't he?

Very sincerely,
ROBERT SCOTT

While Scott waited, and lectured, in Australia, the build-up
of the Expedition proceeded in New Zealand. Meares, in

charge of the ponies (nineteen) and dogs (thirty-one) from
Siberia, and Bruce, who had helped him with them in transit,
had arrived at Lyttelton and were looking after the animals
in quarantine on Quail Island. Bernard Day, the motor sledge
engineer, had reported. Ponting, the cameraman, and three of
the scientists were about to do so. Professor Edgeworth David
wrote from Sydney University to tell Scott that the newly
appointed young geologist, Raymond Priestley, 'is almost beside himself with joy at now being a member of your Expedition, and he is indeed to be envied'. Kinsey was 'very
pleased' to hear that Scott had warned his men that hard work
lay ahead. 'Possibly they would not expect a holiday. But it
would be contrary to my idea of human nature if some of these
young fellows were not looking for a good time in Christchurch, and before they leave for the South.'

At a ball in Melbourne, attended by the Governor and his
staff, Scott and his wife danced in the State quadrille, which she
described as 'very sedate, silly, and rather fun'. At Sydney races,
she had a glimpse of Oates which she transfixed in a diary note:
'In the midst of a most brilliant and over-dressed crowd, I
suddenly espied The Soldier [Oates's nickname in the Expedi-
tion] in Norfolk jacket, such boots, and marvellous trousers
and an indescribable hat, quite unconscious, I think, that he
hadn't a top hat and morning jacket!' (13 October 1910).

Ten minutes before sailing for New Zealand on 22 October,
Scott dashed off a letter to his mother. 'We are doing splendidly—everything goes like clockwork, including our begging.
Kathleen is really wonderful. She has become one of the most
popular people in Australia. Oceans of love.'

As a parting present of his own choosing, he received from
Dr Leeper a volume of Browning's poems. It was inscribed:
'To Capt. Scott, R.N., just starting for the South Pole.' The
Warden added some lines from Tennyson's *Ulysses* that seemed
appropriate: ... *One equal temper of heroic hearts* ... *To
strive, to seek, to find, and not to yield.*

*

Early on the morning of 28 October, loud syren whoops told
the people of Lyttelton, New Zealand, that the harbour board's
tug *Canterbury* had sighted the *Terra Nova* off the Heads.
Those who got up to welcome her as she came into view out of

a rolling white fog were surprised by a trim and tidy ship that did not look as if she had been five months at sea. Except for the dank green marine growth thinly festooning her water-line, the *Terra Nova* might have just come down the Dundee slipway.

'What about Amundsen?' was the first question hurled at Scott by reporters crowding into his hotel at Wellington, where he stayed a night before going on to join the ship. He replied that he was awaiting an opportunity to send the Norwegian explorer a good-luck telegram; for the time being, he did not know where to send it. He explained that there was no question of priority, still less of encroachment. Explorers, he said, usually had a good understanding on such matters.

Answering more questions, he stated the view that Amundsen would make his approach to the Pole from the Weddell Sea coast, which was virtually unknown. Plans for the British Antarctic Expedition remained unchanged. He and his party intended to reach the Pole, but not at the expense of their scientific objectives.

Inevitably, the money problem came up. 'How are you fixed now?' a news agency man wanted to know. Scott seized the chance to announce that he and his officers were prepared for cuts in their salaries, 'or go without them altogether'. When the statement was cabled to London, the *Daily Express* urged that 'the cloud that overhangs the gallant explorer on the threshold of his expedition should be lifted.'

He had left Australia with some assurance that the Federal Government would, after all, increase their initial grant of £2,500. That hope was extinguished by the time he reached New Zealand. The edge was taken off his disappointment by the gift of that amount from Samuel Hordern, the young head of a large store known as 'the Harrods of Sydney'. It was aid and comfort, not relief. The Expedition fund was running dangerously low. Lieutenant Evans told a friend of his in later years: 'We had hardly enough left to pay for our last ton of coal.'

The people of New Zealand, who, as in the *Discovery* days, treated them as visiting kinsmen, gave more in kind than in cash: free meat, free dairy produce, free railway passes, a free Expedition office at Christchurch, and the freedom of their institutions, scientific and social; above all, of their homes. The personal hospitality was prodigious. When Scott, in return, spoke the word gratitude, they knew that he meant it.

He and his wife were the guests of the Kinseys at Christchurch through much of their time in New Zealand. Scott was uplifted by the 'wholly enchanting' view from the house, standing 400 feet above the sea. Far away were the Southern Alps. Gazing at the splendid panorama, 'across a garden which blazes with red and golden flowers', he had feelings of 'inexpressible satisfaction with all things'. Such a depth of contentment was rare in his experience. There, at Clifton, Christchurch, he and his wife had their last taste of home life together.

Te Koraha, Christchurch, N.Z.

7th November 1910.

My own dearest Mother,— ... I quite understood and anticipated your anxiety concerning our spiritual welfare. The Bishop has just gone off to the mountains to recruit his health but will be back in time to have a farewell service. I shall ask him to conduct it on the same lines as before and I am sure he will do so in the same cheerful spirit.

As to the rest, I may tell you that I read the Church Service every Sunday on our journey to Melbourne and that I propose to do the same with equal regularity throughout the voyage—you need not have any anxiety on this point. I hold precisely the same views as I did during the first Expedition, and shall act in a very similar manner. I may add that I invariably read the prayer written by the Bishop of London, which continues to appeal to me as one of the most honest, straightforward requests for assistance that has ever been penned.

My own dearest Mother, there is only one thing that clouds the bright outlook of this venture as far as I am concerned. It is the thought that while we are full of hope and good health you are still a victim of the horrid ailment [sciatica] which has given you so much pain. I shall be thinking of you and that you are once more on your feet and perhaps having a game with Peter.

My dearest Mother, this is the last real letter I can write to you or to the family. Ettie, Rose, Monsie, and all will read it and will understand that my thoughts are often with them.

Also, I hope you will all appreciate that I shall leave with good hope, conscious that I have done my best to deserve success and believing that you will have no cause to regret my having undertaken this venture.

Goodbye, my dear—all my love to you all. Don't ever be anxious. There will be no reason for anxiety.

Goodbye only for the present.

Ever your loving son,

CON

*

His remaining days in the world of civilized men were long and strenuous; ample excuse for neglecting the letter writing task. He did not forget the small daughter of his eldest sister, Ettie Ellison Macartney. 'We are getting ready to sail away and when you are having your Christmas dinner you can imagine the *Terra Nova* all amongst the ice—great pieces larger than the Mint or even the Tower will be all around her and the sea will be full of seals and penguins. Auntie Kathleen will tell you how busy I was before I left and how difficult it was for me to write letters. I shall be thinking of you all at Christmas and hoping that you are having a very merry time—and that you won't forget your loving Uncle Con' (10 November 1910).

His order for unloading the ship at Lyttelton meant officers, crew, and scientists doing stevedores' work. While she was dry docked, everything from her holds was relisted to facilitate the final landing in the Antarctic. Supplies for the two main sledge parties were marked with green and red bands respectively. The base camp huts, complete with beds and other furniture, were set up on waste ground near the wharf. The rehearsal was insurance against later emergencies and delays. Re-stowing posed fresh problems, for New Zealand generosity had added considerably to the cargo weight, which was already well in excess of the ship's normal carrying capacity. Her 'really heavy' deck cargo was another of Scott's worries: 'one is naturally anxious concerning it, particularly in the more stormy seas.'

When all was done, and the signal was given to relax, Petty Officer Evans, who had not begrudged his Herculean strength, was possessed by the drink demon again. Scott wrote stern words in his journal. 'E. Evans disgraced the ship. Saw him at the British Hotel, and spoke straight.' Perhaps to put him beyond the temptations of Lyttelton, Evans was ordered to 'proceed by train' to Port Chalmers, two hundred miles south, where the *Terra Nova* was to take in her last supplies of coal.

On 26 November, the Bishop of Christchurch held a short service on the deck of the *Terra Nova* at noon. It was the last time that Scott wore his gold-laced uniform of a captain in the Royal Navy. What he described in the journal as 'a great mass of people' assembled for the leave-taking. They came by special train from all parts of South Island, making it virtually a public holiday. Pleasure craft weighed down to the water with eager sightseers formed a ramshackle escort for the Expedition ship as, punctually at the advertised hour of 3 p.m., she cast off from the jetty at Lyttelton. Scott and his wife went out in her to the Banks Peninsula, returning in the harbour tug. Ashore again, they watched her from a hillside as she receded 'to a little dot in the S.E.' (Scott).

'My dearest Mother,' he wrote on 28 November, 'this is the last line before sailing and, though short, it is full of good cheer. Kathleen and I are journeying to Dunedin. The *Terra Nova* arrived there last night. I shall leave with high hopes and it's good to feel that all is going well at home.' He mentioned the church service. 'I know you will be glad to hear this. Goodbye, my dear, all love to you. Don't be anxious for me at any time.'

Old unstated family dissensions troubled his eldest sister in that hour of parting. He replied at once that he had forgotten them, 'except in so far as I realize that I was much at fault'. Looking back, it seemed to him that as a family they had 'drifted into an impossibly narrow relationship, which stifled energy and aspiration. I had to revolt, but am conscious that impatience led me to do things harshly.' He begged her to believe that he had 'no resentment left', and bade her an affectionate farewell (28 November).

In the journal for that day he recorded that his second-in-command, Evans, was 'excited by vague and wild grievances, the only reasonable one concerning Evans P.O. The cause of it all is not difficult to guess', an oblique reference to Lieutenant Evans's wife, who dreaded the coming separation. Scott scribbled a footnote: 'Smoothed him down.'

Kathleen Scott's diary notes, written at Dunedin the following day, are more revealing. 'All went well, till on the wharf we met the Evanses, both in a tearful condition. Apparently she had been working him up to insurrection and a volley of childish complaints was let fly. Such as that Con had cut his wife's dance, and many others too puerile to recount, and that therefore he must retire. Their tantrums spoilt the day and prevented us from being happy. If ever Con has another expedition, the wives must be chosen more carefully than the men—better still, have none.'

In the same entry, she referred to Evans as 'a rum little beggar, but there is something very attractive about him' (29 November 1910). She had handed Evans four sealed letters, asking him to see that each was given to her husband on the date shown on the envelope; the first on Christmas Day, the others on personal anniversaries.

For most members of the Expedition the last farewells were said at 2.30 that afternoon, when in bright sunshine the *Terra Nova* began the first part of her Homeric voyage. Lieutenant Rennick hurried aloft to wave good-bye from the crow's nest. Below, on deck, someone waved a tablecloth in humorous response to the massed handkerchief flutterings ashore. The ship was followed by a swarm of small vessels that seemed loath to fall behind and only did so when a tug stood alongside the *Terra Nova* and took off Scott's wife, Wilson's and Evans's, and returned with them to Port Chalmers.

'I decided not to say good-bye to my man,' Kathleen Scott wrote at the end of the day, 'because I didn't want anyone to see him look sad. On the bridge of the tug, Mrs Evans looked ghastly white and said she wanted to have hysterics. Mrs Wilson was plucky and good.' When Kathleen Scott 'tried to muster them for tea' on shore, 'Mrs Wilson sat sphinx-like on the wharf.' By then the *Terra Nova* was out of sight.

Kathleen Scott to Hannah Scott:

> Wellington,
> December 2nd [1910]
>
> ... At last they are off. All in the best of spirits and exceedingly glad to see the last of ports and stopping places. I had a very busy time the last few days marking their clothes. I sewed on 31 dozen tapes!
>
> We had some lovely last days together. Climbing over the hills, we got into great training and very fit and merry.

I haven't begun to realise that he's really gone yet, and I don't want to.

Peter seems slow getting his teeth, but if he's perfectly well of course it doesn't matter.

I am bringing back a lot of photographs that I took the last day of that adorable man and his ship.

CHAPTER FIFTEEN

A RAINBOW IN THE STORM

Two days out of New Zealand, Scott was squaring his shoulders to misfortune. 'A day of great disaster', he wrote in the journal for 2 December 1910. There was a storm, the worst that any in the ship had known. More than once, 'it was touch and go', Scott's own phrase. He was seen standing up to his middle in the green water of waves carefully calculated at thirty-five feet high that came over the deck. 'He might have been at Cowes,' Bowers recalled admiringly. 'He behaved up to our best tradition.'

Logged as 'Force 10', within two units of hurricane strength, the wind rolled and plunged and rocked the ship in a tumult of violence. To Cherry-Garrard, the assistant zoologist, it was 'a howling inferno', to Griffith Taylor, the geologist, 'a wild experience'. Wilson, the senior zoologist, wrote of it as 'a weird night's work with the howling gale and the darkness and the immense sea running over the ship every few minutes, and no engine and no sail.' To Evans, commander of the ship, 'the situation was about as black and as disheartening as it well could be.' Once, 'the lee combings of the main hatch were under the waves. As a rule, if a ship gets that far over she goes' (Cherry-Garrard).

Scott wrote that 'the scene on deck was devastating. The ship was very deeply laden; it did not need the addition of much water to get her waterlogged,' in which condition the worst could have happened. 'The water crept up to the furnaces and put the fires out, and we realized that the ship had met her match and was slowly filling,' Bowers recorded. The pumps were choked by a mixture of oil and coal dust. 'The outlook was grim' (Scott). There was talk of provisioning the boats.

Baling out seemed to be the only means of saving the ship. A chain of men with buckets toiled at it through a night and a day, 'Scott himself working with the best of them and staying with the toughest. It was a sight that one could never forget: everybody saturated, some waist-deep on the floor of the engine-room, oil and coal dust mixing with the water and making everyone filthy, some men clinging to the iron ladder way and passing full buckets up long after their muscles had ceased to work naturally, their grit and spirit keeping them going.'* Griffith Taylor supposed it to be 'something unique in modern times, in a ship of 750 tons—baling with buckets!'

Wilson chose to see the salvation of the *Terra Nova* as a miracle, hallowed by his glimpse of 'a most perfect and brilliant rainbow' that appeared at the height of the storm 'for about half a minute and then suddenly went out'. Seemingly, it was vouchsafed only to his eyes. No one else mentioned it. He was a deeply religious man.

Sea and wind died down in unison after fifty hours of the tempest. Ten tons of coal were lost, sixty-five gallons of petrol, a crate of laboratory spirit, two ponies, two dogs, hardly 'the great disaster' of Scott's journal note. He was worried about the animals from the third day after sailing; not the crew's pet rabbits loping among the hay bales, or the ship's white-whiskered black cat Nigger: the working ponies and dogs of the Expedition. He poured out his compassion for them in the first pages of his journal.

The ponies, 'with sad, patient eyes', swayed in their stalls to the restless motion of the ship, 'a terrible ordeal for these poor beasts'. The dogs whined in wet and shivering misery, ' a picture of wretched dejection; such a life is truly hard for these poor creatures'. When he prayed 'that there may be no more gales,' it was of them that he was thinking. 'I'm anxious, anxious about these animals of ours' (5 December). Such a ready susceptibility to emotional indulgence could be inimical to good judgement.

Not that his anxiety was wholly subjective. He was looking beyond the stresses of the moment. 'Poor patient beasts! One

* Evans: *South With Scott.*

211

wonders how far the memory of such fearful discomfort will remain with them—animals so often remember places and conditions where they have encountered difficulties or hurt. It would seem strangely merciful if nature should blot out these weeks of slow but inevitable torture' (8 December).

In short, would the buffetings of the storm affect the performance of the ponies and dogs in the role he had assigned to them? It was a necessary question. Two or three of the ponies were slow to recover; one looked as if it might not do so. It was a discouraging emergency that he had not foreseen.

*

Lurching across the twelve hundred miles of open ocean that girdles the globe between latitudes 50° and 70° S., the *Terra Nova* was the loneliest ship in the world. She was severed from human society as completely as Captain Cook had been when he crossed the Antarctic Circle two hundred years before, and far more so than any encapsuled astronaut. As for psychological briefings, probably the only significant neurosis in the entire company of sixty-five was the leader's private and profound anxiety that was a constant of his inner life.

Lieutenant Wilfrid Bruce gave a hint of it in a letter written to Kathleen Scott, his sister. The great storm, he said, was Scott's 'first trial after leaving New Zealand'. Their subsequent three weeks in the pack ice 'worried him a lot. He talked very little to anybody.'

They met the ice much farther north than was expected; 'encountering worse conditions than any ship had met before' (Scott). It meant heavy demands on coal for steaming and serious delay in reaching Cape Crozier in latitude 77° S., where it was hoped to establish winter quarters. Scott's exploration of the region in 1903–4 showed that it had several advantages; a good landing beach, sheltered from the fearful southern blizzards, nearness to the Great Ice Barrier, exceptional opportunities for biological work with its proximity to the only known breeding ground of the Emperor penguin, and a more direct approach to the polar route.

'The prospects are alarming from every point of view' (19 December). They were held in the greatest extent of pack ice recorded up to that time. Soon, Scott was writing as if he could not restrain his feelings. 'Oh, but it's mighty trying to be delayed and delayed like this, and coal going all the time. It really is very distressing.' In one morning, they made no more than two and a half miles.

There were icebergs to the leeward. 'We must take our chance of clearing them—we cannot go on wasting coal. We have less than 300 tons left in a ship that simply eats coal. It's alarming—and then there are the ponies going steadily downhill in condition. It looks as though fortune has determined to put every difficulty in our path' (22 December).

*

His wife was back in Australia, awaiting a passage home. On 21 December, in Adelaide, she lunched with Douglas Mawson and his Dutch-born fiancée, aged nineteen. He told Kathleen Scott that he was planning to raise £40,000 for a scientific expedition to the Antarctic, starting in December 1911. 'Made great friends with him,' she wrote in her diary, 'and stayed with him all day.' He told her 'awful tales' about the southern journey that he made with Shackleton's *Nimrod* expedition of 1907–9. 'Stolen food and struggles to possess the only revolver. Shameful yarns.' By her account, Mawson was 'scared to death that Shackleton would try to take over his expedition, once he has got it up'.

While they were lunching, news agency messages came in announcing that Shackleton proposed to circumnavigate the Antarctic continent by landing three separate parties of nine men each and dispatching them at intervals of eight hundred miles. 'Mawson, said: "That's the scheme I laid out for him while I was in England months ago."' He also said, 'with no hesitation or addition', that he did not trust Shackleton. She wished she could help him with his Antarctic plan. 'He looks so very, very nice, and seems so entirely frank. I'd like to do something for him.'

The finances of her husband's Expedition were much on her mind as she embarked for the homeward voyage. She asked herself in the diary: How on earth am I going to get money? 'An exceedingly wealthy Australian spinster, Miss Walker, is on board. They told me to make friends with her and ask her for money, with the terrible result that I can scarcely bring myself to be civil to her.'

Arriving home, she read the letter that Scott had given her

213

at their parting, 'to be opened in England'. It was dated 1 October 1910.

Soon there won't be any post to bring you letters when I am thinking of you, so I write you now for you to read some day in England—and when you read you will know something of what will be in my thoughts and remain in my thoughts till we meet again. Perhaps it needed this first short separation to show me how much happiness you have brought me, and how much I have grown to depend on you, and how sweet to me that dependence is.

I shall be thinking of the wise things you did and made me do until you brought me to a better sense of the fitness of things. You have taught me many things indeed, and, best of all, to value things more rightly.

I am not anxious for the future either for us both or you alone, if you will take care of yourself. If all is well, I know now that we shall always have enough to be happy together because a little will be enough; on the other hand, I know your courage and can picture the gallant independence you would secure for yourself and our boy.

I am sure he is going to be a fine fellow, but I want you to have the makings of his mind as much as you have of his stout little body. It's good to think you have the boy, you being what you are.

I shall be thinking of you always and picturing your daily life, wondering always what you are doing and whether you are thinking of me; and so, goodbye.

God bless you and the boy.

*

On Christmas Day, after joining in the usual celebrations, he had retired at midnight to keep his journal up to date, a contractual obligation. 'We are captured. We do practically nothing under sail to push through, and could do little under steam, and at each step the possibility of advance seems to lessen.'

The next day they 'managed to make 2 or 3 miles under sail'. He was downhearted. 'It is difficult to keep hope alive.' He wrote to his mother: 'You can imagine how often and how restlessly we climb to the crow's nest and study the outlook.

Huge icebergs creep silently towards or past us, and continually we are observing these formidable objects with the range finder and compass to determine the relative movement, sometimes with misgivings as to our ability to clear them.'

Vast sheets of ice broke readily before the iron-shod prow of the ship. 'Sometimes even a thin sheet would resist all our attempts to break it.' Big floes were sheared through without trouble, small ones barred the way with an obstinacy suggesting 'the work of an evil spirit'. The shock of the ship being forced against the floes often startled Scott out of his sleep during the night watches. 'I have seen him hurry up from his cabin to put a stop to it!' (Cherry-Garrard)

Against his impatience with the pack conditions can be set a different aspect of them noted by Wilson in a letter to his wife. 'We have now broad daylight night and day, but the beauty of the day with its lovely blues and greens amongst the bergs and ice-floes is eclipsed altogether by the marvellous beauty of the midnight, when white ice becomes deepest purple and golden rose and the sky is lemon green without a cloud. No scene in the whole world was ever more beautiful than a clear midnight in the pack.'

At last, on 30 December, they were free. They had taken 21 days to cover 380 miles. 'One breathes again,' Scott wrote, 'and hopes that it will be possible to carry out the main part of our programme.' Six hours after: 'We are creeping along at a bare 2 knots. I begin to wonder if fortune will ever turn her wheel. On every possible occasion she seems to have decided against us.'

Answering the Christmas letter from his wife that Evans dutifully handed to him, he did not persist in his enervated mood. Well aware that her invigorating spirit scorned grievances against fate, he boldly claimed: 'I don't take our setbacks too seriously. You needn't worry about my attitude under adversity.' He thought it necessary to tell her, perhaps for his own reassurance too: 'It is doubtful if I could have made myself content to go on in a common rut, dependent on seniority for advancement. Somehow I know that you would rather I was striving for big interesting things, whatever the cost,' as if hers was a siren voice with implacably persuasive undertones.

*

Their great landmark, Mount Erebus, showed up from 115 miles away. As they sailed on under a good spread of canvas, the old hands recognized again the weird white glare, known as ice blink, that irradiated the sky above the still distant Barrier. Ponting's photographs show it glowing along the whole width of the southern horizon.

Sighting the 'remarkably interesting' basalt cliffs of Cape Crozier, they launched a whaler to reconnoitre likely landing places. 'No good! ! Alas! Cape Crozier with all its attractions is denied us' (Scott). 'The swell was too heavy for us; a landing was out of the question' (Wilson). 'It was a great disappointment to us all' (Ponting). To none more than to Wilson, who has high hopes of it as an alternative base—'there is such a heap of interest about the place.' The *Terra Nova*'s course was therefore laid for McMurdo Sound.

The landing was begun on 5 January 1911, fifteen miles north of the *Discovery*'s winter quarters in 1903–4, at what was then briefly named The Skuary, from the number of skua gulls nesting there. Scott now formally designated it Cape Evans, 'in honour of our excellent second in command'. It was reached across more than a mile of sea ice two and a half feet thick, over which a considerable tonnage was borne in the next six days. The men worked stolidly from 5 a.m. to 10 p.m. each day. 'Nothing like it has been done before; nothing so expeditious and complete,' Scott wrote.

When the ponies were led forth, the sight of them moved him to distressful fancies about the miseries of their situation during the months at sea. 'Poor brutes, it is evident all have suffered from skin irritation—one can imagine the horror of suffering from such an ill for weeks without being able to get at the part that itched' (4 January 1911).

Having written in the journal on 5 January: 'Words cannot express the splendid way in which everyone works', he had a reservation to make the following day. 'Gran never does his share of the work, great strong chap as he is.' Yet only a few days earlier he had observed with evident satisfaction that Gran 'is wonderfully good and gives ski instruction well'. Now he thought him 'a lazy, and posing fellow', who lost no chance of being in the picture if anyone produced a camera.

The unpublished parts of Scott's journal show that he looked on Gran with a coldly critical eye in those weeks after the landing. The question here is, was his attitude prejudiced by Amundsen's appearance in the Antarctic arena? One of the Expedition's scientists put it to the present biographer that Scott at that time 'rather disliked Norwegian matters'.* There are journal entries indicating that while he was irritated by the foibles of some other members of the party, he reserved his harshest judgements for the young Norwegian ski expert.

Unloading the ship provided an opportunity to test the motor tractors, which Scott reported 'are working well, but not very well'. He 'rather feared' that they would not draw the loads expected of them. He noted that 'at a little distance, without silencers, they sounded exactly like threshing machines'. Then on 8 January there occurred what he wrote down as a *disaster* (his italics). The ice gave way under the third tractor, which sank at once in a hundred fathoms, beyond recovery.

His relative unconcern at the loss was noted as a sign of regained composure after the frustrations of the past weeks. 'Having landed, and feeling a bit more settled,' his brother-in-law, Lieutenant Bruce, wrote home, 'he bucked up a lot and said many pretty things to all of us.' Bruce referred to the 'awful strain' on Scott of bearing 'the responsibility for a show like this'.

Scott to J. J. Kinsey:

Winter Quarters,
Cape Evans.
12 January, 1911.

My dear Kinsey,—Here we are, safe and sound, on land with all stores. Fortune has been variable, but, on the whole, kind. I won't go into our adventures, as you will be in an exceptionally good position to hear of them first-hand from members of the ship's party.

They will tell you of the gale which cost us something, and very nearly cost us all—of the fearful extent of the pack ice—of our disappointment at Cape Crozier—of our selection of a camp site, and its good promise—of the losses we have sustained, and of the events which are yet to happen before the ship leaves us.

* Professor T. Griffith Taylor, the geologist.

The speed with which our winter station has been set up is a record, and one to be proud of. In a week from our arrival we had landed all our stores, and nearly completed the erection of the hut, though every package had to be transported across $1\frac{1}{4}$ miles of sea ice. We could never have accomplished the work so promptly had it not been for the preliminary practice in working stores which all hands obtained at Lyttelton, and for the wonderful way in which they stuck to the work here. I have never known work conducted with such vigour or in such harmony.

I have every hope of success with such support, but here, of course, one is face to face with possibilities which are beyond human guidance.

The loss of one of our motor sledges was a bad blow, as the other two have proved themselves efficient by dragging big loads of stores on shore, but, even so, as I watch them working here I feel rather than know that I was right not to place serious reliance on these machines. . . .

I shall write again as things develop, but I fear the letters may be scant.

Yours ever sincerely,

R. F. SCOTT

The immediate surroundings of the winter camp were akin to those of a Norwegian fjord bare of all vegetation. The coast line extending from it on either side was indented by glaciers; some looked like frozen Amazons awaiting a cataclysmic melting. They intersected enormous snow slopes that descended to black and chocolate-brown foothills near the sea. Out in the Sound was a scattering of conical islands standing pillar-wise 300 or 400 feet above the ice. Beyond them, far away, were the Western Mountains with cloud-raking peaks and deep glacial valleys forming 'a vision of mountain scenery that can have few rivals' (Scott). Wilson wrote of 'its unimaginable beauty. The peace of God which passeth all understanding reigns here.' Scott wrote in a letter to his wife for posting when the *Terra Nova* returned to New Zealand: 'Fortune has been kind after all, and every day shows the advantages of the spot we have chosen for our winter station. Of course the elements are going to be troublesome, but it is good to know them as the only adversary and to feel that there is so small a chance of internal friction. When shall I hear of you again? What weary months must elapse ...' (12 January 1911).

The days were bright and warm. The men washed in pools made by the melted snow, and drank from cupped hands the clear water bubbling up between the rocks. Ponting, the photographer, wrote: 'It filled one with a sensation of delight to throw back the arms, expand the chest, and, opening wide the lungs, inhale great draughts of the sweet exhilarating air. It made one thrill and tingle to be alive, to have health and strength, and to feel the marvel of it all.' For Evans, 'those were such happy days,' marred for Scott by a visit to the old *Discovery* quarters at Hut Point on 14 January. Shackleton and his *Nimrod* party had used it last, in 1907–9.

He found it full of snow, and blamed Shackleton for the neglect leading to that result. Digging out the hut was a disheartening experience. 'I went to bed thoroughly depressed. It seems a fundamental expression of civilized human sentiment that men who come to such places as this should leave what comfort they can to welcome those who follow, and finding that such a simple duty had been neglected by our immediate predecessors oppressed me horribly. Boxes full of excrement and other filth. It is extraordinary that people could have lived in such horrible manner with such absence of regard for those to follow.'

Scott to Major-General Sir Douglas Haig, K.C.V.O., C.B., Chief of Staff, British Army H.Q., Simla:

> Winter Quarters,
> Cape Evans,
> Antarctic Regions.
> 22 January 1911.

Dear Sir,—I hope you will forgive the liberty I take, as a stranger, in writing to you, in view of the very exceptional nature of the request which I have to make.

You will perhaps have heard of this Expedition and know that we are here with the hope of reaching the South Pole.

I have 15 ponies with which to make the attempt and Captain Oates, of the Inniskilling Dragoons, has charge of them.

Before directing more ponies to be sent down, I have thoroughly discussed the situation with Captain Oates, and he has suggested that mules would be better than ponies for our work and that trained Indian Transport mules would be ideal. It is evident already that some of our ponies have not a uniform walking pace and that in other small ways they will be troublesome to us.

I understand that the system of the Indian Transport Department produces the most excellently trained mules in the world.

I am aware that it must be most unusual to dispose of such animals outside the Service, but I feel that you will consider that the circumstances are altogether exceptional.

I have asked for seven to allow wastage in planning a team of six. I send this letter by my ship, the *Terra Nova*, but of course can receive no reply to it till she returns, with or without the mules, next year!

I think you will appreciate the urgency of such a case as this and be in sympathy with the object of the expedition. We are all very much in earnest here and feel that it *must* be an Englishman who first gets to the Pole. Pray help us if you can.

I must apologise for the length of this letter, and once more urge the importance of the business in extenuation.

Hoping to have the pleasure of thanking you by our next mail in a year's time,

Yours very truly,

R. F. SCOTT

Captain, R.N.

Sending a draft of the letter to Haig for Kinsey to see, Scott asked him: 'Will you do your best? We must get them', the mules. 'I cannot tell you how perfect our station arrangements are. Everything goes like clockwork; the scientific work is being done under the most admirable conditions. Our cooking is so good that we actually *prefer* seal and penguin to mutton', an admission that may not have been thought tactful by Kinsey, whose fellow countrymen made a gift to the Expedition of a hundred and fifty carcases of Canterbury lamb. 'Life is absolutely comfortable', Scott's letter assured him. 'The ship ran ashore today, by way of providing some excitement. The ice is breaking up, and we are desperately busy getting the depot party away' (22 January).

CHAPTER SIXTEEN

ANGRY ABOUT AMUNDSEN

'THERE is nothing I would not do for him, he is just splendid.'
Wilson was writing to Scott's wife. 'I am sure he feels as I do,
that it was only yesterday that we were here, and that the
seven years which have passed over us have left no trace,
except, in your husband, a very much more confident grasp of
conditions and possibilities, in which he simply excels.' Cherry-
Garrard wrote in his diary: 'Scott seems very cheery about
things,' commenting later; 'And well he might be. A man
could hardly be better served. We slaved until we were dead-
beat, and then we found something else to do until we were
quite dead-beat. The way men worked was fierce.'*

Assessing their qualities and merits weighed heavily on
Scott. Each day brought him nearer the point at which he must
make crucial decisions affecting them individually. It troubled
him to tell Lieutenant Rennick, before they left New Zealand,
that he would have to resign his provisional place in the Shore
Party to Bowers. Scott had come to the conclusion that Rennick
'lacked Bowers's brains. I wasn't quite sure what to make of
him,' he told Kinsey. His relief that Rennick took the verdict
against him in a manly way is evident from the journal. 'He is
a good fellow and one feels for him much—it must be rather
dreadful for him to be returning.'

A similar *contretemps* arose when Scott put Ponting in charge
of the Western Geological Party that was to be sent out as
soon as possible after the landing. Griffith Taylor, the geologist, did not hide his disappointment at the decision, which
Scott then reversed in Taylor's favour. 'Ponting at once dis-
claimed any right. I'm sure he's a very nice fellow,' Scott
wrote.

Ponting was 'entranced with everything', Scott told Kinsey,
'and is producing some remarkable work.' Simpson, the meteorologist, was also 'certain to do some very good work', while
Wright, described by Evans as 'the lusty young Canadian
physicist', was 'taking his ice study very seriously', and was
'pretty sure to make a good thing of it'.

* A. Cherry-Garrard: *The Worst Journey in the World.*

All the ship's officers were 'doing wonders'. Pennell, in command of the *Terra Nova*, had gained a high place in Scott's regard: 'the ablest man I have met for many a long day. He has a remarkable headpiece, and what is of more importance, any amount of common sense, resource and good judgement.' Endorsing that tribute to Pennell, Wilson wrote that he was 'by far the most capable man in the whole Expedition'.

Wilson was 'to the fore in everything,' Scott wrote; his experience 'always in demand, his opinions always consulted, the most valued and valuable of all. He is a positive wonder.'* Oates, who spent the greater part of his time in caring for the ponies, was classed as 'a treasure', like Bowers, with the qualification added three days later, 'he is not an optimist'. Summarizing his judgements, with omissions that may or may not have been significant, Scott told Kinsey: 'They are a fine lot all round. I could not wish for a better.'

Scott to his mother:

> Glacier Tongue,
> McMurdo Sound.
> Jan 25 [1911]

My own dearest Mother,—... I think of you so often. Spring will be with you as our winter approaches. We are off on a longish sledge trip and as each week brings us a colder temperature I shall be consoling myself with the thought that it will be bringing you better and warmer conditions. It is good to know that you will be taken care of and free of many small worries that must have harassed you in times gone by.

My companions are a far abler lot of men than I had in the *Discovery*, and all are devoted to the work and loyal to me. We are expecting to be cut off from our base at Cape Evans for a long time, and have therefore to transport a large quantity of food. Just now we are getting this food safely away from the sea with ponies and dogs.

You will know when you get this how little cause there is for anxiety and how successfully we have begun our work. Goodbye, my dearest Mother. Mind you take every care of yourself, so that I may find you fit and well when I return.

> Your loving son,
> CON

* From a letter to Scott's sister, 25 January 1911.

He objected to the term 'hut' for the winter headquarters. 'It is misleading. It is really a house of considerable size, in every respect the finest that has ever been erected in the Polar regions; 50 ft. long by 25 ft. wide, and 9 ft. to the eaves.' Its double walls of tongue-and-grooved boards were insulated with 'excellent quilted seaweed', and lined with felt. The roof was covered with 'three-ply ruberoid', the floor laid with linoleum. Volcanic sand made a good draught excluder, and compressed forage bales piled against the east and south sides gave extra weather protection. It was divided into two compartments, the wardroom for Scott and his officers and the scientific staff, and the mess deck for the rest.

'It is a first-rate building' (Scott), housing a fully equipped scientific establishment that was as competent to report on the radio-activity of rocks as it was to investigate the incidence of parasites in fish. Proud of it as a manifestation of the contemporary spirit of his Expedition, Scott wondered about the future of the building in relation to the timeless Antarctic perspectives.* He noted that the hut built by William Barents in Novaya Zemlya in 1596 was found by Captain Carlsen in 1871, 'two hundred and seventy-five years later, intact with everything inside as left'. Against the same entry in the journal, he inserted a quotation:

'He is not worthy to live at all who, for fear and danger of death shunneth his country's service, or his own honour, since death is inevitable and the fame of virtue immortal.—Sir Humphrey Gilbert.'

*

He was to lead a party of 12, with 8 pony sledges and 2 dog sledges, to lay reserve supplies in latitude 80° S. for the coming polar journey. Lieutenant Campbell was to take a party of 5 to explore the coast of King Edward VII Land, for the purpose of finding a possible take-off point nearer the Pole. Griffith Taylor, with 3 others, was assigned to a geological reconnaissance of the mountains and glaciers of Victoria Land.

Having landed Griffith Taylor, his fellow geologist, Debenham, Wright, the physicist, and Petty Officer Evans, on the

* When Sir Edmund Hillary visited Cape Evans in 1957, he found rubbish, empty tins, and seal carcases strewn round the hut—'a complete shambles. It seemed a poor monument to a great man!' The hut has since been restored to its original state by the New Zealanders at Scott Base.

western side of the Sound, the *Terra Nova* was to disembark Campbell, Priestley (geologist), Levick (medical officer), and three Royal Navy seamen, Abbott, Dickason, and Browning, on King Edward VII Land, four hundred miles to the east, at the farthest extremity of the Great Ice Barrier. She was then to return to New Zealand. It would be the parting of the ways for the ship and shore sections of the Expedition.

Scott's party started out on 24 January 1911. With him were Evans, the second-in-command, Wilson, Atkinson, and Cherry-Garrard, as scientists, Bowers and Oates, responsible for stores and ponies respectively, Meares, in charge of the sledge dogs, three petty officers, R.N., Crean, Forde and Keohane, and a young Russian dog driver, Dimitri Gerof.

Known in the annals as the Depot-Laying Party, they went off in a flurry of agitation, for the sea ice, that provided the only direct route to the Barrier, was fast receding. It was crossed with only hours to spare—'in a state bordering upon panic', by Cherry-Garrard's account. Had the start been delayed, the programme of the Expedition might have been gravely affected, possibly to the extent of a year's postponement.

Besides his habitual daily wear, each man carried 12 lb. of 'private gear', mostly extra clothing. The list of permissible items included 'perhaps one small book'. The supplies they were transporting consisted of pony fodder, dog biscuits, sledging rations, and paraffin. Their march was plotted to take them as far south as possible over the Great Ice Barrier, where the reserve depot was to be laid.

Farewells were exchanged between ship and shore parties on 25 January. For the final rendezvous, the *Terra Nova* had been worked round to Glacier Tongue, a jutting ice formation six miles south-east of the winter quarters at Cape Evans (it broke off a few months later and was seen grounded, 'a huge flat iceberg two miles long', forty miles away). For an hour or two before the respective exploring parties set off, they foregathered in the ship to write letters for posting in New Zealand. Scott wrote to his mother, his wife, his sister Ettie, and to the wife of his second-in-command, comforting her with the tribute: 'I daily grow more grateful to you for sparing him for this venture,' a compliment revoked in a later letter to Kinsey.

By 29 January, the great weight of reserve stores was relayed to what was thereafter known as Safety Camp, two miles over the Great Ice Barrier. The *Terra Nova* left with Campbell and his small Eastern Party (eventually known as the Northern Party because of an enforced change of direction) to sail eastward along the Barrier to King Edward VII Land.

Before the ship cast off, Pennell, her commander, called the company aft to be addressed by Scott, who thanked them for their 'splendid work'. In his journal he wrote that 'it was a little sad to say farewell to all these good fellows and to Campbell and his men. I do most heartily trust that all will be successful in their ventures, for indeed their unselfishness and their generous high spirit deserve reward. God bless them!' Noticeably, in those last months of the Expedition it was God he invoked, not Providence, as had long been his habit.

The Depot-Laying Party soon ran into difficulties. Atkinson, the surgeon who was also the Expedition's parasitologist, developed a suppurating foot from chafing and had to be sent back to base, with Petty Officer Crean to look after him. The Barrier surface was softer than they had anticipated.

Describing the conditions in a letter to Kinsey, Scott wrote: 'Our arrival here has revealed a fact which I had not taken into account. Our ponies have been floundering badly. In every respect, other than this difficulty with the surface, we are doing well. The fellows I have with me are splendid. Wilson is wonderful, and is my right hand throughout, but it would be impossible to better any of them, and such people as Bowers, Oates, and Meares, will take a lot of stopping when they have the hang of this business.'

For Scott and Wilson, the start of the Barrier journey had the interest of reviving shared memories. They passed again under the shadow of Mount Terror, behind Erebus; saw Castle Rock, where the *Discovery* had so nearly come to grief in the squall, and the wooden cross for Able Seaman Vince who glissaded helplessly to his death over the cliff. Tins discarded by the *Discovery* men lay glinting in the shallows round Hut Point. Stakes they had placed to mark the movement of minor glaciers were still there; old footprints still visible on the frozen slopes.

The sun was above the horizon all through the twenty-four hours, and marching by night was decided on, sleep in the afternoon and evening, breakfast at 10 p.m. The temperature fall at night, it was thought, would improve the surface. The difference was hardly appreciable, and the ponies were frequently brought to a standstill by the depth of snow. The average daily distance was no more than ten miles. They never knew when they would come on a snow-bridged crevasse. 'No hunter could conceal his snare so perfectly' (Scott).

They met their first blizzard early in February. Outside the tents, it was 'raging chaos', Cherry-Garrard recorded. The wind was at gale strength, driving the snow before it in blinding clouds. It was dangerous to venture more than a yard or two in the open. 'Lose your sense of direction and there is nothing to guide you back.' They were held up three days; three crucial days in the history of the Expedition.

On the march again, the animals suffered more than the men; and Scott's anxiety for them is imprinted on the pages of his journal. 'It is horrid to see them half engulfed in the snow, panting and heaving from the strain. Now and again one falls and lies trembling and temporarily exhausted.... What extraordinary uncertainties this work exhibits! Every day some new fact comes to light—some new obstacle which threatens the gravest obstruction. I suppose this is the reason which makes the game so well worth playing' (3 February 1911).

The dog teams were pulling 'very well', and Scott made notes, as he did during his first expedition, of the instinctive canine behaviour that to him was 'almost alarming'. Two white dogs in Meares's sledge team had been trained to attack strangers. They broke into vicious barking when anyone but their driver approached. Suddenly Scott realized that he was a potential victim. 'I had no stick, and there is no doubt that if Meares had not been on the sledge the whole team, following the lead of the white dogs, would have been at me in a moment.'

On 14 February, one of the ponies sank exhausted into the snow as they were making camp. Instantly, it was set on and terribly mauled by the dogs. That atavistic display prompted Scott to reflect that 'it is such stern facts that resign one to the sacrifice of animal life in the effort to advance such human projects as this'.

Possibly because of the absence of the familiar sounds of

urban life, he was the more sensitive to those of the 'vast and godlike spaces' of the Antarctic. The patter of dog pads, the shuffle of ponies' hoofs, the rhythmic crunch of marching men, echo eerily in his journal pages, along with the 'deep booming' of the wind against the tent canvas, and the hissing of the Primus stoves. His recurring adjectives for the all-pervading stillness were 'deep', 'vast', 'eternal'. He confirmed Meares's claim that the barking of their dogs at Cape Evans had been heard in calm weather at a distance of seven or eight miles. Ponting heard a whale spouting—'a loud, hollow-sounding blast'—at Cape Royds, seven miles from where he stood. The silence of the Antarctic world could be so *vast*, he wrote, that 'the voices of men talking in ordinary outdoor tones can be heard for a mile or more'. Sounds like random revolver shots startled the ear—'the ice contracting on the glaciers of Erebus' (Cherry-Garrard).

*

Reaching the 79th parallel, Scott agreed with Oates that some of the ponies were giving out. Oates proposed that they should be taken to the last mile they were capable of and then killed as dog food, to be left at the depot for the final journey. Having allegedly resigned himself to the sacrifice of animal life, Scott could not face the prospect. 'I think he felt the sufferings of the ponies more than the animals themselves' (Cherry-Garrard). Reproaching himself for not 'supervising these matters more closely', he ordered 'Teddy' Evans and the two petty officers, Forde and Keohane, to take the three weakest of the animals back to winter quarters at Cape Evans, where, presumably, he expected that they would recover under care.

As soon as Scott and his diminished party were out of sight, Evans had the weakest of the three ponies killed, 'for humanity's sake', the animal was so obviously failing. Lieutenant Evans said that 'poor old Forde,' who did the deed, 'was practically in tears.' A second pony struggled on with them for thirty miles, 'looking like a spectre', and then fell and died. The third completed the journey and was soon ready to work again.

Marching south, Scott kept records of their laborious daily distances in miles and yards: 14 February, 7 miles 650 yards; 15 February, 7 miles 775 yards; 16 February, 6 miles 1450 yards. The limit of the Depot-Laying Journey was decided by the rapid decline in the strength of the remaining ponies. By 17 February, the temperature was down to minus 20 degrees F. 'Bowers's ears were quite white.' Oates's nose was giving him trouble. 'The Soldier takes a gloomy view of everything,' Scott wrote, 'but I've come to see that this is a characteristic of his. In spite of it he pays every attention to the weaker horses.' Meares had 'a refractory toe'. Scott's face was lightly frost-bitten.

The load-pulling power of the ponies was declining fast. The snow surface was too deep; for the animals, every yard was a struggle. At 79° 29′ S. Scott ordered the final halt and selected the site for the depot, 130 miles across the Great Ice Barrier, 670 miles from the Pole. 'It is a pity we couldn't get up to 80°, but as it is we shall have a good leg up for next year' (Journal).

Shifting 'considerably over a ton of stuff', a hoard of fodder, dog biscuits, and paraffin for cooking, was packed into a round solid cairn of snow, six feet high. Biscuit tins, some full, some empty were let into the sides as reflectors, making it a more conspicuous landmark on light days. They built what was to be a tragic monument in the history of polar logistics. It was given the name of One Ton Depot. Over it, on a bamboo pole, there waved a black flag.

*

Disappointed at having failed to reach his planned objective of the 80th parallel, Scott showed a not quite characteristic eagerness to get back to Hut Point, fifteen miles from the winter camp, where the *Terra Nova*, on her way back to New Zealand, was to touch in with news of Campbell's party. Scott hurried on ahead with the two dog teams, one with himself and Meares, the other with Wilson and Cherry-Garrard, leaving Bowers, Oates, and Gran to follow with the ponies.

The dog teams made good going, travelling over eighty miles in the first three days, the men alternately riding and running. With what seems to have been impulsive judgement, Scott decided on a short cut. Disregarding Wilson's advice, 'he shaved things rather fine,' as Evans put it, and soon ran into trouble. Wilson's diary gives a more vivid account than Scott's of the near-disaster that followed.

'I was running my team abreast of Meares, when I suddenly

saw his whole team disappear one dog after another, as they ran down a crevasse in the Barrier surface. Ten of his thirteen dogs disappeared as I watched, they looked exactly like rats running down a hole; only I saw no hole: they simply went into the white surface and disappeared.' Hurrying forward to investigate, Wilson looked down into 'a great blue chasm in which hung the team of dogs in a festoon, whining and yapping and trying to get a foothold on each other and on the crumbly snow sides of the crevasse'. Two of the thirteen dogs had fallen out of the harness and were lying on a snow ledge sixty feet down, 'where they curled up and went to sleep!' Cherry-Garrard said they could see 'nothingness below'. The miracle was, said Wilson, that 'the sledge hadn't followed with Meares and Capt. Scott.'

The dogs hung in the void for an hour and a half, while all the efforts of the men were devoted to getting them out. The two on the ledge far below still had to be rescued. Cherry-Garrard wrote: 'Scott proposed going down on the Alpine rope to get them; all his instincts of kindness were aroused. Wilson thought it was a mad idea and very dangerous, and said so. We lowered Scott, who stood on the ledge while we hauled up the two dogs in turn. They were glad to see him and little wonder!'

The crevasse episode, the news of the loss of two of the ponies that he had sent back for recuperation, depressed Scott, whose morale was about to be tested still more severely. After vainly searching for the mail that was to have been left for him at Hut Point, he made for Safety Camp, near the Barrier edge, where Atkinson handed him a mailbag 'that contained but one letter'. The letter was from Campbell: 'I have just learnt the startling fact of Amundsen's establishment of his party of 8 with 130 dogs in the Bay of Whales.' Scott hurriedly copied out the message into his diary. His comment that followed was suppressed from the published journal: 'I cannot help feeling disgusted because Amundsen's action is secret and deliberate.'

Scott went on to say: 'I hope and think it would have been outside my code of honour under any circumstances, but that will not necessarily condemn it from a public point of view and it is pretty certain to be justified if success attends his effort. Some things are clear already; firstly, I will not be betrayed into a public expression of my opinion; secondly, I will make no alteration in own plans because of this' (22 February 1911).

*

On 27 February, Lieutenant Wilfrid Bruce, on board the *Terra Nova,* wrote a long letter to his sister, Kathleen Scott, describing the unexpected meeting with Amundsen. They had sailed eastward beyond the Great Ice Barrier, looking for a place to land Campbell and his party for their exploration of King Edward VII Land. 'Of all the desolate places in the world,' Bruce wrote, 'none can compare with this. Sheer 100 ft. cliffs of ice, rolling smooth hills behind, all, all in white. Not a dark speck or a break of any kind could we see. Nowhere could we find an even possible landing place, so we had to come back, coasting and surveying all the way.'

It was decided to make for the Bay of Whales, along the Great Barrier, the inlet from which Scott had made his balloon ascent in 1902. 'All Campbell's stores were got ready to land. We turned the corner into the Bay just after midnight on 4 February. I had just got on the bridge and you can imagine our excitement when we found a ship there, which in two minutes we recognised as the *Fram*! Curses loud and deep were heard everywhere, and we ran close by her and made fast to the floe ahead without them knowing.'

The crews exchanged visits in the course of the *Terra Nova*'s twelve-hours' stay in the Bay. Few questions were asked on either side. An extraordinary punctilio prevailed. 'Individually, they all seemed charming men, even the perfidious Amundsen. They had 120 dogs and are going for the Pole; No science, no nothing, just the Pole!'

Bruce's letter tells of the rigours of the *Terra Nova*'s return journey to Cape Evans, before she sailed north for New Zealand. Every man in the ship was hurt during the gale that swept over her. 'We were all bleeding. Sometimes we were all inclined to scream.'

The effect of the news of Amundsen's arrival on Scott and his shore party was described by Cherry-Garrard. 'For an hour or so we were furiously angry, and were possessed with an insane sense that we must go straight to the Bay of Whales and have it out with Amundsen and his men.' In after years, Cherry-Garrard told his Hertfordshire neighbour, George Bernard

230

Shaw, that 'in a burst of temper, Scott wanted to go to the Bay of Whales and fight Amundsen'. That does not square with the temper shown in Scott's journal, where he wrote: 'One thing only fixes itself definitely in my mind. The proper, as well as the wiser, course for us is to proceed exactly as though this had not happened. To go forward and do our best for the honour of the country without fear or panic' (22 February 1911).

Raymond Priestley,* the geologist of Campbell's Eastern Party, kept a diary in which he noted the meeting with the Norwegians that day. To him, they seemed to be men of distinctive personalities, physically and mentally tough, and likeable, though 'dangerous rivals'. He observed that they refrained from asking for information. His impression of Amundsen as a simple, blunt Norwegian sailor was considered to be 'very erroneous' by Cherry-Garrard, who wrote of him as 'an explorer of the markedly intellectual type, rather Jewish than Scandinavian'.† In fact, he was using words put into his mouth by Shaw, to whom he had shown a photograph of Amundsen, and subsequently repeated by Shaw in a letter.‡

'Captain Scott took it very bravely, better than any of us, I think.' His second-in-command was writing about the news of Amundsen's proximity. 'It was he [Scott] who initiated and founded Antarctic sledge travelling, it was he who had blazed the trail, and we were very, very sorry for him, for such news could hardly be expected to give him a happy winter.'§ Scott himself wrote that 'Amundsen's plan is a very serious menace to ours'. He was shadowed from that day by the possibility of a shattering anti-climax of all his effort so far, mental and physical, and of all that had yet to be.

*

Getting the five remaining ponies, and the two dog teams, of the Depot-Laying Party back to winter quarters was of itself a major worry for Scott, impelling Evans to write that 'if ever a man's footsteps were dogged by misfortune, they were surely

* Sir Raymond Priestley, M.C., M.A.
† A. Cherry-Garrard: *The Worst Journey in the World*.
‡ To Lord Kennet, 2 February 1948: "To my amazement I saw a portrait of a Jewish aristocrat, no Hittite with a number six nose, but a handsome Philistine of the highest type, much more intellectual than Scott.'
§ Evans: *South With Scott*.

231

our leader's.' The immediate place of assembly was to be Hut Point. Scott had pony mortality much on his mind. He sent Bowers, with Cherry-Garrard and Crean, to guide four of the ponies across the sea ice at the foot of Mount Erebus. He himself stayed with Oates and Gran to look after the fifth pony, which was in a bad way. Advancing over the ice, Bowers realized that it was on the move. He ordered an about-turn, only to find that they were being floated out to sea. The ponies, described as 'tired and listless' after the hard journey across the Barrier, showed a sudden surprising nimbleness in jumping the cracks in the floe. Where the cracks were too wide, the men bridged them with the sledges.

After an hour and a half of skipping from one piece of floe to another, they came to what they took to be fast ice. Exhausted, they pitched a tent for food and sleep. 'It was very dark,' Bowers said, 'and I mistook a small bag of curry powder for the cocoa bag, and made cocoa with that, mixed with sugar. Crean drank his right down before discovering anything was wrong.'

At 4.30 a.m. they were awakened by 'a strange noise'. Opening the tent, Bowers saw water all round them. One of the ponies had gone. He wrote: 'I cannot describe the scene or my feelings. Our camp was on a floe not more than 30 yards across'. The men were in their socks. They rushed out to save the sledges, drifting out of reach. Then their own piece of ice cracked under them. Bowers was remembered as having remarked: 'We've been in a few tight places. This is about the limit.'

The only way of escape was southward. There was by now so much movement that as soon as a crack opened up it was often as quickly closed. Progress was made by judging the critical moment at which men and ponies could be sure of going on together. They were frequently separated, and reunited after agonizing pauses.

What Bowers called 'a further unpleasantness' occurred in the arrival of a host of 'killer' whales, *Orca gladiator*, probably the most ferocious beast of the sea. Scott had been a witness of their 'deliberate cunning', which showed, he noted in the journal, 'that they are endowed with singular intelligence, which in future we shall treat with every respect'. He had seen them diving beneath a floe on which some of the dogs were

232

tethered, and breaking it up by heaving against its underside, 'fiendish activity' of which Bowers and his two marooned companions were acutely aware as they watched 'the immense black fins sticking up', and heard the monsters 'blowing with a terrific roar'. Cherry-Garrard said that 'they were undisguisedly interested in the ponies'.

It took Bowers and his party six hours to get back to the Barrier edge, where there was a floe that promised safety. Arriving on it, they saw between it and the Barrier a lane of water forty feet wide, filled with brash ice that heaved in the swell 'like the contents of a cauldron'. Killer whales were cruising amid the turmoil. Then the floe broke in two and once again they had to scramble for safety. Crean was sent to find a way of getting up on the Barrier, where he could make contact with Scott. Bowers and Cherry-Garrard waited with the ponies.

'I felt that having been delivered so wonderfully so far, the same Hand would not forsake us at the last,' Bowers wrote. His most 'disconcerting recollection' was of the killer whales. 'They had a habit of bobbing up and down perpendicularly, so as to see over the edge of a floe. The huge black and yellow heads with sickening pig eyes were only a few yards from us at times.' He and Cherry-Garrard could have reached safe ice on the Barrier by using a sledge as a ladder, 'but there was the consideration of the ponies, so we waited'.

Wilson, who was making first for Safety Camp, near the Barrier edge, with Meares and the dogs, saw Crean through his glasses leaping from floe to floe towards the Barrier. At the camp, Wilson found Scott 'in a dreadful state of anxiety'. Later in the day, having surmounted the Barrier by using a ski stick for digging footholds, Crean reported to Scott, who at once returned with Oates and Crean to give what help he could to Bowers and Cherry-Garrard. 'My dear chaps, you can't think how glad I am to see you safe!' he called down to them from the top of the ice cliffs. Cherry-Garrard said that he well understood Scott's feelings. 'He had been blaming himself for our deaths.'

How to get the ponies up the Barrier face was the problem. Oates and Bowers began digging a ramp up which they might be hauled to safety. 'It would have taken hours. We dug like fury,' until Scott peremptorily ordered the two men to be pulled to the top by Alpine rope, he having seen that the water

233

lane between the Barrier and the floe was widening. It meant leaving the ponies on the ice until some other means of salvation was found for them. Meanwhile, the whales were 'chasing up and down like racehorses' (Bowers).

They watched the ponies slowly drifting away again on their floe. Scott and the others had 'a mournful meal', considering what to do. When the rest of the party settled down to snatch some sleep after their exertions, Bowers descended the Barrier again and managed to reach the ponies huddled on the ice.

'Poor trustful creatures! If I could have done it then, I would gladly have killed them rather than picture them starving on that floe out on the Ross Sea,' where eventually they might have drifted, 'or eaten by the exultant killers that cruised around.'

An attempt by him and Oates to get the animals away met with disaster. The first pony fell in the water as it was being jumped across a crack and had to be killed where it vainly struggled. 'It was awful,' Scott wrote. A second pony was jumping, 'when suddenly a school of over a dozen of the terrible whales arose'. Frightened, the pony became unmanageable.

Scott was for abandoning it: 'he was afraid of something happening to us with those devilish whales so close.' Bowers had no thought 'for anything but the horse', which suddenly collapsed and could not rise again. Oates said: 'I shall be sick if I have to kill another.' It was Bowers who carried the blood-stained ice-axe up the Barrier. 'These incidents are too terrible,' Scott wrote in his journal at the end of the day. The third pony was brought back safely.

For Scott it was a time of deep dejection. 'This is the end of the Pole,' was his disconsolate remark to Cherry-Garrard as they prepared to leave the Barrier edge. He had lost confidence in the motors; the dogs had failed him; and he now felt that he had little to hope for from what he had regarded as his 'most solid asset', the ponies. He wrote in the journal on 2 March: 'The events of the past 48 hours bid fair to wreck the Expedition.' Considering them retrospectively, he made the rare and revealing admission: 'I could not rid myself of the fear that misfortune was in the air.'

*

The split-up Depot-Laying Party began converging on Hut

Point on 5 March. The Eastern Party, under Lieutenant Victor Campbell, had become the Northern Party in consequence of the frustration of his hope of getting ashore on King Edward VII Land, and of his finding Amundsen in the Bay of Whales. Describing Campbell as 'a very queer bird and awfully full of his own importance', Kathleen Scott's brother Wilfrid told her in his letter of 27 February 1911 that Campbell's disappointment at not being put ashore 'was almost pitiful and when we eventually landed him at Cape Adare he was in the depths of misery'. Cape Adare was on the far side of the Ross Sea, north of McMurdo Sound. 'He was quite sure that his King Edward VII Land show was going to be *the* thing of the whole Expedition.'

Instead, Campbell and his companions disappeared into the unknown for many months, with the result that they were deprived of conspicuous mention in Scott's journals. The consolation awaited Campbell of being the leader of a party that made valuable additions to scientific knowledge, especially in geology and glaciology.

Having reassembled at Hut Point, fifteen miles from the main base at Cape Evans, the Depot-Laying Party faced the prospect of being cut off there indefinitely until the sea ice formed again, when they could make the crossing. They had no boat; and the route over the ice-falls at the foot of Mount Erebus, towering above them, was too heavily crevassed, even up to 3,000 feet, to be safe for a procession of men, ponies, and dogs. Again and again, the sea froze to a depth that looked as if a crossing would soon be feasible; equally often, the ice broke up as the party was preparing to set out. There was nothing to be done but to ensure that life would be tolerable for several weeks in a space thirty-six feet square.

The situation was complicated by the return on 14 March of the geological reconnaissance party of 4 headed by Griffith Taylor, bringing the number in the hut up to 16. The field work of Taylor and his companions was a further enhancement of the Expedition's scientific reputation. They had even washed hopefully for gold. Recording their return, Scott wrote that 'the main part of their work seems to be the rediscovery of many facts which were noted but perhaps passed over too lightly in the *Discovery*' (13 March 1911). Their exploration of the strange, impenetrable ice formation known as the Koettlitz

Glacier entitled them to claim to have done more original research than Scott then seemed willing to concede.

The day after Griffith Taylor's return, Scott was remarking in the journal: 'He is full of good spirits and anecdote, an addition to the party but not very practically useful' (15 March). Wilfrid Bruce had already written of Taylor as 'a wild sort of person, very keen on geology, and a bit grumpy'.

What appears to have been Scott's exasperation 'with Norwegian matters', as Griffith Taylor put it, recurred in the journal at that time. In a reference to his having given Tryggve Gran a task, he wrote: 'I felt there was nothing for it but to tell the young man exactly what I thought of him, and I did so.' Citing the occasion of his grievance, he added: 'A terrible mistake to bring him' (17 March). Sir Charles Wright, the physicist of the party, remembers 'thinking that Scott's public castigation of Gran was unfortunate'. Evans had found Gran 'a most entertaining assistant in the survey work'.

The young Norwegian became for Scott at that time a subject of troubled preoccupation, as the journal pages show. 'He worries me, since he is only really a boy, and a very nice boy under ordinary conditions, good-natured, good-tempered, helpful. I am inclined to think that the cold and the exceptionally hard conditions of this season's work have affected him mentally as well as physically ... I feel angry, but extremely glad it is not one of our own people who thus behaves.'

Life in the hut was not congenial to Scott. He resented having 'to sit still and contemplate the ruin which has assailed our transport. The Pole is a very long way off, alas!' After sixteen days, they were living as comfortably as possible in quarters that inhibited privacy and had no ventilation. An open blubber fire in the middle of the floor made it 'impossible to see your neighbour, to speak without coughing, or to open your eyes long before they began to smart. We were as smutty as sweeps', wrote Cherry-Garrard, while in Scott's view: 'We look a fearful gang of ruffians.' The wind howled unceasingly, 'and to say that the hut was cold is a very mild expression of the reality' (Cherry-Garrard). Wilson, rising early one morning, 'shivered for seven hours' (Diary).

'Phenomenally terrible weather' caused suffering and deterioration in the dog teams. 'Well, well,' Scott was ruminating again, 'fortune is not being very kind to us,' while granting that 'things might be worse'. The outlook on 24 March was grey enough to set him 'counting our resources and arranging for another twenty days' stay'.

Evans, stepping out to gaze on the twilight scene, thought it 'beautiful in a sad sort of way,' but was convinced that without companionship 'one could very soon go mad down here. The stillness is awful.' On 30 March, Scott wrote: 'It is trying—trying—but we can live, which is something.' Cherry-Garrard was more explicitly philosophic. 'Just enough to eat and keep us warm, no more—no frills or trimmings: there is many a worse and more elaborate life. The luxuries of civilization satisfy only those wants which they themselves create.'

They sat on packing cases. Their chief meal was fried seal liver, eaten with 'hunks of bread and butter', washed down with cocoa made in a bucket. Their talk was of many lands, there being hardened travellers among them. Sleeping, seven of them lay on the main floor; the others disposed themselves in the store room and the ponies' annexe. The dreams their diaries recorded were of tempting dishes. Some snored loudly, 'but none so loud as Bowers'. Some, haunted by the anguish of recent peril, cried out in their sleep.

By the second week of April 1911, the sea had frozen again, and Scott, impatient to be away, set off in overcast weather and a razor-edged wind for Cape Evans and winter quarters. He had with him Bowers, Griffith Taylor and Petty Officer Evans. Lieutenant Evans was ordered to follow with Wright, Deben-ham, Gran, and Crean. Seven men, with the dogs and the rem-nant of the Depot-Laying Party's pony team, were left at the Hut until it was safe for the animals to cross.

It was a hazardous proceeding. Men and sledges had to be lowered by Alpine rope over a cornice on an ice-cliff on the lower slopes of Erebus. 'I admired Scott's decision to go over; a more nervous man would have fought shy because, once down on the sea ice, there was little chance of our getting back.'*

Down on the ice, Scott halted his two parties to discuss the advisability of continuing through the night. There was no dissent, but Bowers wrote later that to him 'it seemed folly to venture upon a piece of untried, newly frozen sea-ice in inky darkness'. When, at 10 p.m., they were compelled to halt by a snowy mist 'in which we could literally see nothing', Bowers

* Evans: *South With Scott.*

decided that he, 'for one, would lie awake. You knew that there was only about six or ten inches of precarious ice between you and the black waters underneath.'

The next forty-eight hours were spent on a ledge just wide enough to accommodate two tents, on the steep lava slopes of Inaccessible Island, four miles off Cape Evans. They were held there by a blizzard, which 'yelled all round,' Evans wrote. Their situation was doubly precarious, for there was a chance that the sea ice would break up and drift away before the force of the wind. In that event, 'we should have been left to starve'.

They reached the winter station on 13 April. At first, they were not recognized. They had not washed or shaved for eighty days. Ponting mistook them for 'some of the Norwegians'.

*

At home in London, Kathleen Scott had begun keeping a diary in which the entries took the form of letters to her huband. Apparently it gave her a sense of more intimate communication. On 28 March 1911 she received a cable from New Zealand giving the news of Amundsen's arrival in the Antarctic. 'In a state of frenzy all day. I was of course bombarded with reporters but I wouldn't see them. One or two, however, caught me. I told them we still needed money! ! !' On 30 March she put off another dinner engagement to dine with Reginald Smith, the publisher (Smith, Elder & Co.), thinking that 'there might be Expeditionary useful people there but there weren't.' On 3 April 'do you remember the rival baby who was 4 days older than Peter? Well, she is rival no more. She is the poorest, puniest, spottiest little creature. Peter looks quite coarse beside her.'

Mawson, the young Australian explorer, lunched with her on 8 April. 'He was in a rather bad frame of mind, having finally persuaded himself that you had "done him in the eye," and had always intended to land a party at Cape Adare, and hadn't made a fair try for King E. Land, and so on galore. I explained a little to him of his absurdity and when he went he said he was very much happier. It prevented him from saying anything foolish at his lecture. He begged me not to associate him in my mind with Shackleton. I told him that I wanted to champion him, but he must play the game better. We parted excellently good friends.'

At Mawson's lecture on 10 April, 'he enunciated the work of previous explorers and showed all their photos, including my Con, a very nice one in uniform. His only references to you were right and nice. Shackleton was there and inoffensive when he spoke, saying he was sorry you hadn't been able to land on King E's Land in the same way as he had been unable, as there is valuable work to be done. I shook hands with him but didn't speak.' Shackleton, she noted in a wry aside, was 'without exaggerated discretion'.

She noted on 13 April that Sir Henry Lucy, *Toby M.P.* of *Punch*, had appealed in that paper for subscriptions to the Expedition fund. 'It only brought one guinea!'

CHAPTER SEVENTEEN

MAN OF UNCONQUERABLE SPIRIT

SUNRISE on 23 April was the last that the men at Cape Evans would see for four months. During that period their daylight would be a kind of bilious after-glow. Scott saw it more poetically: 'the long mild twilight which like a silver clasp unites today with yesterday.'

Evans observed that 'different people took the winter in different fashion,' and mentioned that 'there were some who never could have faced a second winter'. One of the two Russian grooms was unnerved by the absence of the sun and had to be sent home the following year.

At the winter station it was a time of vigorous specialized activities. 'Uncle Bill' Wilson, the leader of the scientific staff, was amplifying his numerous notebooks of zoological observations, diagrams, and sketches, for later publication, and adding to his already extensive collection of Antarctic watercolours, in which he combined beauty with accuracy. 'Sunny Jim' Simpson was assembling a complex network of meteorological equipment, including instrument bearing hydrogen balloons, that would have long-distance effects on his branch of science. 'Atch' Atkinson, the surgeon parasitologist, was busy with sterilizers, test tubes, and microscope slides. Wright was studying ice physics, 'a somewhat new line of research'. Nelson, nicknamed Marie, was surrounded by the enamel trays and dishes of his marine biology studies. 'Griff' Taylor, Debenham ('Deb'), and Priestley stooped over their specimens of hornblende, felspar, and kenyte, while in his 8 ft. by 6 ft. darkroom, Ponting experimented with Autochrome plates 'for photographing in natural colour'.

Scott worked all day at the linoleum-covered collapsible table in his six feet square bunk, to an accompaniment of ticking chronometers and sledge watches. Fur mittens, fur boots, woollen undergarments, draped the walls. His old navy greatcoat was his bedspread. 'It is twenty-three years old and I confess an affection for it.' Under the bed, as if he were a transient visitor to the region, was a brown leather suitcase, labelled. Around him at eye level were photographs of his wife and son, his mother, his sisters, and nieces. His books were by Hardy and Galsworthy, and the little Browning volume.

Cherry-Garrard left an impression of Scott in the bunk, 'quietly organizing, working out masses of figures, taking the greatest interest in the scientific work of the station, and perhaps turning out, quite by the way, an elaborate paper on an abstruse problem.' * At the top of one of his pages of notes he wrote: 'Think—think—think!' Sincerely dedicated to the cause of science, lamenting that he had not had a scientific training, he liked no intellectual exercise better than discussions with the scientific staff.

A cryptic entry appears in his journal for that time, unrelated to adjacent topics. 'Science cannot be served by "dilettante" methods, but demands a mind spurred by ambition or the satisfaction of ideals' (13 July 1911). He was prompted to that reflection by 'one young man who is idle', namely, Nelson, the biologist. 'I scarcely know how to deal with the case.' He considered whether the lack of outside work, 'and no adequate technical library,' could be held to justify Nelson's laziness. Scott did not think so. 'The practical point to me is that here are a fine opportunity and a not inconsiderable outlay wasted on a young man whose habit of life is that of a pot-house politician.' It was later remarked that Nelson was 'a good talker who liked to air his Conservative politics even in those outlandish parts'.†

* *The Worst Journey in the World.*
† *Evans of the Broke* (Oxford University Press, 1963).

Sir Charles Wright, looking back to his time as physicist of the Expedition, thinks that 'despite his very considerable interest in our scientific activities, Scott had a difficulty in understanding the mental make-up of the scientists.' * It was they who sustained the course of three lectures a week that he instituted during the long darkness: Wilson on aspects of zoology, including taxidermy; Atkinson on scurvy; Evans on polar surveying; Wright on glaciology; Bowers on polar clothing; Nelson on biology; Debenham on volcanoes; Oates on horse *mis*management. . . .

As in the *Discovery* days, 'he could analyse statements and theories in a very embarrassing manner'.† It was invariably Scott who asked the most perceptive questions. His mind was a keen-bladed instrument that could dissect a proposition or lay bare an argument with intimidating precision. Afterwards, he would return to his bunk to make notes of what he had heard: '*Corona*, caused by diffraction of light round drops of water or ice crystals; *Halos*, caused by refraction and reflection through and from ice crystals; *Rainbows*, caused by reflections and refraction from and through *drops of water*—colours vary with size of drops; *Auroras*, most frequent and intense in years of maximum sunspots; this argues connection with the sun' (3 May 1911).

He still often seemed coldly unapproachable, when the mood of self-withdrawal was on him. Evans said that, *vis-à-vis* Scott, he never knew when he was going to be called 'Teddy' or Evans. Scott never encouraged easy familiarity. There was no one in the Expedition to call him 'Scottie', a liberty permitted only to a few old friends in the Navy.

What none in the Expedition knew (and few thereafter) was how closely he was observing their individual performances, and assessing them as likely supporters of his final effort to reach the Pole. Sparing the feelings of his surviving colleagues, the editor of his published journals omitted his more critical comments, though they may have been equally revealing of Scott himself.

He wrote about Simpson, the meteorologist: 'Admirable as a worker, admirable as a scientist, admirable as a lecturer, but irritating as a companion. Irritation caused by want of worldly

---

* Letter to the biographer, 26 September 1965.
† L. C. Bernacchi: *Saga of the 'Discovery'*.

241

wisdom and not at all through lack of good nature, its manifestation occasioned by the display of cocksureness and by unconscious facial expression, such as a contemptuous pursing of
the lips, suggesting derision of argument even before the
argument has begun. His is an example of a manner to be
avoided, but he wouldn't be grateful to be told so. Yet I begin
to think it would be a kindly office.'

He set the qualities of Griffith Taylor against those of his
fellow geologist, Debenham. 'Taylor's intellect is omnivorous
and versatile, his mind unceasingly active, his grasp wide. Yet
on a different plane he strikes doubt. Will he just fail to stamp
his work with originality? I confess a difficulty to grasp his full
meaning to the Expedition. Debenham is clearer. Here we
have a well-trained, sturdy worker who realizes the conception of thoroughness, conscientiousness but not brilliancy.'

Wright, 'his mind saturated with the ice problems of this
wonderful region', was good-hearted, strong and keen, 'a hard
and conscientious worker who has an excellent knowledge of
physics, but not a great aptitude for applying that knowledge'. Ponting, the cameraman, impressed him as charming,
generous, highly strung, artistic. 'But his wrestling for existence with the very materialistic conditions in California and
elsewhere has had its effect.'

He thought his second-in-command, 'Teddy' Evans, 'a queer
study', and compared him unfavourably with Bowers. 'His
boyish enthusiasm carries all along till one sees clearly the
childish limitations of its foundation and appreciates that it is
not a rock to be built upon.' Gran, the young Norwegian, he
could admit had 'a certain amount of intelligence and a great
fund of good nature under his thick crust of vanity'. Day, the
motor engineer, was 'more sanguine in temperament than his
sledge is reliable in action'.

*

Scott's journal repeatedly records his satisfaction with the
goodwill prevailing among the members of the Expedition.
He thought it a fine inspiriting thing. Cherry-Garrard has
some comments on the same theme on page 226 of his book,
The Worst Journey in the World. 'Before we went South
people were always saying, "You will get fed up with one
another." If I say that we lived this life for nearly three years

without any friction of any kind, I shall be supposed to be making a formal statement of a somewhat limited truth. To be absolutely accurate, I must admit to having seen a man in a very "prickly" state on one occasion. That was all.' On page 227 he recalls 'how the greatest friends were so much on one another's nerves that they did not speak for days for fear of quarrelling'.

Up to the time of the departure of the *Terra Nova*, for example, Meares and Bruce, Scott's brother-in-law, were not on speaking terms. 'We got sick of each other,' Bruce wrote to his sister. 'He wasn't a bit my style. We just avoided each other and there was no rupture.' Bruce was also at odds for a time with Wilson. It was held against Ponting that whereas he constantly solicited help with his photographic work, he seldom showed a wish to reciprocate, except to Scott and Wilson. Another private criticism of him was that he had no general conversation. Wilson wrote to his wife: 'Grievances there are bound to be and disagreements; but as long as everyone can keep them from boiling over I think we can rightly say that we have been extraordinarily free from any want of unity.'

The persisting general harmony, if it owed most to the good sense of those who sustained it, was continually inspired by the presence of two men, Scott himself, 'certainly the most dominating character in our not uninteresting community' (Cherry-Garrard), and Edward Wilson, of whom Scott wrote: 'There is no member of our party so universally esteemed. He stands very high in the scale of human beings.' In some of the Expedition's emergencies, Wilson's judgement was pre-eminent, deferred to by Scott as by the others. Wilson could change Scott's mind, as no one else could. Each was a tower of strength to the other, the two buttressing the Expedition with a weight of experience and a force of character that accounted for a large part of its dynamic impulse and unity.

By then Scott's personal ascendancy was complete. His petulant impatience, his moods of isolating aloofness, his constrained sense of humour, were discounted by his power of self-command, his deep abiding regard for justice and truth, and his wholly unaffected charm, as to which there is the ardent testimony of Cherry-Garrard: 'I have never known anybody, man or woman, who could be so attractive when he chose.'

With doubtful validity, Scott maintained that there was no way of life 'quite so demonstrative of character as an Antarctic expedition. One sees a remarkable reassessment of values. Here the outward show is nothing, it is the inward purpose that counts. So the "gods" dwindle and the humble supplant them. Pretence is useless.'

One of the secrets of his successful leadership was his ability 'to keep going', though he was senior in years. Cherry-Garrard said that men did not know Scott until they had been sledging with him. 'He went harder than any of us,' a supremacy that he was to show many times in the months to come. His early physical discouragements, the languor that he assumed to be inherited, the untoward depressions, even the indigestion that at a later stage he thought as ominous for his plans as Amundsen—he mastered them all. Scott's conquest of the South Pole was also a triumph of self-conquest.

On 8 May 1911 he lectured to the full company on his plans for the coming polar journey. 'Everyone was interested, naturally.' He tentatively affirmed his opinion that 'the problem of reaching the Pole' would be solved by reliance on ponies and man-haulage. There was general concurrence in his mistrust of dogs. 'It's going to be a tough job; that is better realized the more one dives into it.'

*

That day, Kathleen Scott wrote in one of her unposted letters that 'there is a long appeal in the papers from Shackleton for Mawson's expedition. Sir Clements Markham was furious.' The following day, she wrote: 'The *Daily Mail* printed Sir Clement's letter and a letter from Shackleton. Sir Clements wrote another and sent it round to me before sending it to the *Daily Mail*. Such a letter! With all the tact I could muster I wrote back and prevented him publishing it. It was an attack on Shackleton and a eulogy of you which, though I could gloat over it in private, would not have helped us, I fear. I followed up my note by a trembling visit, to find the dear old man not the least offended. He said, talking of Amundsen, "I suppose if Con meets him he will give him a motor-sledge." He knows your precious nature very well, does that old man; he is a dear.'

One of the first women air passengers, she was at a flying

display at Hendon on 12 May. 'Whole Cabinet seemed to be there. Mawson was talking to me and suddenly said: "I must go. I see Shackleton!" I took a lot of trouble to get Mawson a good aeroplane and a good pilot and now he tries to make out that he could have done better, not a fact in the first place, and bad manners in the second. I'm afraid he's an ass. I'm sorry, as I've championed him throughout. Grahame White threw bombs with great accuracy, but only from 1000 ft.'

Meeting Admiral Sir Lewis Beaumont, principal naval aide-de-camp to the King, she noted on 24 May: 'He seems rather against Mawson, but, curiously enough, doesn't seem much against Shackleton and *doesn't know* Shackleton dislikes you.' Dining with the Darwins, she met Jean Charcot, the French explorer of the Antarctic, who remarked: 'You know, I *love* your husband.' She told him: 'He loves you.' She also recorded 'a curious dream about Seaman [meaning Petty Officer] Evans. How silly.'

Noting the growing number of 'ill-assorted couples' in their social circle, she was moved to reflect: 'It makes one feel very lucky some days and apprehensive other days.' She wrote down the question: 'Do you remember how Peter used to climb up your legs in spite of all opposition: He is developing that instinct and I like to see your disposition coming out in him. Schopenhauer says somewhere: "In the overcoming of obstacles one feels the full delight of existence." Do you like him for knowing that, and what lots you will have overcome before you read this, if you ever do?' (25 May 1911)

At the President's reception at the Royal Geographical Society, she learnt that the Society was making a grant of £1,000–£1,500 in the autumn. 'I followed up with a letter saying that £1,500 was a magnificent sum, and other nice things. Shackleton came in alone, took a furtive look at me and shook hands. I said I hadn't seen him since he sent us off. He reminded me that I had (at the Mawson lecture), where I couldn't make myself speak to him.' When she inquired about his son, 'he sat down and talked and talked without a pause for 20 minutes. He began to abuse Wilson. I said: "Don't let's talk about Dr Wilson. You know we all love him." He said: "So used I, but he has behaved——" I said: "We won't talk about Dr Wilson," and he, "I must defer to your demand." '

Shackleton told her, she wrote, that he knew her husband

very well, '"perhaps better than any man. I have never seen him hesitate. He is the most daring man I ever met—extraordinarily brave." I said: "Yes, he's brave morally as well as physically," and he said, "Yes, indeed, I agree" (quite decently). I couldn't stop the stream of his talk. I scarcely had to reply at all, he streamed on. He said: "Of course Scott had £60,000 before he left." I said you had not. "Oh, yes, £60,000." "No," I said, "barely £40,000." "Oh, then he can't have got the response he expected." (I think I will ask Sir Edgar Speyer if it might not be well to publish a balance sheet.) Then he proceeded: "If Scott had £60,000,000 it would not make his achievement of the Pole any more possible. His equipment lacked nothing for money." Of course there is much truth in that. Throughout this tirade (all at a terrific pace) I said practically no word, but was quite polite and attentive. My goodness, what an Irishman!' (14 June)

She went to see Sir Clements Markham. 'He had sent another long letter of eulogy of you and covert abuse of everyone else to the *Geographical Journal*.' The new President of the Royal Geographical Society, Lord Curzon, 'begged him to withdraw it, which he did. Dear old fellow, I suppose his friendship for you leads him astray; but I must say he is a relief after these phlegmatic and debonair people who are afraid to say or even think a word lest it should be tactless' (15 June).

Calling at Mawson's expedition office, she found Shackleton there, 'as bad luck would have it. He was egregiously pleasant to me.' She thought it 'positively shocking' that Mawson 'expects in 15 days to have an aeroplane transposed into a reliable motor sledge,' finding it amusing to see 'Mawson at work after having been used to your thoroughness' (17 June).

She watched the coronation procession of King George V and Queen Mary from Admiralty House. 'Sat next to the Egertons on one side and Mrs Algood on the other, who abused Teddy Evans. I told her I loved him fondly.' As for the grand occasion, 'I don't really think pageants of this sort thrill me much and royalty doesn't affect me at all. I liked the horses rather. On the whole, I don't think it a very good show. We all drank your health at lunch and tried to imagine your midsummer [sic] festivities' (22 June).

*

At Cape Evans, storms were frequent as Midwinter Day.

22 June, drew near. High velocity winds came roaring up from the south without warning, shaking the fabric of the hut with what seemed like sentient fury. The day was observed with the 'festivity customary at Christmas at home'. Champagne was served instead of cocoa. At 7 p.m. they sat down to 'an extravagant bill of fare', starting with seal soup and ending with liqueurs. Scott was presented with the third edition of the *South Polar Times*, edited by Cherry-Garrard, 'a very good little volume', Scott thought. Its fifty pages (typewritten) of anonymous contributions in prose and verse were bound in venesta boards covered with sealskin. The first two copies had been produced by Shackleton during the *Discovery* expedition ten years before.

Scott had felt 'obliged to request the omission of compliments' from the evening's speeches. What he appreciated, none the less, was the 'really genuine recognition' of his attitude to the scientific work of the Expedition. A day of goodwill and happy fellowship was brought to a close on a note of awe. The eastern sky was 'massed with swaying auroral light', the most vividly beautiful display in Scott's experience. 'There is infinite suggestion in this phenomenon, and in that lies its charm; the suggestion of life, form, colour, and movement never less than evanescent, mysterious—no reality. It is the language of mystic signs and portents—the inspiration of the gods—wholly spiritual—divine signalling. Might not the inhabitants of some other world (Mars) controlling mighty forces thus surround our globe with fiery symbols, a golden writing which we have not the key to decipher?'

Aurora Australis did not always stir his imagination to lyrical flight. It is easier to picture him watching the stupendous show and brooding on the dilemma of man's free will trapped in the seemingly mindless machinery of the universe. The mysterious light incessantly rolled and rippled, as if proclaiming the doctrine of eternal recurrence, interrupted by sudden agitations suggesting encephalic recordings on the cosmic scale. We leave him standing there solitary in the polar night, a man of unconquerable spirit asking himself his perennial conundrum: What is it all about?

> *Who is man and what his place,*
> *Anxious asks the heart perplext,*
> *In the recklessness of space,*

Worlds with worlds thus intermixt,
What is he, this atom creature,
In the infinitude of nature?

—F. T. Palgrave *

CHAPTER EIGHTEEN

END OF THE MOTOR DREAM

THE new season's work was inaugurated in midwinter darkness, when on 27 June Wilson, Bowers, and Cherry-Garrard started for Cape Crozier,† at the eastern extremity of Ross Island, sixty-seven miles from Cape Evans. Their mission was a strange one. They were to collect eggs of the Emperor penguin at a precise stage of incubation. By studying the embryos of what was thought to be the world's most primitive bird, it was hoped that more knowledge of the evolutionary links, particularly regarding the origin of feathers, would be forthcoming.

It was Wilson's project, and Scott, while being sensible of its implications, tried to dissuade him from it, no one ever having ventured on such a journey at that time of the year before. Cape Crozier had been visited only in daylight and then always in conditions of hazard. Scott could at least agree that' the right men have gone to attempt it'. Before their return, the Crozier Party, as they were called, were to endure the uttermost privations of the Antarctic.

Beginning a new manuscript volume of his journal the following day, Scott wrote out a quotation on the flyleaf: 'So far as I can venture to offer an opinion on such a matter, the purpose of our being in existence, the highest object that human beings can set before themselves, is not the pursuit of any such chimera as the annihilation of the unknown; but it is simply the unwearied endeavour to remove its boundaries a little further from our sphere of action.—Huxley.' He may have remembered that the Victorian scientist's grandson, Julian

* Lines copied out by Scott on the last page of his journal for that period.

† Named after the captain of Sir James Ross's expedition ship *Terror*.

Huxley, had applied for a post as biologist with the Expedition, unsuccessfully, as he was considered too young.

On 4 July, Scott was seen 'looking pale and dejected and in a great state of anxiety' (Ponting), because of the prolonged absence of Atkinson, the surgeon, who had gone out to inspect a thermometer on the floes. One of the unaccountable blizzards of the region blew up, confusing his sense of direction. Search parties had failed to find him. 'I grew more than ever alarmed,' Scott wrote. 'Atkinson had started for a point a little more than a mile away; he had been five hours away; what conclusion could be drawn?'

Atkinson reappeared with a frightfully frost-bitten hand, his fingers distended by enormous carapace-like blisters, and unable to give more than a rambling account of what had happened to him. 'There can be no doubt,' Scott wrote, 'that in a blizzard a man has not only to safeguard the circulation in his limbs, but must struggle with a sluggishness of brain and an absence of reasoning power which is far more likely to undo him. Everything goes to confirm the fact that Atkinson had a very close shave of being lost altogether.'

It was the worst blizzard Scott had known on the Antarctic mainland. Going outside to clear the anemometer vane, he was 'struck with the impossibility of enduring such conditions for any length of time. One seemed to be robbed of breath; ten paces against the wind were sufficient to reduce one's face to the very verge of frostbite. Twice I had literally to lean against the wind with head bent and face averted and so stagger crablike on my course' (10 July).

He recorded having been 'the victim of a very curious illusion', in which, touching cold metal, he withdrew his hand sharply, thinking that his fingers were burned. He repeated the action, with the same effect. When he warned the others, Meares pointed out: 'But it's cold, sir.' 'And so it was,' Scott noting that while there was 'nothing intrinsically new in the observation, it is none the less an interesting variant of the common fact.'

From 'curious illusion' he passes to 'horrible fright', when one of the best of the remaining ten ponies 'suddenly went off his feed'. There followed a page of description of the pathos of a suffering animal, 'his misery indicated by those distressing spasms and by dumb movements of the head turned with a patient expression always suggestive of appeal.... Towards midnight I felt very downcast.' Visiting the sick animal at 2.30 a.m., 'it suddenly raised its head and rose without effort to its legs'. Scott went to bed 'with much relief' (14 July).

Two days later, another pony showed similar symptoms. Scott was mystified by 'what it is that is disturbing these poor beasts'. Not all was well, either, on the human plane. Ponting's temperament was 'of the quality to take this wintering experience badly'. Scott concluded that neglect of exercise was partly at fault. 'Taylor is another backslider, and is not looking well. Anyway, the return of the light should cure all ailments, physical and mental.' Still the great blizzard went on raging. On 24 July the wind reached 'a record force' of 82 m.p.h.

The Crozier Party staggered back on 2 August, 'after enduring for five weeks the hardest conditions on record. They look more weather-worn than anyone I have yet seen. Their faces are scarred and wrinkled, their eyes dull,' Scott observed. There was a general rush from the hut to welcome them; still more to give them the first-aid they obviously needed, for their clothes were frozen on them. 'Their looks haunted me for days' (Ponting).

On 6 July they had experienced 108 degrees of frost; for ten days running the temperature was not above minus 56 degrees; on seven of those days it was minus 65 degrees. When the canvas roof of their storm shelter was blown away in a hurricane, they lay in their sleeping-bags under snow for forty-eight hours. And there was Cherry-Garrard's hint of other perils: 'Crevasses in the dark *do* put your nerves on edge.' There were days when they travelled no more than two miles, so chaotic were the conditions.

For Cherry-Garrard it was 'the weirdest birds'-nesting expedition that ever was or ever will be; no words can express its horror.' It yielded three Emperor penguin eggs in an advanced stage of incubation, at which 'Wilson's joy was great' (Ponting). The scientists of the Natural History Museum, South Kensington, agreed that while the eggs did not yield the new information hoped for, 'the worst journey in the world in the interest of science was not made in vain'.* Scott wrote his appreciation in the journal:

'To me and to everyone who has remained here the result of this effort is the appeal it makes to our imagination as one of

* Professor J. Cossar Ewart, M.D., F.R.S. (1851–1933), Regius Professor of Natural History, Edinburgh University.

the most gallant stories in Polar history. That men should wander forth in the depth of a Polar night to face the most dismal cold and the fiercest gales in darkness is something new; that they should have persisted in this effort in spite of every adversity for five full weeks is heroic. It makes a tale for our generation which I hope may not be lost in the telling.'

He put it on record that Wilson (39) returned 'very thin', that Cherry-Garrard, the youngest of the three (26), 'has suffered most severely, but his spirit never wavered for a moment,' and that Bowers (29) had come through best—'a sturdy, active, undefeatable little man', whose astonishing energy and physique 'enables him to continue to work under conditions which are absolutely paralysing to others' (2 August). All three hobbled about on crippled feet. Impenetrated by ice, their clothing weighed 66 lb. more than when they started out. Their tent had acquired an extra weight of 25 lb. They learnt things about sledging rations that were basically useful for the polar march to come.

*

Kathleen Scott was telling her husband *via* her diary: 'It's going to be an immense thing, this cinematography.... For the first time in my life, I have an overdraft on my banking account. It gives me sensations as tho' I were going down in a lift every time I think of it' (26 June 1911). She had called on his mother, as he wished. 'She looks so young, and is very full of life. Really, she is wonderful' (16 July). Visiting the Garvins [J. L. Garvin was editor of The *Observer*], 'she told me you had told her of all your hopes and ideas for your son and then confessed he wasn't born yet!!' (17 July).

She was at the cottage on the Kent coast in August, happy with her boy. 'It is all very delicious in its simplicity.' She felt 'the need of a man' down there in that lonely place, 'but hesitate to ask one, because I am afraid I should make love to him if I had one. One has so much time here and one is so idle. So, though it seems rather a waste, perhaps I'd better not,' concluding that, after all, she was 'very happy alone' (31 August).

On 1 September she reminded herself: 'Tomorrow will be our wedding day. We shall have been married 3 years. I bet anything you won't remember it. What fun we've had one way and another since, haven't we? I used to say I would like a baby but not a husband and I've got it, but with a difference. One hasn't got one's husband in the body but one has him so firm in the spirit that it spoils everything!' Her whole being was crying out, she wrote: 'You are young, you are healthy, go out and love.' She counselled herself: 'I think decidedly I had better get back to work.'

One night she walked out along the beach, 'along to where you and I once went. You won't remember, right along to where the river flows into the sea. I saw the very tuft of grass on the sand that we sat upon. That was a long time ago. It was more beautiful today than then, for there was an exquisite sunset over the marshes, the moon was rising, and not a sound but only my bare toes on the ground. I wonder if you will be here with me next year' (3 September).

Ponting's films of the first stage of the Expedition had reached London. 'The Gaumont people say they have never seen anything so good. They very much want to delay showing them till the news of the arrival at the Pole comes through' (12 September). Expedition money problems rose up to haunt her again. She had received 'a most distressing letter' from Admiral Sir Lewis Beaumont, Vice-President of the Royal Geographical Society.

'He says he's heard from Sir Edgar Speyer that the money is getting very short and only enough to meet outgoing expenses at the end of October, that Kinsey writes for £1,000, and the London agent £500. Sir Lewis wanted to know what's to be done. I wrote him a long letter saying he had better make the Geographical [Royal Geographical Society] give £1,500 and I would try Mortimer Singer and Lord Howard de Walden, and then they'd better publish the accounts and say how urgent the need is, etc. Sir Edgar said we were to ask for £15,000. I told Sir Lewis you said £8,000, but that was before there was much talk of a third year' (13 September).

*

'We felt very young, sang and cheered.' Scott was recording the return of the sun of 25 August 1911. 'We were reminded of a frosty morning in England—everything sparkled and the air had the same crisp feel.' Champagne was drunk in celebration. 'It is such a very real and important event that one cannot pass it in silence. It changes the outlook on life of every individual.' Evans wrote that 'the animals went half dotty over it', and mentioned, above all, the grins on the faces of the Russian grooms. 'Yes, we were all smiling when the sun came back.'

Scott basked as joyfully as the others in the boon of daylight renewed. Once again, his appreciative eye assured him that for all its forbidding remoteness, McMurdo Sound at certain times was a dramatically beautiful setting for a polar ship's anchorage. Winter's monochrome was succeeded by the magical palette of the sun spilling many shades of colour, soft violet to blood red, from the mountain tops down to the snow slopes and out to the floes far below. The effect, under a rose-pink sky, could be breath-taking.

His journal pages radiate his optimism. 'Of hopeful signs for the future none are more remarkable than the health and spirit of our people. It would be impossible to imagine a more vigorous community. The animals are in splendid form' (10 September). He could convince himself that 'nothing, not even priority at the Pole, can prevent the Expedition ranking as one of the most important that ever entered the polar regions.'

As the obverse of his rare euphoria, his wife wrote in her diary for 20 September 1911: 'Rather a horrid day today. I woke up having had a bad dream about you, and then Peter came very close to me and said emphatically: "Daddy won't come back," as tho' in answer to my silly thoughts. Happily I am not often silly.'

With 'Birdie' Bowers's help—and Scott noted yet again that Bowers was 'a treasure all round'—he completed down to the smallest particular his arrangements for the Expedition's climacteric phase. He then drafted, as part of that task of many days and nights, instructions for the maintenance of the winter station during his absence, the work of the Western Party under Griffith Taylor, and the disposition of Campbell's Northern Party when they returned. Included in the document was a long and detailed memorandum for the captain of the *Terra Nova*. Without yet naming them, he also made his choice of the 'good men and true' (his phrase) who were to accompany him on the great final journey.

He wrote supplementary orders for Simpson, Griffith Taylor, Meares, who had charge of the dog teams, and Campbell. Those strictly formulated instructions were variously addressed: e.g., 'My dear Simpson,' to the meteorologist, and 'My dear Campbell,' whereas Meares was 'Dear Meares', and Taylor and Lieutenant Evans were not saluted by name. The commanding officer of the *Terra Nova*, Lieutenant Pennell, was wished 'every sort of good fortune'. Griffith Taylor, leader of the Western Party, was also wished well, and Scott expressed similar sentiments in concluding his orders to Campbell of the Northern Party. He allowed himself no lapse from formality in issuing his instructions to others.

*

'If the motors are successful,' he considered in writing, 'we shall have no difficulty in getting to the Glacier,' the mighty polar highway discovered by Shackleton and named after his principal backer, William Beardmore, a Glasgow industrialist. 'If they fail, we shall still get there with any ordinary degree of good fortune.'

It seemed that he had only to use the phrase to call down the fickle goddess's displeasure. Three men were disabled, one after another: Petty Officer Forde with a badly frost-bitten hand that irritated Scott too: 'it argues want of care'; Clissold, the cook, seriously concussed by a fall; Debenham, a knee injury at football, 'wasting precious hours'.

There was a passing diversion from those minor worries when, for the first time in the Antarctic, the telephone bell rang and Scott heard speech from Hut Point. The aluminium-sheathed cable had been laid across the intervening fifteen miles of sea ice. 'I had quite a talk with Meares and afterwards with Oates. Not a very wonderful fact, perhaps, but it seems wonderful in this primitive land.'

When another pony appeared to be cracking up, and a dog died of 'a mysterious disease', Scott retired to his bunk to write: 'It is trying, but I am past despondency. Things must take their course.' He was 'secretly convinced', he wrote on 17 October, that the motors would not be of much help. Then, seeing them moving ponderously under loads on 24 October, he felt that 'it is impossible not to be convinced of their value'. He was 'immensely eager' that they should succeed. They represented 'a unique effort', one that could 'revolutionise Polar transport'. A major unresolved problem was how the engines would behave in the steeply falling temperatures of the Barrier. As always, he foresaw failure, a Sophoclean hero whose fate is decided not by the gods but by some powerful inimical force in his own nature.

*

Beyond the reach of the claims and exactions of the commercial world, he still could not dissociate himself from his liabilities. The money side of things continued to be a source of vexatious cares, a shadow following him into the solitudes. It was central to his character to comply with his bargains. No man was more firmly resolved to do so.

Towards the middle of October 1911 he called the men together in the Hut at Cape Evans and told them frankly of the financial situation, which required an overdraft at the bank. Having explained matters, he invited all who could to forego their Expedition pay for the next twelve months. There was a generally warm response; only a few refrained on the ground of imperative need.

He signed a formal note of indemnity relieving the Expedition fund of liability for a number of salaries, including his own. The document was to be sent to London, with other mail, when the *Terra Nova* returned from New Zealand. At the same time, he drew up a list of potential assets for the eye of the Expedition treasurer, Sir Edgar Speyer. It included contracts with the Central News Agency and the Gaumont Film Company, the value of the *Terra Nova,* and proceeds from literary work and lectures. He also proposed a special stamp issue that might attract the world's philatelists.

Scott to J. J. Kinsey:

Winter Quarters,
28th October, 1911.

My dear Kinsey,—I write on the eve of our departure for the South. We shall leave with high hopes of accomplishing our object in spite of the reverses of last season.

I am fully alive to the complication of the situation by Amundsen, but as any attempt at a race might have been fatal to our chance of getting to the Pole at all, I decided long ago to do exactly as I should have done had Amundsen not been down here. If he gets to the Pole, he is bound to do it rapidly with dogs, but one guesses that success will justify him, and that our venture will be 'out of it'. If he fails, he ought to hide! Anyway, he is taking a big risk, and perhaps deserves his luck if he gets through—but he is not

255

there yet! Meanwhile, you may be sure we shall be doing the best we can to carry out my plan.

The only worry I can foresee for you and others interested in the Expedition is the financial question. I think when you have read my letter to Speyer you will agree that I have done my best to put that right.

Of course I write in ignorance of everything outside our own little circle. I haven't a notion where Campbell is landed, or how he is getting on. I have little but the highest praise for everyone here. I am surrounded by men whom I can thoroughly trust. Wilson is positively splendid, Bowers a perfect treasure, Oates, Cherry-Garrard, Wright and the rest, are not very far behind.

Teddy Evans is a thoroughly well-meaning little man, but proves on close acquaintance to be rather a duffer in anything but his own particular work. All this is *entre nous*, but he is not at all fitted to be 'second-in-command', as I was foolish enough to name him. I am going to take some steps concerning this, as it would not do to leave him in charge here in case I am late returning.

Nelson is also a disappointment. A clever little fellow, but idle. I think the biologist honours will all be with Lillie.

On the whole, I am greatly pleased with the work done so far. If not journalistically exciting, it is far more scientifically interesting than that of our previous Expedition. We shall have an enormous mass of scientific data.

Taylor, a remarkable character, has done some remarkable work in his own line. So also has Simpson; and, in fact, so have the rest in their several departments.

It would be impossible to exaggerate the extraordinarily happy conditions under which we have lived here. There have been no quarrels or troubles of any sort. I sincerely hope I may have as good an account to render to you when I next communicate (I trust in person).

Please give my very kindest regards and remembrances to Mrs Kinsey.

Yours ever sincerely,
R. F. SCOTT

He wrote letters to his wife, his mother, his eldest sister, a schoolboy nephew and a schoolgirl niece, his publisher, Reginald Smith (of Smith, Elder & Co.), and the wife of Petty

Officer Edgar Evans. His letter to his wife filled seventeen pages. 'My own darling, I'm charged with love, news, and business, and scarce know which to let out first....' Having disposed of more prosaic matters, he returned to those nearest his heart.

I am quite on my feet now. I feel both mentally and physically fit for the work, and I realise that others know it and have full confidence in me. But it is a certain fact that it was not so in London or indeed until we reached this spot.

The root of the trouble was that I had lost confidence in myself. I don't know if it was noticed by others consciously, but it was acted on unconsciously, as a dozen incidents in my memory remind me. Had I been what I am now, many things would have been avoided. I can trace these things to myself very clearly and can only hope that others do not, but you see, with this knowledge I cannot but regard it as lucky that things have come as right as they have.

Of course all sorts of things may have gone wrong with matters which are not under my control, but which are within the limits of my responsibilities, such as Campbell's party, the ship, etc., but it is significant of my recovery that I do not allow anxieties to press on me where I deem my actions to have been justified.

Evans, he told his wife, had 'faithfully delivered' the anniversary letters which she had entrusted to him in New Zealand. He wanted her to know that he treasured the 'inspiriting thoughts' they contained.

At such a time as this it thrills me to think of your courage. It is the greatest comfort to know that you possess it, and therefore by nature can never sit down and bewail misfortune. I can imagine you nothing but sturdily independent and determined to make the most of the life you possess.

It seems a woeful long time since I saw your face and there is the likelihood of a woefuller time ahead, and then what? I want to come back having done something, but work here is horribly uncertain and now of course there is the chance of another man getting ahead.

I don't know what to think of Amundsen's chances. If he gets to the Pole it must be before we do, as he is bound to travel fast with dogs, and pretty certain to start early. On this account I decided at a very early date to act exactly as I should have done had he not existed. Any attempt to race must have wrecked my plan, beside which it doesn't appear the sort of thing one is out for. You can rely on my not doing or saying anything foolish, only I am afraid you must be prepared for the chance of finding our venture much belittled. After all, it is the work that counts, not the applause that follows.

Repeating that he had never felt 'better or fitter for hard work in all my life', he concluded: 'I am not going to desert you if I can help it. I can see you setting off on your various missions in a wholly practical manner. The antithesis of the pathetic grass widow. Bless you.'

Scott to his mother:

Winter Quarters,
Oct. 1911.

My own dear Mother,—...I hope, I do so very much hope, that you are well and happy and that I shall find you so when I return. In regard to that, you must remember that in any case it will be less by some months than the *Discovery* absence. As that came out all well you may be sure that this will also.

I could not possibly be in better health. I am a thousand times fitter than I was in London. You see, my dear, we know all about things down here now. Exactly how to feed and clothe ourselves and how to set to work. It is a simple life and therefore very healthy. I could not wish for better companions than I have got. Wilson, as you know, is a perfect treasure, and the rest are of much the same calibre. Oh, we are doing remarkably well, so that you need not have a moment's anxiety about me.

In a very few days now we start off on the long Southern journey, such a big party. Four are already on the road and there are twelve more to follow, besides motor sledges, ponies and dogs—such a cavalcade!

I can't say how it is all going to work out, but I have taken a lot of pains over the plans, so I hope for the best.

Now that we know what to do and how to do it, everyone is ridiculously happy on this sledging work, and you can imagine us having a regular picnic most of the way. Of course, there will be a tough bit at the end, but I have the right people with me to undertake it, and I believe we shall pull through.

I am afraid Kathleen will have robbed you of our Peter and that you will miss him. I hope she brings him to see you sometimes. I've got his photographs at one year, as you may suppose, and he really looks rather a jolly little chap, doesn't he? Dear me, how I wish I could see you all.

Well, my own dear, dear Mother, you must take care of yourself and remember there is no one to whom I shall be prouder to tell my successes or more willing to confess my failures. In any case, I want you to be looking well and happy when I come home again. It will not be very long now.

Meanwhile, with my very best love, my dear, dear Mother,
I remain,
Your loving son,
CON

He wrote to assure the wife of Petty Officer Evans, at Rhossily, Gower, Swansea, that her husband was 'in the best of health, very strong, and in very good condition'. He hoped that, on the completion of his present engagement, her husband would return to suitable employment at home, and that he would never again be parted from her or their children. 'He is such an old friend of mine, and has done so well on this Expedition, that he deserves all I can do for him. So I hope you won't be anxious or worried.'

Scott to Admiral Sir George Egerton: *

Winter Quarters,
October 31st, 1911.

My dear Admiral,—It seems a very long time since you wished me God-speed in Government House, Pretoria, but the memory of all your kindness and friendship is ever fresh.

This is our last night in our very comfortable Hut. We leave for the South tomorrow.

My motors left some days ago and we saw them disappear over the surface of the Barrier, one twenty miles away going strong. They may not get very far because the trials were

* Admiral Egerton was one of Scott's principal sponsors for the leadership of the Expedition.

quite inadequate, but they have already justified their exist-ence, shown the future possibilities of motor traction in these regions, and falsified the prophets who gloomily pre-dicted total failure.

We start with the ponies tomorrow. In spite of a bad blow which cost us some of the best last year, the others are in such good form that I think they will do what we require of them. The dogs, also in splendid form, will follow a few days later. I don't know if we shall get through. You know the chances of this sort of game. All I can say is that I have laid the plans with care and that I believe I have as fine a set of supporters as ever man had for such a venture.

Ever yours sincerely and gratefully,

R. SCOTT

Also writing on the eve of 'the great journey', Bowers told Scott's wife of the 'almost unparalleled succession of initial reverses', and said that 'Capt Scott had endured the trials of Job again', including the news of 'Amundsen's low down game to the Eastward'. Bowers was delighted, he wrote, by Scott's decision to rely on man-hauling for 'the final dash'. Though slow, it was sure and 'after all, it will be a fine thing to do that plateau with man haulage in these days of the supposed deca-dence of the British race'.

There was a discussion in Ponting's darkroom between Oates and Nelson, the biologist, on what should be done if a member of the final polar party suffered an injury, or col-lapsed from some other cause. 'Oates emphatically expressed the opinion that there was only one possible course—self-sacrifice.' He thought that a revolver should be available, 'so that if anyone broke down, he should have the privilege of using it'.*

Tuesday, October 31. Under that date in the journal, Scott wrote that 'if the weather holds, we shall all get off tomorrow'. The Motor Party, consisting of Teddy Evans, Day, the en-gineer, Chief Stoker Lashly, and Hooper, the steward, had already been away six days with the two mechanical sledges drawing fuel and forage.

The Main Party, consisting of Scott, Wilson, Oates, Bowers, Cherry-Garrard, Atkinson, Wright, Petty Officers Evans, Crean and Keohane, set out at 11 p.m. on 1 November 1911. With

---

* Herbert G. Ponting: *The Great White South* (1923).

them went ten ponies and twenty-three dogs. Scott wrote that night: 'The future is in the lap of the gods; I can think of nothing left undone to deserve success.'

*

The two motors, each drawing three loaded sledges, had conked out in a week, and were abandoned on the Barrier. If their collapse was not unexpected, it must have been an uncomfortable reminder to Scott of the fallibility of his judgement, for it was by his long persistence that they appeared on that scene. 'So the dream of great help from the machines is at an end!' (4 November) The second motor had travelled nearly fifty miles under load; a possibly always forlorn pioneering effort vindicated in our later time by the Sno-cats used by Fuchs and Hillary as leaders of the Commonwealth Trans-Antarctic Expedition 1955–8.

Scott wrote to his friend Lord Howard de Walden: 'This is written on our way South to tell you that there is *nothing whatever* the matter with this principle of propulsion of which you hold the patents. Had you seen them sailing over the snow down here as we did you would understand what I mean. The breakdown was solely due to the overheating of those wretched air-cooled engines. I am quite sure that there is a big future for traction motors of this sort in Canada and other places. I therefore write most urgently to you to see that the patents are clear and safe in all countries. Hoping to tell you all about it some day....' What had been the Motor Party, under Lieutenant Evans, was reconstituted as a man-hauling team, pulling 740 lb. on a 10 ft. sledge.

By that time, Amundsen was beyond the 80th parallel, his food depots guaranteeing him support two hundred miles beyond One Ton Depot, on which Scott so greatly depended. Amundsen and his team of four were all expert skiers. His fifty-two dogs were to serve as food as well as transport. 'In my calculations,' he afterwards wrote, 'I figured out exactly the precise day on which I planned to kill each dog as its usefulness should end for drawing the diminishing supplies on the sleds and its usefulness should begin as food for the men.'* Those were the logistics of a raid rather than of a scientific exploration, to which Amundsen did not aspire. As for killing dogs, apart from his English prejudice, the fate of

*Roald Amundsen: *My Life as an Explorer.*

261

the dogs used on Scott's first Expedition was still painful in his memory.

*

Kathleen Scott met Nansen at lunch in London on 17 November. H. G. Wells also was present, 'a disgusting little bounder, yet certainly very clever and amusing today'. Nansen assured her that he knew nothing of Amundsen's intentions until he received a letter from Madeira in which Amundsen had said: 'I wish I had told Scott,' presumably meaning that he would have wished to be more frank about his polar plan. 'Nansen said that when he saw Amundsen off he asked him why he had so many dogs, and A. had been rather evasive.' Kathleen Scott went on to say that she was quite confident that Nansen 'was absolutely innocent about it all', and that he upheld Amundsen as an old friend. 'He told me that he himself had meant to go South in 1905, but Amundsen had wanted the *Fram*, so he relinquished her as a favour, 'and now he has gone South himself'.

The *Daily Mirror*, to support a new appeal for funds, wanted to print an explanatory letter from her and with it a photograph of her son. 'My dear, I humbly beg your pardon if I have done wrong, but I said "No!" Not only can I not bear my weeny being bandied about in the halfpenny press but also I doubt greatly whether any considerable sum would be got. I couldn't bear the thought. The young people don't care and the old people don't feel' (19 November).

Kathleen Scott thought the appeal 'a stuffy affair'. It bore a number of distinguished signatures, and was published on 20 November, after revision by Sir Arthur Conan Doyle, who subscribed another £10. It drew attention to the new factor of Amundsen's intervention, surmising that it would necessarily stimulate the effort of Scott and his men 'to secure for their country the prize on which their hearts have been set for so long'. They were attempting 'a great geographical feat', that had for its hazardous and difficult object 'the penetration of the vast ice-bound continent to its very heart. In scientific results, it should surpass all that have gone before it.'

If the £15,000 asked for was not subscribed, the Expedition's scientific work would be halted, and there would be other doleful consequences, including hardship for wives and families. The appeal committee earnestly desired to be able to send a heartening message to Scott by the *Terra Nova* on her return to McMurdo Sound.

Nansen lunched alone with Kathleen Scott at 174 Buckingham Palace Road on 28 November. 'He came at 1.30 and stayed till 5.30! He is the most charming individual imaginable. We talked about the most unexpected things,' including obstetrics. 'He told me so much about his own self. How inexperienced he was when he married at 29.' He disclosed that he made his notable journey across Greenland 'to get away because he was overworked and unhappy'. They parted on the best of terms. 'I think we are very great friends.'

The following day she had 'an amazing letter' from Nansen. He told her: 'It is nice to know there is a woman so like what one has dreamt of but never met,' and she reflected that 'it does my work good to have the admiration of a person like Nansen. I worked hard and well all day.'

*

In those November weeks, Scott was moving forward over the Great Ice Barrier with growing apprehension. 'The weather was horrid, overcast, gloomy, snowy. Our spirits became very low' (12 November). The snow portended a possibly severe change in the conditions. 'If this should follow, our luck will be truly awful. The camp is very silent and cheerless, signs that things are going awry' (13 November). Oates reported that the ponies, each carrying about 500 lb., were not doing as well as he expected. Scott was inclined to think the Soldier too pessimistic, as usual. On 17 November, just after leaving One Ton Depot, Scott himself doubted whether 'the little beasts will last; the weakness of breeding and age is showing itself already'.

The Main Party overtook what had been the Motor Party on 21 November. 'We haven't seen Amundsen yet!' Day, the engineer, called out in greeting. By then, the Norwegians had surmounted a hitherto unknown glacier and were in latitude 83° 30' S., on the polar plateau, 10,000 feet up. Amundsen later revealed that he and his men were much exercised at that stage about Scott's progress, and were the more determined to push on, knowing that 'the Englishman would not be idle'.

The Motor Party was disbanded and Day and Hooper returned under orders to the winter base, taking letters. Scott to his wife: (*November 24th*, 1911. Lat 81° 15' S.)—'Just a little note from the Barrier to say that I love you. There are long hours in which to think of you and the boy. Everything is going pretty well for the present, though we had a bad scare about the condition of the ponies last week. The animals are not well selected. I knew this in New Zealand, though I didn't tell you. That they are going well now and bidding fair to carry us through the first stage of the journey is entirely due to Oates. He is another treasure. Take great care of yourself and bless you. The sun shines.—C.'

Lieutenant Evans was given charge of what was thereafter called the Man-hauling Party, with Atkinson (the surgeon), Wright (the physicist), and Chief Stoker Lashly. They were instructed to go forward fifteen miles and maintain that distance ahead of the Main Party, to erect marker cairns, select camp sites, and carry out surveying and navigation work.

The Main Party were to march at night and rest when the sun was high and the air warm. Behind them, by some hours, came the dog teams driven by Meares and Dimitri, the Russian groom. Depots containing a week's rations for each returning party were laid every 65 miles. They were made as conspicuous as possible with flags flown from bamboo poles. One was seen from nine miles away.

The snow that had made Scott uneasy 'fell as thick as a hedge', as he put it, in the last days of November, making the going exceedingly hard for the weaker ponies; and 'tired animals mean tired men'. Three ponies had to be shot during the next eight days. True, they supplied meat for men and dogs, but it was a distressing business, especially for Scott, who shrank from taking part in it and shuddered when the shots were fired.

Minor blizzards had swept over them. There was worse to come. In the first week of December, normally a month of calm and settled weather, they were held fast in their two tents for four days while the tempest raged with a violence suggesting cosmic disturbance. Evans considered it 'a knock-down blow, the biggest in the history of the expedition to date. It tore to ribbons our chances of any great success,'[*] because it meant a profitless consumption of food by men and animals as well as delay. It was the greatest snowfall in Scott's experience as an Antarctic explorer. With it came a tempera-

[*] Evans: *South With Scott.*

264

ture rise that brought its own sequel of misery—slush eighteen inches deep everywhere, dripping tents, wet sleeping-bags.

'Our luck in weather is preposterous,' he wrote dismally on 3 December, remembering resentfully that Shackleton, arriving at the foot of the Beardmore Glacier, had been more favourably treated by fortune. Scott's repeated journal grievances about the weather indicate the strain he was under, culminating in the near despair of the four-day blizzard.

He was now accenting luck, as if he felt that the organized momentum of the Expedition might soon be spent. 'It is really time that the luck turned in our favour—we have had far too little of it.' He visualized Amundsen having 'a stroke of luck' that might reduce his distance to the Pole by a hundred miles or so. 'What on earth does such weather mean at this time of year?' he asked in the journal. 'It is more than our share of ill-fortune, I think, but the luck may turn yet.' There was 'food for thought', he ruminated, 'in picturing our small party struggling against adversity in one place whilst others go smilingly forward in the sunshine. How great may be the element of luck! No foresight—no procedure—could have prepared us for this state of affairs' (5 December). The warm blizzard, he complained again, was 'real hard luck'.

They were wet through, day and night. They lay in pools of water formed by the warmth of their bodies. Their sleeping-bags, 'which are the objects of our greatest care' (Bowers), were soaked through. Their food was damp. The ponies shivered more than they would have in a temperature many degrees lower. On 6 December Scott wrote: 'Miserable, utterly miserable. We have camped in the Slough of Despond.... Oh! but this is too crushing. A hopeless feeling descends on one and is hard to fight off.'

Scott's analytical mind played up and down the scale of his plans and preparations without finding any aspect of them that could have been altered to meet, far less avert, the crisis that had come upon them. 'Resignation to misfortune is the only attitude, but not an easy one to adopt. It seems undeserved where plans were well laid and so nearly crowned with a first success' (7 December).

'A little hope revived' on 8 December, only to be extinguished by another thick fall of snow. 'Our case is growing desperate. The snow all about us is terribly deep,' hindering all movement. 'I cannot load the animals heavily on such snow' (9 December). It looked as if the end of pony transport was at hand; 'but one wonders what the dogs can do on such a surface. I much fear they also will prove inadequate.' The outlook was hopeful again that night, 'but nothing can recall our four lost days'.

Amundsen in latitude 87° was keeping up an extraordinary rate of progress in spite of snowstorms in that first week of December. His worst day was 2 December: 'Dangerous to proceed; crevasses; blizzard,' when their mileage was down to two and a half. Some days they travelled twenty-eight miles with comparative ease. At no time was the weather the insuperable handicap to Amundsen that it was to Scott. On the other hand, his route up the Heiberg Glacier, and from there up the heavily crevassed Devil's Glacier, was reckoned by some experts to have been more difficult than Scott's up the Beardmore Glacier.

While Scott was toiling over the last twelve miles of the Barrier to the foot of the Beardmore, his wife was loyally busy about Expedition affairs, telling him in her diary that she had addressed two hundred and fifty envelopes for appeal letters, and that 'it seems absurd not to have a paid person to do them' (5 December). She was 'concocting a letter' to Lloyd George, Chancellor of the Exchequer, asking him to guarantee £10,000. 'Of course, nothing will happen, but I don't care. We thought nothing would happen in Australia and it did. So one may as well have a shot' (10 December).

The next day she went to Downing Street, 'to find Ll.G. or a secretary, then to the Treasury. No luck. Came home and wrote to Carnegie,' at his castle in Scotland. On 14 December, she made a personal approach to Lord Strathcona, Canadian High Commissioner in London. 'He would only give £200 and nothing would induce him to give any more. Said he hadn't got it, wicked old man.'

The Chancellor of the Exchequer to Kathleen Scott:

11 Downing Street,
Whitehall, S.W.
12th December, 1911.

Dear Mrs Scott,—It is with the utmost regret that I have to refuse such an appeal as you make to me. But you must remember that it is not my own money with which we are concerned and that I cannot consider my personal feelings in dealing with it.

I am forced most reluctantly to the conclusion that I should not be justified in going beyond the very liberal treatment that the Government have already accorded to the Expedition.

Yours sincerely,

D. LLOYD GEORGE

*

Scott wrote mournfully on 9 December that the remaining ponies had been shot. 'Poor beasts!' Sinking well above their hocks in the deep snow, they could hardly move and had to be driven on by the lash. 'It was a grim business. There was not one man there who would willingly have caused pain to a living thing,' wrote Cherry-Garrard. It was with a heavy heart that Scott watched groups of men gathered round the weaker ponies, trying to force them forward. As a final act of mercy, the men halved their biscuit ration and fed it to the animals. Then each was led to the place of execution—'the slaughter of the innocents' (Evans). Horrid crimson stains marked the spot. 'Thank God!' Wilson wrote fervently in his diary. 'We can now begin the heavy work ourselves,' and he was not alone in his relief that the ponies were spared further suffering.

Wilson was privately speculating on the leader's decision concerning the composition of the Polar Party. 'We shall have another party returning in ten or twelve days' time, reducing us to 8. I expect to be one of the 8; but whether I shall have the good fortune to be considered strong enough to be one of the final 4 or not—why, I don't know. No one knows yet who they will be' (10 December).

The subject can hardly have been other than a desperately preoccupying one for Scott, in view of the testing time through which they had all lately passed. To deliver judgement on individual capabilities in that terribly isolated context of propinquity and risk was a responsibility to try the soul of any leader. Cherry-Garrard did not doubt that 'the mental strain was very grave'.

Scott's journal entry for 10 December is not the only one from which anxiety on that score can be deduced. Having divided the party into three sledging teams of four men each, he was disturbed to hear from Wilson that Wright, the young Canadian physicist, showed signs of 'getting played out'.

Lashly, also, was not at his peak of fitness. 'It is a very serious business,' Scott wrote, 'if the men are going to crock up,' as if the notion of infirmity came as a disagreeable surprise to him.

He blamed Lieutenant Evans for the decline in the powers of those two members of his team. 'He shows a terrible lack of judgement.' In his own team Scott had Wilson, Oates, and Petty Officer Evans. With Bowers went Cherry-Garrard, Crean and Keohane. Each man pulled 170 lb.

Bowers told his mother in a letter written from the Barrier: 'One gets down to bedrock with everybody, sledging under trying conditions. The character of a man comes out and you see things that were never expected. You get to know each other inside out and respect some more and, unfortunately, some less. I think more highly than ever of our leader,' and less highly, he added, of 'Teddy' Evans. 'We all notice the change in him so much. I must say I am sorry to see it.'

A good start on 11 December supplied one of the more cheerful entries in the journal for that period. 'I was very jubilant; all difficulties seemed to be vanishing.' It was a fleeting mood of exhilaration. 'Unfortunately, our history was not repeated with other parties.' Evans's team annoyed him by not being 'trim and drilled'. Evans was summoned for a talk in the leader's tent, and wrote later: 'He was disappointed with our inability to keep up, but I pointed out that we could not expect to do the same as fresh men—the others had only put on sledge harness for the first time the day before. Scott agreed, but seemed worried and fretful.'*

Evans and Atkinson had been pulling a loaded sledge for weeks, since the breakdown of the motors, 'bearing the brunt of the hard work' (Evans). When, on 14 December, seeing their dragging steps, Scott offered to take over part of the load pulled by Evans's men, Evans shook his head. 'His pride would not allow such help' (Scott).

That day, the dog teams with Meares and Dimitri turned back, having carried out their task of bringing up 200 lb. of stores for the Lower Glacier Depot. They had travelled farther South than their food allowance warranted. Meares undertook that he and his fellow driver would cut their daily ration on the 450 miles journey back. Evans alone noted 'Meares's generosity'. Scott had written in the journal: 'Bit by bit I am

* Evans: South With Scott.

losing all faith in the dogs and much in Meares.' On that day, Amundsen and his dogs reached the Pole.

Scott gave Meares a letter to be sent home in due course by the *Terra Nova*. It was for his wife. 'Just a tiny note to be taken back by the dogs. Things are not so rosy as they might be, but we keep our spirits up and say the luck must turn. So far every turn shows the extraordinary good fortune that Shackleton had. This is only to tell you that I can keep up with the rest as well as of old, and that I think of you whenever I stretch tired limbs in a very comfortable sleeping-bag.—C. P.S. The thought of you is *very* pleasant' (10 December 1911).

CHAPTER NINETEEN

HEARTBREAK AT THE POLE

AFTER the 400 miles and more of the white, shadowless Barrier, where no horizons lured the eye, there was refreshment in the sight of the rugged granite cliffs of the gateway to the Beardmore Glacier. It took them six hours to traverse the last mile in the deep soft snow of the lower slopes; frequently they were up to the thighs in it. 'Due to incaution' half the party were smitten by snow-blindness, evoking querulous comment from Scott about his 'tiresome fellow countrymen'. He was suffering from bouts of acute indigestion that no one else seemed to know about until he mentioned it to Cherry-Garrard. 'He told me that at the bottom of the Glacier he was hardly expecting to go on himself.'

Ascending the Beardmore Glacier, the 'great glittering river of ice', which extends 120 miles through the Queen Alexandra Mountains, bordering the polar plateau, and widens between ten and twenty miles, involved them in 'dozens of critical moments'. With the departure of the dogs the sledge loads were increased to 800 lb. each. 'Could we pull them or not? It was a very anxious business,' Scott wrote. The distance for their first day on the Glacier was seven miles. On succeeding days the going got worse; one forenoon they covered half a mile; another day it took them nine hours to travel the same distance. 'I have never pulled so hard,' Cherry-Garrard remembered, 'or so nearly crushed my inside into my backbone by the everlasting jerking with all my strength on the canvas round my unfortunate tummy. We were all in the same boat.' They were hauling sledges subscribed for by the Old Boys of Sidcot School; factory workers at Rowntree's of York; and officers and men of H.M.S. *Invincible*.

The 'exceptional exercise' gave Scott bad attacks of cramp. His indigestion kept him awake at night. Their lips, 'raw and blistered', were festooned with strips of sticking plaster. The aneroids showed a rise of about 500 ft. a day; and by 17 December they were at 3,500 feet. They hauled the sledges up huge pressure ridges and tobogganed down the reverse slopes, so recovering part of their time schedule. The Mid-Glacier Depot was laid in latitude 84° 33′ S., marked with a red flag. Weather and surface were at last in their favour. 'It is splendid to be getting along and to find some adequate return for the work we are putting into the business' (Scott).

On 20 December, the first Returning Party was named: Atkinson, Wright, Cherry-Garrard, and Keohane. They were to turn back after the next day's march. 'All are disappointed— poor Wright rather bitterly, I fear.' Scott 'dreaded this necessity of choosing—nothing could be more heart-rending.' Cherry-Garrard wrote that 'Scott was very put about, said that he had been thinking a lot about it but had come to the conclusion that the seamen with their special knowledge would be needed. I said I hoped I had not disappointed him, and he caught hold of me and said "No—no—no." '

On the night of 21 December, 'There is a very mournful air. Bill [Dr Wilson] came in while I was cooking to say goodbye. He told me he fully expected to come back with the next party; that he could see Scott was going to take the strongest fellows, perhaps three seamen' (Cherry-Garrard). When the moment of parting came, 'affecting farewells were exchanged: dear good fellows as they are' (Scott).

Scott to his wife:

Lat. 85 S.
December 21st, 1911.

We are struggling on, considering all things, against odds. The weather is a constant anxiety, otherwise arrangements are working exactly as planned, but this will reach you months after you have got the public news, and so there is

270

only the old thing to add, I love you very much and all the time.

Four your own ear also, I am exceedingly fit and can go on with the best of them, so that I am not ashamed to belong to you.

I write this sitting in our tent waiting for the fog to clear —an exasperating position as we are in the worst crevassed region. Teddy Evans and Atkinson were down for the length of their harness this morning, and we have all been half way down. As first man I get first chance, and it is decidedly exciting not knowing which step will give way. Still all this is interesting enough if one could only go on.

Since writing the above I made a dash for it, got out of the valley, out of the fog, and away from crevasses. So here we are, practically on the summit and up to date in the provision line; we ought to get through.

But we shan't catch the ship except by a miracle, so take care of yourself and the boy. How I should love to see you.

c.

*

Starting a new journal volume on 22 December, he noted on the flyleaf: 'Ages, self 43, Wilson 39, Evans (P.O.) 37, Oates 32, Bowers 28. Average 36.' It appears that he had already decided who were to be his comrades on the last march to the Pole.

'Great vicissitudes of fortune in the afternoon march' (22 December). 'We got on the most extraordinary surface— narrow crevasses in all directions. They were quite invisible. We all fell in one after another and sometimes two together. It was like breaking through a glasshouse at every step.' There was sometimes the weird feeling that the great Mississippi of ice called the Beardmore Glacier covered mountain tops and filled valleys.

Christmas Day 1911 was spent amid 'a scene of wild desolation', and the tone of Scott's long journal entry is more practical than festive, though at night he felt 'almost too replete' to write. On the day's march they had to tack frequently to avoid crevasse dangers. 'Lashly went down very suddenly, spinning round at the full length of his harness, with 80 feet of clear space beneath him' (Evans).

At home, Scott's wife took their small son to Henley for Christmas. 'Your Mother is marvellous in health, but she would talk religion, and said how sad it was that Peter didn't know the divine meaning of Christmas Day. I had to be a little stern, and told her that Peter knew that there was a little baby in history born in a stable who grew up to be a very wonderful man, and that was more than most babies of two knew. Poor old Mummy!'

*

Breasting the Glacier, with its often cruelly steep ice surface, its forbidding pressure ridges, its gigantic snow drifts, its tributary glaciers, its overhanging ice-falls, compelled admiration of Shackleton's 'fine performance', as its discoverer and first explorer. Unlike Shackleton, who did not shrink from styling himself 'a representative of the British people', Scott had none of the sensations of a conqueror as he reached the summit in the last days of 1911. His satisfaction was the lesser one of having 'caught up Shackleton's dates' (30 December).

He had been spurred by Shackleton's feat in surmounting the Beardmore to emulate and if possible to excel it. In spite of the great blizzard, he matched Shackleton's daily averages, largely by uncannily intuitive leadership in difficult places. 'Everything would be cheerful,' he wrote, 'if I could persuade myself that the second party were quite fit to go forward.' Those overworked men, 'Teddy' Evans and Lashly, with Bowers and Crean, were showing a loss of stamina.

They were now up on the polar plateau, at around 10,000 ft., more than a thousand feet, as they later discovered, above the level of the Pole. It was a stark and sterile region of ridges fifty feet high, with one-in-three gradients and between them, crevasses 'as big as Regent Street'. Far-off mountains made a magnificent prospect, east and west. Scott and his men marched forward with little speech in that rarefied air, using their breath for a more necessary purpose. A stinging wind, howling like an ironic chorus, forced them to bend their heads as they marched.

Nothing impeded Scott's will and energy in those New Year days as he neared latitude 88°, Shackleton's farthest distance south, and the way seemed clear for triumph. Leaning against the knife-edged blast, he toiled on as if yards mattered more than miles. Presently, with the levelling of the horizon, his spirits soared. 'For the first time our goal seems really in sight.' His confidence restored, he made known on the evening of

3 January 1912 what was in his mind for the last stage of the southward quest. Wilson wrote in his pocket diary: 'Scott told us what the plans were for the S.P. Scott, Oates, Bowers, Petty Officer Evans, and I, are to go to the Pole. Teddy Evans is re-returning from here tomorrow with Crean and Lashly. I feel very sorry for him, as he has spent 2½ years in working for a place on this polar journey. We are now 5 and we have only 4 pairs of ski, Bowers has to go on foot just behind Scott and myself.'

On the memoranda pages at the end of his diary, Wilson wrote: 'Paint 2 Pole pictures. "The Queen's Flag at the British Pole," and "The South Pole for King George."' Beneath the reminder he drew two postage-stamp size sketches of the compositions he had in view.* By then, his loyal intentions had been nullified by Amundsen's success. The Norwegian flag had been flying at the Pole since 14 December. Back in 85° S., Amundsen was about to begin the return crossing of the Barrier. On New Year's Day the two expeditions had passed within a hundred miles of each other.

Scott tore a perforated leaf from his little notebook and pencilled another message to his wife. It was to be taken back by the last Returning Party: Lieutenant Evans, Lashly, and Crean. Evans had been asked to cede Bowers from his team, so that Scott could lead a five-man unit to the Pole.

Lat 87·32.
January 3rd 1912.

A last note from a hopeful position. I think it is going to be all right. We have a fine party going forward and arrangements are all going well. So this is simply to say that I love you and that you needn't be ashamed of me, or the boy either. I have led this business—not nominally but actually—so that no man will or can say I wasn't fit to lead through the last lap that is before us.

I shall have to keep wondering how you are and thinking of you constantly, as I have done all along. But it will be good to see you when this business is through.

P.S. Bless you, bless you.

C.

The three dismissed men kept company with the Polar Party for a further five miles. Then Scott called a halt. He

* Wilson made two drawings at the Pole. They were sent to King George V.

noted that 'poor old Crean wept and Lashly was affected'. Teddy Evans did not disguise his disappointment, and 'behaved like a man'. The two parties then separated, to go their opposite ways. At intervals they turned to wave farewell.

Rarely have the mutations of individual fortune been more starkly illustrated. After suffering great privation on the way back down the Beardmore Glacier and across the Great Ice Barrier, Evans returned to England to live life more abundantly than he could ever have dreamed of,* while Scott was probably already doomed to the fate so soon to overtake him.

His change in the organization of the Polar Party was never convincingly explained. It was thought that he wanted as many of his comrades as possible to share in the success he felt by then was assured. Cherry-Garrard and Debenham agreed with that view. Lieutenant Evans believed that in adding Bowers to the Party, Scott was thinking above all, of the long and exhausting march that would face them when they turned north again from the Pole. The addition of Bowers meant an access of physical and psychological strength; but it also meant an imbalance of food supplies, more tent discomfort, and an excess load on the sledge.

'Only a march from Shackleton's final camp' (Scott on 3 January); but their pace was reduced by *sastrugi*. 'We go little over a mile and a quarter an hour now.' Conditions worsened; the *sastrugi* developed barbs of ice that tore at their ankles. 'The vicissitudes of this work are bewildering' (7 January). 'Evans has a nasty cut on his hand (sledge-making). I hope it won't give trouble.'

Petty Officer Evans's cut hand figured prominently in histories of the Expedition as one of the likely contributory causes of his breakdown. In 1965, Professor Frank Debenham who sledged with him some months before the start of the Southern Journey, gave the new information that Evans incurred the damage at that earlier time. It appears, then, that Evans nursed and perhaps concealed the injury in that climate uncongenial to healing, if also to sepsis, long before it came to Scott's attention. The effect on Evans may have been psychologically rather

* In August 1929 'a scene of unrestrained emotion' was witnessed at a luncheon at a Sydney club, where Evans, by then a rear-admiral and Commander-in-Chief of the Royal Australian Navy, spoke about how he and Scott 'had been served differently by Providence'. A local newspaper reported that 'twice Admiral Evans broke down, and was unable to continue'.

than physically lowering, as Dr Wilson observed in a wider context five weeks later.

At that stage of the journey Scott wrote of Evans as 'a giant worker with a really remarkable headpiece'. Bowers was praised again too—'a little marvel'. Wilson was 'tough as steel, never wavering'. Oates stood the hardships as well as any: 'I would not like to be without either.' Scott was sure that 'our five people are perhaps as happily selected as it is possible to imagine' (8 January). As an appraisal it was prejudiced by tradition and obstinacy, as events were soon to show.

Reaching latitude 88° 25′ S. on 9 January, he was careful to note that they were 'beyond the record of Shackleton's walk', and that all was *terra incognita* ahead. 'Only 85 miles from the Pole, but it's going to be a stiff pull *both ways* apparently.' Soon his 'happily selected' team was failing to meet the demands made on it. 'The work was distressingly hard' (10 January). 'The rest of the forenoon was agonizing. I never had such pulling. It takes it out of us like anything' (11 January). It was like having to drag a weighted plough through heavy clay.

They were 'only 51 miles from the Pole' on 13 January, but the margin of physical strength left to them was also diminishing. Scott had never previously allowed himself to be cast down by the monotony of the march. 'One grows horribly sick, of it,' he was now writing, and also that 'one can easily imagine oneself getting played out'. It was a rare admission: his ability to 'keep going' had been a source of private gratification, as the journal shows.

Then, suddenly, he was overwhelmed by 'the appalling possibility' that they had been forestalled by the Norwegians (15 January), bringing home to him the shattering implications in terms of personal prestige. His ardour for scientific achievement had never finally displaced his hope of crowning it by the distinction of priority at the Pole. Haunted by the spectre of anti-climax as he had been since Amundsen's appearance in the Bay of Whales, he may not have considered its full consequences: the devaluation of his journalistic and publishing commitments, the dismay of his backers, the decline of public interest in his fortunes. Disdainful of the plaudits of the crowd, ready as he was to revert to the anonymity of naval life, he none the less preferred admiration to sympathy.

Disappointment struck him full in the face on 16 January.

They reached latitude 98° 42′ S. at midday. 'Feeling that to-morrow would see us at our destination,' they started out on the afternoon march with revived spirits. Two hours later, Bowers's sharp eye spotted ahead of them a black speck that seemed alien to its immediate configuration. Gradually it came into focus as a flag over a cairn. Trailing to and from the site were sledge tracks and the paired imprints of dogs' feet. 'This told us the whole story,' Scott wrote in the journal. 'I am very sorry for my loyal companions,' an expression of noble regret that was to ring down the years.

At the head of his journal page for Wednesday 17 January 1912, he pencilled THE POLE in shaky inch-high capital letters, and recorded that 'none of us slept much after the shock of our discovery'. His revelation of dismay is important in the light of later claims that he was unmoved by his eclipse. It seems likely that his personal disappointment was more profound than he or anyone else realized. In crushing out zest and hope, it may have inflicted injury at deeper levels of his being. 'Well, we have turned our backs on the goal of our ambition with sore feelings, and must face 800 miles of solid dragging—and good-bye to most of the daydreams! Great God! This is an awful place.'

They hoisted the 'poor slighted Union Jack,' given them by Queen Alexandra, and, by controlling the shutter release of the camera with a long thread, took a photograph of them-selves that became historic. There were handshakes all round and even smiles, faintly recorded in another photograph. Scott collected a note left for him by Amundsen. 'He asks me to forward it to King Haakon! I am puzzled,' not immediately grasping that Amundsen was taking a precaution in case of calamity to his returning party.

There was subsequent editorial tampering with Scott's journal account of the events of that day. The printed volume quotes Scott as writing: 'I fancy the Norwegians arrived at the Pole on the 15th Dec. and left on the 17th, ahead of a date quoted by me in London as ideal, *viz* Dec. 22nd.' What he wrote was more pointed: 'I think it quite evident they aimed to forestall a date quoted by me in London as ideal, *viz* Dec. 22nd.' He was apparently referring to old newspaper inter-views in which he indicated the Expedition's time schedule. Intelligent anticipation now had the aspect of blazing indis-cretion, intensifying the discomfiture of the day.

Editorial caution was brought to bear on the paragraph in which Scott wrote that 'it looks as though the Norwegian party expected colder weather at the summit than they got; it could hardly be otherwise from Shackleton's overdrawn account.' The word 'overdrawn' does not appear in the printed version. Part of another entry for the same day was also omitted. As printed, Scott was made to say: 'Now for the run home and a desperate struggle.' What he wrote was: 'Now for the run home and a desperate struggle to get the news through first.' It seems that he was clinging to a hope that he might still supply the Central News Agency with the 'scoop' that was so confidently expected from him.

Soon after starting the return journey they came on the Norwegian cairn from which flew 'the ominous black flag which had first apprised us of our predecessors' success. We had packed the flag up, using the staff for our sledge sail. So that is the last of the Norwegians for the present.' They pressed on again, Scott fearing that 'the return journey is going to be dreadfully tiring and monotonous' (19 January).

*

Oates was the first to show signs of faltering. 'I think he is feeling the cold and fatigue more than any of us' (Scott, 20 January). In three more days the leader was noting that 'there is no doubt that Evans is a good deal run down. His fingers are badly blistered and his nose is rather seriously congested with frostbites.' Evans had amused them by speaking habitually of his nose as 'my old blossom'. Now cheerfulness was beyond him. 'He is very much annoyed with himself, which is not a good sign' (Scott).

On 24 January, with a full gale screaming round them, the question arose: 'Is the weather breaking up? If so, God help us. I don't like the look of it.' Heavy shadows fall across the journal pages again. Wilson was a casualty—'suffering tortures from his eyes'. Evans's nose and fingers were 'in a bad state'. One of Oates's feet was giving trouble. The faces of all of them were 'much cut up by the winds' on the plateau. 'A long way to go, and, by Jove, this is tremendous labour' (27 January). They were pulling a high-packed sledge loaded with five full kitbags, the cooker, an instrument box, biscuit boxes, a paraffin tank, with their tent laid on top.

Misfortunes crowded in on them after two moderately good

marching days, Evans's hands were 'really bad, and he shows signs of losing heart over it'. Wilson's diary records that 'Evans's fingernails are all coming off' (31 January). Wilson himself, still half blinded by snow glare, strained a leg tendon, and Scott wrote: 'It will be a mighty serious thing if Wilson's leg doesn't improve.' On 2 February, Scott came 'an awful purler' and damaged the point of his right shoulder. 'Three out of five injured, and the most troublesome surfaces to come.' He was foreseeing the perils of the Beardmore Glacier.

*

In the week that he began the descent, the *Terra Nova* returned to McMurdo Sound. She sent out boats at Cape Adare to pick up the Northern Party, under Lieutenant Campbell, returning to Cape Evans after having spent seven hard winter months huddled in a snow-burrow, 13 ft. by 9ft.; an incredible experience, the more so as they were wearing their light summer sledging clothes. The ship also brought 7 Indian mules supplied at Scott's request by Major General Sir Douglas Haig, at Simla. As Scott had not yet declared his intention to stay a further year in the Antarctic, it was thought necessary to expedite his return from the Pole, so that he might catch the ship if he wanted to do so. Cherry-Garrard and Gerof, the Russian, set out with a dog team in the hope of meeting the Polar Party at One Ton Camp.

For the first time, going down the Beardmore, Scott suffered from loss of sleep. Evans's condition was a source of mounting worry. From the beginning, he had been regarded as a tower of strength to the Expedition, physically its strongest member. Now Scott seemed to be losing patience with him. 'He is becoming rather stupid and incapable' (4 February). 'Evans is a good deal crocked up and very stupid about himself' (5 February). The references to Evans's 'stupidity' are deleted from the published journal.

He became mentally confused. Wilson saw him fumbling helplessly with his ski shoes, which 'kept coming off'. He was 'told to wait and get them right and follow on and catch us up,' evidently an order from Scott. There was a sense in which the chief petty officer was out of scale. He was the most muscular member of the party and he had to subsist on the same amount of food as his fellows. He was a martyr to Scott's loyalty, rooted in old and tried association on sea and land.

Scott had a fondness for him as a Royal Navy shipmate of generous heart and great good humour. Above all, Evans personified the man-hauling power and steadfastness that Scott misguidedly thought paramount in Antarctic transport, a Herculean figure on whose strength and reliability he staked more than they could support. 'I think another week might have a very bad effect on Evans, who is going steadily downhill' (7 February).

They found a depot note from Lieutenant Evans informing them that his Returning Party had 'passed through safely' three weeks earlier. Scott noted: 'They have taken their full allowance of food. First panic, certainly that biscuit box was short. Great doubt as to how this has come about, as we certainly haven't over-issued allowances. Bowers is dreadfully disturbed about it,' perhaps fearing that it presaged further disquieting discoveries as they proceeded.

*

Scott's account of their descent of the Beardmore Glacier communicates the horrific character of the journey as they neared the Mid-Glacier Depot. 'For three hours we plunged on on ski, first thinking that we were too much to the right, then too much to the left; meanwhile, the disturbance got worse and my spirits received a very crude shock.' There were times when it seemed that they would not find a way down through 'the awful turmoil'. They could no longer manage on ski. 'The turmoil changed in character, irregularly crevassed surface giving way to huge chasms, closely packed and most difficult to cross. It was very heavy work, but we had grown desperate. We won through at 10 p.m., and I write after 12 hours on the march' (11 February). Cherry-Garrard said that 'days and nights spent coming down the Beardmore will give you nightmare after nightmare, and wake you shrieking in years after'.

Their food supply was thinning: 'we have two full days' food left.' Yet in spite of it all Scott and Wilson found it 'extremely interesting' to note geological features of the Glacier. Wilson collected rare specimens; for example, a piece of coal with fossil leaf impressions. 'A lot could be written on the delight of setting foot on rock after 14 weeks of snow and ice and nearly 7 out of sight of aught else' (Scott).

On 12 February they 'arrived in a horrid maze of crevasses and fissures—the worst place of all,' referred to in the journal the next day as 'the worst experience of this trip,' one that gave them 'a horrible feeling of insecurity. We mustn't get into a hole like this again.' Bowers was afflicted by 'a very bad attack of snow blindness, and Wilson another almost as bad'. Evans was no longer capable of 'camping work'. Scott addressed himself with the plain truth on 14 February: 'There is no getting away from the fact that we are not going strong.'

When, two days after, Evans collapsed with giddiness and vomiting, Wilson noted in his 'Wellcome's Medical Diary' that it was unfortunate for Evans 'that he has never been sick in his life'. Deprived of his normal vigour, the big sailor was pathetically lacking in self-reliance. Scott thought that he had 'nearly broken down in brain' (16 February).

Saturday 17 February was 'a very terrible day' (Scott). Evans pronounced himself fit to continue again and took his place in the traces. After no more than half an hour, he fell out. Wilson's diary says that 'he lagged far behind'. They went back for him, Scott being first at his side. 'He had fallen and had his hands frostbitten,' Wilson wrote. 'He was rapidly losing the use of his legs, so we fetched him in on the sledge. He was comatose when we got him into the tent and he died without recovering consciousness at 10 p.m.'

Wilson had nothing to say about concussion, though Scott's journal states that Wilson suggested it as a possible cause of Evans's death. 'It is a terrible thing to lose a companion in this way, but calm reflection shows that there could not have been a better ending to the terrible anxieties of the past week.' What was done by way of last rites for Evans is nowhere recorded, except that Scott, Wilson, Oates, and Bowers kept a vigil by the body for two hours after all hope for him had gone.

They gave themselves the luxury of a good sleep at the Lower Glacier Depot, where pony meat was added to the ration. 'New life seems to come with greater food almost immediately,' but Scott could not surrender himself to the sensations of well-being. 'I am anxious about Barrier surfaces,' which had surprised them to their grievous disadvantage on the outward journey.

*

On the day that he made that entry in his journal, 18 February 1912, his wife noted in her diary: 'I was very taken up with you all evening. I wonder if anything special is happening to you. Something odd happened to the clocks and watches between nine and ten p.m.' The following day, Scott recorded that they had 'struggled 4.6 miles over a really terrible surface,' rounding off his account of a particularly frustrating day with the speculation: 'I wonder what is in store for us.' His wife, under the same date, wrote: 'I was still rather taken up by you and a wee bit depressed. As you ought about now to be returning to the ship I see no reason for depression. I wonder.'

Captain (later Admiral) Philip Dumas, R.N., made a diary note of Kathleen Scott telling him and his wife that young Peter, aged three, playing on his rocking horse in the dining-room, asked to be lifted down. He then went towards the door, holding up his hands, saying: 'Hullo, daddy!' Peter Scott remembers the incident. He does not think his mother attached any supernatural significance to it.

One of her sitters at the time was Compton Mackenzie, the novelist, who has lately recalled her telling him that she did not believe that Scott would reach the South Pole. 'He has always been unlucky. If he has an important engagement, the train or the bus breaks down, and he misses something that might have made all the difference. I try to put away this doubt, but it's no use. I cannot somehow believe that he will reach the Pole.' *

She was noting in the diary which she continued to keep in the form of messages written for him to read later that she had lunched with Asquith, the Prime Minister, who was 'extraordinarily pleasant'. It was the prelude to a friendship in the course of which Asquith considered himself at liberty to drop in at her studio whenever he chose. He became one of Kathleen Scott's several eminent admirers. At the lunch, he talked about Haldane's impending pacific mission to Berlin.

J. M. Barrie was frequently at 174 Buckingham Palace Road that year and after. He had a parlour trick to amuse his small godson, Peter Scott, flipping licked postage stamps on pennies up to the blue ceiling of the drawing-room. Three stuck there until the house was demolished in 1928.

In February 1912 Kathleen Scott was preparing to send twenty of her sculptures to an exhibition of women's art at the Grafton Gallieries, 'although I hate being among women'.

* Sir Compton Mackenzie: *My Life and Times: Octave Four* (Chatto & Windus, 1965).

The centre-piece was her bronze figure of the Hon. C. S. Rolls, the young flying pioneer who crashed to his death at a Bournemouth aviation meeting in 1910. 'I *think* it looks stunning.' Taking tea with Admiral Sir Edward Seymour, some time Commander-in-Chief, Devonport, 'I told him you wanted to go straight back into the Navy and that your whole heart was in the Navy. I tell all admirals that.'

*

Scott was not thinking of Buckingham Palace Road when he wrote on 22 February: 'There is little doubt we are in for a rotten critical time going home.' The haven of his hopes for the time being was the Hut at Cape Evans, four hundred miles away northward across the Barrier. The next day he wrote more cheerfully, 'Things are looking up, as we are on the regular line of cairns, with no gaps right home, I hope.'

It was an all too brief respite from anxiety, which was renewed in full measure by the rapidly falling temperature. By the last day of February it was minus 37 degrees, a drastic change for weakened men to endure. The pulling became exhausting, and not only by reason of the bad surface which had no glide on it. Apart from the small supplementary ration of pony meat, their food was deficient in vitamins and calorie values.*

They prayed that March would come in like a lion. 'A blizzard, a succession of blizzards, would have been the salvation of them all,' was the verdict pronounced later by the Expedition's meteorologist, Dr George Simpson. It would have meant a temperature rise. It would have improved the sledging surface of the Barrier. It would have provided an opportunity of hoisting a sledge sail, thus conserving energy. Yet on 2 March, 'in spite of a strong wind and a full sail', they covered only five and a half miles. Clearly, other factors were at work against them.

The oil shortage, which meant fewer hot meals, was one of them. There was less paraffin at the depots than they reckoned to find. The allowance per man per day on the return journey had been fixed at one forty-eighth of a gallon. It was intended to ensure a margin against delays, but not against any considerable loss from evaporation or seepages. Both those

* As confirmed by A. P. Thomson, M.D.: see *Antarctica* by J. Gordon Hayes (1927).

causes operated in the case of the depot supplies. It is evident from Scott's journal that he did not accept them as solely accountable for the diminished quantities he found. Having recorded on 26 February, 'fuel woefully short', he confirmed it on arriving at the Middle Barrier Depot on 2 March. 'First we found a bare half gallon of oil,' a plain statement of fact that was rendered differently in the printed version of Scott's journal, 'arranged by Leonard Huxley,'* where it reads: 'First we found a shortage of oil.'

Scott cited it as the first of 'three distinct blows which have placed us in a bad position'. The other two were the bad state of Oates's feet, and the 'dark overcast weather'. In the same entry he referred to their being 'in queer street', and to 'feeling the cold horribly', in some degree undoubtedly due to the lack of hot meals.

Sunday March 4.—Things looking *very* black indeed. All the morning we had to pull with all our strength, and in 4½ hours we covered 3½ miles. We are about 42 miles from the next depot and have a week's food, but only about 3 to 4 days' fuel—we are as economical of the latter as we can possibly be, and we cannot afford to save food and pull as we are pulling.

We are in a very tight place indeed, but none of us is despondent *yet*, or at least we preserve every semblance of good cheer. Providence to our aid! We can expect little from man now except the possibility of extra food at the next depot. It will be real bad if we get there and find the same shortage of oil.

The following day, 'our fuel dreadfully low and the poor Soldier nearly done. It is pathetic enough because we can do little for him.' Scott thought that more hot food might do a little, 'but only a little, I fear'. He knew the importance of hot food on the march from his experiences of ten years before. 'The habit of heating his food is about the only one possessed by the sledge traveller which can be said to go beyond the bare necessity of life. Theoretically, I believe, the food would be as nourishing and sustaining were it swallowed cold; it would only lose its immediate stimulating effect. As regards the heating of food, I can only say that I should prefer to be absent from a party that had decided to forego it. The prospect of a

* Published by Smith, Elder & Co., 1913.

cold supper after a long and tiring march through the snow, with the thermometer below zero, would hold out no allurements; and, indeed, I believe that few, if any, sledge travellers could continue long without hot food.' *

The next depot was the one named Mt Hooper, 16 miles on. 'If there is a shortage of oil again we can have little hope' (7 March). 'If there is another short allowance of fuel, God help us indeed. We are in a very bad way, I fear, in any case' (8 March). Reaching the depot, after fearful effort, Scott must have felt that the dark powers were finally arrayed against him.

'We marched up to the depot, Mt Hooper. Cold comfort. Shortage on our allowance all round. I don't know that anyone is to blame' (10 March). Presumably in deference to the feelings of members of the Returning Parties, Scott's amplified comment was edited out of the published journal. He had written: 'Generosity and thoughtfulness have not been abundant.'

The implication is damning. It seems clear that, allowing for natural wastage, there was grave mishandling of the oil supplies at the depots. A permissible observation here is that in no such circumstances would Scott have jeopardized his companions' chances of survival. His sense of responsibility remained firm to the end.

How great a force it was in his personal life is shown by the faithfully kept daily record of the journey to and from the Pole. Obviously, there were many times when sheer weariness of mind and body incited him to neglect of a duty to which he was formally committed. He had written during his first Antarctic expedition that 'a diary is a great nuisance', especially when the light was uncertain and the tent was being shaken by the wind. 'As he pores over his task, the writer's breath forms a film of ice over the paper on which the pencil frequently skids. Now and again his bare fingers will refuse duty, and he must wait until they are nursed back to life. Altogether, the keeping of diaries and records is no joke in cold weather.' *

Wilson, who was under no contractual obligation, stopped writing his diary on 27 February. Scott went on entering up his journal for another month, until his fingers could no longer hold the pencil. It showed more than estimable self-

* *The Voyage of the 'Discovery'.*

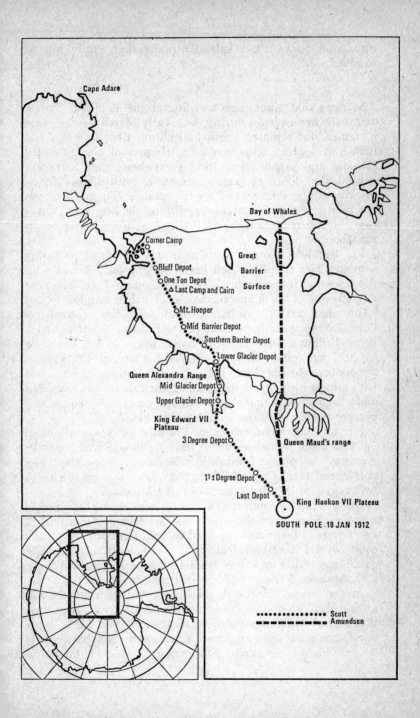

Cape Adare

Bay of Whales

Corner Camp

Great

Barrier

Surface

Bluff Depot

One Ton Depot

Last Camp and Cairn

Mt. Hooper

Mid Barrier Depot

Southern Barrier Depot

Lower Glacier Depot

Queen Alexandra Range

Mid Glacier Depot

Upper Glacier Depot

King Edward VII
Plateau

Queen Maud's range

3 Degree Depot

1 1/2 Degree Depot

Last Depot

King Haakon VII Plateau

SOUTH POLE - 18 JAN 1912

•••••••••••• Scott
▬ ▬ ▬ ▬ ▬ Amundsen

command; above all, a splendid sanity that would not be subdued.

*

The news that Amundsen was first at the Pole was flashed across the hemispheres during those early March days of 1912, a tremendous topic of world journalism. Everywhere it was hailed as a great achievement, a triumph of single-minded purpose and organizing ability; everywhere, that is, except behind the doors of certain scientific institutions. There, priority at the Pole was of no importance. To many of the specialists, it was a barren expedition, yielding not even a chart for future users of the route that Amundsen had so boldly pioneered.

For Kathleen Scott in London it was a week of confusing rumours. Her telephone bell began ringing on 6 March with the news that it was Scott who had reached the Pole. The next day was one of 'clash and turmoil, cables right and left to say, "Amundsen arrived Hobart: states Scott has reached the Pole."' Newspaper boys shrieked the tidings: 'Scott at South Pole—Brilliant Victory!' Scott's wife wrote in her diary for him: 'I was certain there was something wrong. The various papers brought me their cables, but I told them at once and with all the insistence I could that those cables were worthless and unsigned, and that they would only make themselves and everybody else ridiculous by publishing them.'

Her warnings went unheeded. The false news was published far and wide. 'I had an awful day; the house was a pandemonium—telephone, front door, telegrams, and reporters.' She announced through *The Times* that there was no reason to believe the cables. 'But I tasted of hell all the same.'

On 9 March, Amundsen's success was confirmed. Scott's name vanished from the headlines. 'My friends are afraid of me. I worked badly and my head rocked. I'm not going to recount what I have been feeling. It's better only to record the gay things of life and thro' it all I have hope and confidence and assurance. I know out of it great good will come.'

At the meeting of the Royal Geographical Society the following day, when the President, Major Darwin, announced that he had sent congratulations to Amundsen in the Society's name, 'there was scant applause'. Little Peter asked his mother: 'Is Amundsen a good man?' She answered: 'Yes, I think he is.'

Then the boy said: 'Amundsen and Daddy have both got to the Pole. Daddy has stopped working now' (11 March 1912).

She received a letter from the President of the Royal Geographical Society explaining why he had felt bound to send the message to Amundsen. She replied: 'But *of course*. Let us at any rate, if we don't win, be good losers.' Copying that reply into her diary letter to Scott, she appended to it the note: 'As you would be, my only man.' When she asked Darwin, the President, whether she should send congratulations to Amundsen, he wrote to her from his private address, 12 Egerton Place, S.W.: 'I like your spirit in wishing to send congratulations. On the whole, I think your friends are right in advising against it. He has not played the game, and, such being the case, he might make unfair use of your generosity.'

She wrote in her diary that she had seen Shackleton at the Royal Geographical Society meeting, and was sure that he was 'delighted at the turn things have taken'. Sir Clements Markham had written sympathetically to her, 'dear old chap'. To him, Amundsen was 'that interloper'. Her mind throbbed incessantly with the question, she wrote: 'Is my man unhappy?'

A letter from Nansen begged her to believe that she would know 'indescribable joy.' His fellow Norwegians, he told her, 'take much interest in Scott'. When he spoke to the King of Norway about Amundsen's success, 'the first thing he said was that he thought of you, and that he wished it had been Scott, and the Queen said the same, though they both admire Amundsen very much'. People in England were wrong, Nansen said, 'to think that Amundsen has been mean and dishonourable. They do not understand that the only reason he did not mention his plan was because of the difficulties he then was afraid of meeting at home. He is in every way a fine and noble fellow and is really a man' (19 March).

Professor Edgeworth David wrote from Sydney University to Kinsey on 12 April: 'I do so hope that there will be no kind of bitter feeling at all between Scott and Amundsen. If Amundsen's ideas of "polar etiquette" don't agree with ours, we can surely have the generosity to waive any grievance, and congratulate him.'

*

Hardly able to drag himself over the frozen miles, Oates was asking what he should do. Scott urged him 'to march on as long as he could'. His state had become pitiable; one foot hideously swollen, his legs weakened beyond supporting him more than a few yards at a time.

On 11 March a point of crisis was reached at which Scott faced the alternative of suicide. He virtually ordered Wilson to hand over to each man the supply of thirty opium tablets apiece that had been consigned to his care as the Polar Party's doctor. Wilson himself was to retain a phial of morphine.

Oates had declared some time before what he conceived to be the duty of any member of the Polar Party who was incapable of completing the journey.* That he was sensible of what passed between Scott and Wilson cannot be doubted. But he had not earned the sobriquet of 'No Surrender Oates' in the South African war for nothing. He had ordered the men of his patrol to crawl to safety when their ammunition was spent, leaving him to face a Boer commando alone. Their rifle bullets shattered his thigh bone. Now, limping from that old wound, he was being forced by fate into a greater extremity; and this time there was no way out.

What cannot be fairly surmised is the extent to which he was influenced by Scott in taking the step that gave him an imperishable name. The two men were of the same fibre. They had been trained in similar schools of discipline. They shared the same values. The direful effect on their fortunes of Petty Officer Edgar Evans's protracted breakdown was all too fresh in their memories.

Behind the silent drama was the fact that Oates had not wanted to be included in the Polar Party. He did not believe himself to be fit enough for the final test. Scott desired to show his appreciation of Oates's services to the Expedition; more especially, he wanted the British Army to be represented at the Pole with the Royal Navy. Oates's unpublished diary was destroyed after his mother's death, by her wish.

On 16 March, 'or 17'—Scott had 'lost track of dates'—Oates begged the others to go forward, leaving him in his sleeping-bag. 'That we could not do.' In spite of 'the awful nature' of the going, he struggled bravely on. 'We made a few miles.' At night he was nearing *extremis*. Scott wrote: 'We knew the end had come.'

*

* See page 260.

288

Eleven miles away to the north, Cherry-Garrard and the dog team were making ready to leave One Ton Depot to go back to the winter base at Cape Evans. They had waited a week without a sign of the homecoming Polar Party, until provisioning and a blizzard compelled them to retrace their steps. That day, Fortune irrevocably turned her back on Scott. For him thenceforward hope was but a flickering candle flame.

'Tragedy all along the line,' he wrote with the extraordinary composure that makes his last journal entries one of the great human documents. Oates had slept, praying not to wake again. 'But he woke in the morning—yesterday. It was blowing a blizzard. He said, "I am just going outside and may be some time." He went out into the blizzard and we have not seen him since. Though we tried to dissuade him, we knew it was the act of a brave man and an English gentleman.'

Emotion was quelled by the resolve 'to meet the end with a similar spirit'. Instead of despair, 'my companions are unendingly cheerful'. They even sang songs, though Scott doubted whether either Wilson or Bowers believed there was a chance of salvation. 'We move dreadfully slowly,' yet they would not abandon the 35 lb. of geological specimens from the Beardmore Glacier that were to help date a continent.

Scott was crippled by frostbite in his right foot, where only two days previously he was the 'proud possessor' of the best feet in the team. He now conceded the palm for fitness to Bowers; 'but there is not much to choose. The others are still confident of getting through—or pretend to be—I don't know! We have the last *half* fill of oil in our primus.' On 19 March he emphasized their need of hot food. Without it, 'there's no chance to nurse one's feet. All our feet are getting bad.' Contemplating the state of his own, he concluded stoically that 'amputation is the least I can hope for now'. His avoidance of self-pity was as heroic as his patience under suffering. 'Must be near the end. Have decided it shall be natural.'

For eight days the tent was shaken by a gale-force blizzard. Wilson and Bowers were waiting for a chance to make for One Ton Depot for fuel. When it came they were too far gone to seize it. Scott made no journal notes between 23 and 29 March. Instead, immured in the tent with the temperature at minus 40 degrees F., he wrote letters of farewell to the two women who meant most to him, his wife and his mother, and to the wives and mothers of those who, like him, would never return, to old Admiralty colleagues, to the Expedition treasurer, to J. M. Barrie, to his publisher, Reginald Smith, to Kinsey, in New Zealand. His letter to his wife was addressed with what now seems sublime detachment: 'To my Widow,' telling her how pleasant were his recollections of her as he was preparing to depart.

I shall not have suffered any pain, but leave the world fresh from harness and full of good health and vigour. When provisions come to an end we simply stop unless we are within easy distance of another depot. Therefore you must not imagine a great tragedy.

I want you to take the whole thing very sensibly, as I am sure you will. The boy will be your comfort. I had looked forward to helping you to bring him up, but it is a satisfaction to know that he will be safe with you.

You know I cherish no sentimental rubbish about remarriage. When the right man comes to help you in life you ought to be your happy self again—I wasn't a very good husband, but I hope I shall be a good memory. Certainly the end is nothing for you to be ashamed of, and I like to think that the boy will have a good start in his parentage of which he may be proud.

You must know that quite the worst aspect of this situation is the thought that I shall not see you again. The inevitable must be faced, you urged me to be the leader of this party, and I know you felt it would be dangerous. I have taken my place throughout, haven't I? God bless you. I shall try and write more later—I go on across the back pages.

I think the last chance has gone. We have decided not to kill ourselves but to fight to the last for that depot, but in fighting there is a painless end, so don't worry. Make the boy interested in natural history if you can. It is better than games. They encourage it in some schools. I know you will keep him in the open air. Try and make him believe in a God, it is comforting——

What lots and lots I could tell you of this journey. How much better it has been than lounging about in too great comfort at home. What tales you would have had for the boy, but oh, what a price to pay. Dear, you will be good to the old Mother.... Oh, but you'll put a strong face to the world, only don't be too proud to accept help for the boy's sake. He ought to have a fine career and do something in the world.

I haven't time to write to Sir Clements. Tell him I thought much of him, and never regretted his putting me in charge of the *Discovery*.

To his 'dear, dear Mother', he wrote with the tender compassion of a fellow mourner. Above all, he was concerned that she should have the comfort of knowing that he clung to the substance of the religious faith that meant so much to her—'not perhaps believing in all that you hold to so splendidly, but still believing that there is a God—a merciful God'. He wished that he had been a better son; 'but I think you will know that you were always very much in my heart and that I strove to put you into more comfortable circumstances'.

The letter he wrote in those last hours to Sir James Barrie, the dramatist, was subsequently cited as a rare testament of friendship. Extracts from it were given prominence in the introduction Barrie contributed to an edition of *Scott's Last Expedition*. In the letter Scott made the moving avowal: 'I never met a man in my life whom I admired and loved more than you, but I never could show you how much your friendship meant to me. You had so much to give and I nothing.'

What was not disclosed by the printed extracts was that, in thus laying bare his feelings, Scott was distracted by the knowledge that a distance not comprised in latitudes had come between him and that famous friend of his. He summoned his failing powers to repair a misunderstanding. 'We are pegging out in a very comfortless spot. Hoping this letter may be found and sent to you, I write a word of farewell. It hurt me grievously when you partially withdrew your friendship or seemed to do so. I want to tell you I never gave you cause. If you thought or heard ill of me it was unjust. Calumny is ever to the fore. My attitude towards you and everyone connected with you was always one of respect and admiration. Under these circumstances, I want you to think well of me and my end.'

Of the reason for Barrie's seeming coolness, Scott gave no hint in the letter, which was an eloquent appeal for aid and comfort for his dependants. That it deeply troubled him in his last hours of consciousness is shown by the heartrending postscript. 'As a dying man, my dear friend, be good to my wife and child. Give the boy a chance in life, if the State won't do it—he ought to have good stuff in him—and give my memory back the friendship which you suspended.'

He told Kinsey, writing on 24 March: 'I'm afraid we are pretty well done, four days of blizzard just as we were getting to the last depot. My thoughts have been with you often. You have been a brick. You will pull the Expedition together, I'm sure. Teddy Evans,' he wrote, 'is not to be trusted overmuch', implying, it may be presumed, that Evans was not competent to wind up affairs, 'though he means well.' Scott continued: 'My thoughts are for my wife and boy. Will you do what you can for them, if the country won't?' If he knew they were in safe keeping, he would have little regret in leaving the world, 'for I feel that the country need not be ashamed of us. Our journey has been the biggest on record, and nothing but the most exceptional hard luck at the end would have caused us to fail to return.' He reminded Kinsey that they had been to the South Pole, as they had set out to do. 'God bless you and dear Mrs Kinsey. It is good to remember you and your kindness.— Your friend, R.S.'

Finally, Scott wrote out his Message to the Public, setting forth the causes of the disaster, including 'a shortage of fuel in our depots for which I cannot account'. He maintained that the arrangements for returning were 'quite adequate', and that 'no one in the world would have expected the temperatures and surfaces which we encountered at this time of the year. . . . Our wreck is certainly due to this sudden advent of severe weather. I do not think human beings ever came through such a month as we have come through.'

The Message ended with the reverberating affirmation: 'Had we lived, I should have had a tale to tell of the hardihood, endurance, and courage of my companions which would have stirred the heart of every Englishman. These rough notes and our dead bodies must tell the tale. . . .' He then returned to the last page of his journal, to write there on Thursday 29 March 1912:

Since the 21st we have had a continuous gale from W.S.W. and S.W. We had fuel to make two cups of tea apiece and bare food for two days on the 20th. Every day we have been ready to start for our depot *11 miles away*, but outside the door of the tent it remains a scene of whirling drift. I do not think we can hope for any better things now. We shall stick it out to the end, but we are getting weaker, of course, and the end cannot be far.

It seems a pity, but I do not think I can write more.

R. SCOTT

For Gods sake look after our people.

His handwriting was strikingly clear and decisive. It was as if, looking back over his life, in which there had been as much frustration as fulfilment, he realized that it was his sovereign vocation to show men how to die. With Wilson and Bowers already dead beside him, he lay in the tent alone, probably conscious for another day, or more. He was the oldest, and he had held out the longest. The tablets of release remained untouched in the bottle. Outside, the abating gale sobbed and sighed like lamentation music.

On 31 March his wife was rung up at midnight from Fleet Street with the news that he was staying another year in the Antarctic. 'I didn't enjoy the rest of the night very much,' she wrote in her diary. 'I can quite well bear your staying away another year, but it is difficult to bear the thought of your disappointment about Amundsen. Also, it's hard to think of you out so late in the season, but there, I suppose you know your job and wouldn't take too awful risks.' In after years she pencilled alongside that diary passage: 'He had been dead two days at least.'

CHAPTER TWENTY

'... AND NOT TO YIELD'

A MONTH after the world heard of Amundsen's great exploit, the Central News Agency distributed the news that on 3 January Scott was within 150 miles of the Pole, and that he was staying in the Antarctic another year 'to complete the work'. The announcement was followed by a long dispatch, signed by Scott, giving a full account of the Expedition up to the time of the departure of the last Returning Party. The narrative filled many columns of the newspapers, and inspired almost as many leading articles. Scott's wife thought that 'Garvin's in the *Pall Mall Gazette* last night was magnificent' (2 April 1912).

That renowned editor had written in the course of one of his wide-measure dissertations on topics of the day: 'There has been no "dash" for the Pole, or "race" to the Pole, or any of the other follies dear to a generation of sensation-lovers and "record" maniacs. Captain Scott set out to do the work which was worthy of him as a British naval officer; he was not lent by the Admiralty to take part in a Marathon race.'

Kathleen Scott wrote in her diary: 'My dear, I have no words to express how fine and simple and splendid that magnificent tale is. The hardy, straightforward spirit in it is most inspiring. I thought surely the disappointment of being in a race you hadn't entered for will soon be dispersed by the joy of having been of use to humanity and a lasting credit to the country. I have never read a more uplifting document. It seems of a sudden to restore all the romance, all the prestige, all the *worth*, of Polar exploration. With all one's heart one feels: "Well done!"'

Having made a gesture to the comity of nations by sending, after all, a telegram of personal congratulation to Amundsen, she dined with Reginald McKenna, a future Chancellor of the Exchequer, and returned to Buckingham Palace Road, to find a letter awaiting her from Scott, written from winter quarters nearly six months before. 'I must say I loved every word of it—almost.' She was pleased because it confirmed her private judgement of the men on whom he particularly relied, Bowers, Oates, and Atkinson: he referred to them in the letter as 'treasures'. She reminded him, *via* the diary, that she had 'spotted them' (her phrase) before the Expedition sailed from New Zealand. It was a surprise to her, she wrote, that Meares had fallen short of his expectations. 'I am not a bit surprised about Teddy Evans, or Wilson, tho' I always hoped he might improve with hardening,' an allusion that appears to connect with Wilson's remarks to Cherry-Garrard that he expected to be sent back with the last Returning Party.*

She was especially pleased with Scott for resigning his Expedition pay. 'I remember your once saying that you believed a man always did his best when there was no financial gain to confuse the issue. I believe you are right, and I am profoundly

* See page 270.

we shall stick it out
to the end but we
are getting weaker of
course and the end
cannot be far

It seems a pity but
I do not think I can
write more—

R Scott

Last Entry

For Gods Sake look
after our people

grateful to you and happy that we shall not make money out of the Expedition. As regards me, you must never worry. I make £300 a year on sculpture now and want for nothing, nor does, nor shall, Peter' (10 May 1912).

She disclosed in another of her unposted letters that she had taken a step which she hoped Scott would commend. 'I have in the event of you and I dying before you return (I like to leave nothing to chance) made Peter the property of Sydney Holland. I can think of no surroundings I would rather see my son grow up in'* (13 August 1912).

She, who also was soon to be shatteringly acquainted with grief, was the bearer of bad news for the wife of Leading Stoker Robert Brissenden, R.N., serving with the *Terra Nova* on hydrographic survey work in New Zealand waters. He was drowned on 17 August. 'Con, dear, it was just terrible. She was a dear, quiet little woman with a fine boy of seven. I don't suppose anybody could have felt her blow more poignantly than I, but I doubt if my sympathy was any help. It seemed so terrible to descend on her gay, neat little house, to drop a bombshell like that, and depart. I wrote to her when I got home, but it all seems so paltry in the face of her sorrow.'

Amundsen's gaunt shadow fell across her path that autumn. Lord Curzon, as President of the Royal Geographical Society, was invited to meet him at dinner at the Norwegian embassy in London. He asked Darwin, the ex-President, whether he should accept. Darwin sought Kathleen Scott's opinion. 'I said that Lord Curzon must of course be civil, but that there was no reason why he should not plead another engagement.' Sir Clements Markham told her that he 'did not know how Major Darwin would have the impertinence to speak to you, after shaking hands with Amundsen. He was really rather absurd.' Half-heartedly, she 'tried to stop' Amundsen lecturing in London, and declined the ticket offered her by the council of the Royal Geographical Society. 'I do not feel sociable about Amundsen' (7 November).

*

At near midday on 12 November, in latitude 80° S., a hundred and forty-eight miles from the Cape Evans base, silent figures

* Sydney Holland, 2nd Viscount Knutsford (1855–1931), of Kneesworth Hall, Royston, Hertfordshire. As chairman of London Hospital, his fund-raising ingenuities made him famous as 'The Prince of Beggars'.

tracking across the Great Ice Barrier converged, as if by signal, on a point ten miles due South of One Ton Depot. They were the search party which, under Surgeon-Lieutenant E. L. Atkinson, R.N., had gone out on 29 October to try to find Scott and his companions, who for some months past had been presumed lost. It was Atkinson's guess that they had come to grief in a Beardmore Glacier crevasse. His party was provisioned to go on searching for three months over a range of 600 miles.

Wright, the Canadian physicist, who was in charge of the Indian mules that formed the search party's advance transport and who was also the navigator, saw 'a dark patch' on his right, about a quarter of a mile away. 'I left the column and ski'd over to investigate. It turned out to be about six inches of the top of the tent at their last camp.' He recalls his initial attempts to attract the rest of the party's attention by hand movements. 'I was most conscious of a feeling that to do so by shouting would be like desecration. For the same reason, I had camp made about a couple of hundred yards away from the tent. We waited for "Atch" [Atkinson] with the dog team to come up and take charge. Until then, about two hours later, no one was allowed to approach the tent.' It was drifted by snow and looked like one of the guide cairns built along the route to the Pole.

When the tent was dug out and opened, under Atkinson's supervision, Scott was found lying in his sleeping-bag (subscribed for by the pupils of the County School, Cardigan), with Wilson and Bowers lying on either side of him. Wilson's hands were clasped on his chest, like a knight recumbent. 'Birdie' Bower's great nose curved like a scimitar out of his Jaeger helmet. Their gabardine overalls were stiff as armour. With their cross-gartered Burberry leggings, they could have been disentombed Vikings.

Sir Charles Wright remembers that 'they looked surprisingly peaceful'. For another member of the search party, Tryggve Gran, it was 'all ghastly. I will never forget it as long as I live; a terrible nightmare could not have shown more horror.' Cherry-Garrard wrote in his diary: 'It is all too horrible—I am almost afraid to go to sleep now' (Midnight, 12–13 November).

Atkinson read out extracts from the last pages of Scott's journal, specially emphasizing, as Scott wished, the self-sacrifice of Oates. Cherry-Garrard wrote: 'We learnt that Amundsen had been to the Pole, and that they too had been to the Pole, and both items of news seemed to be of no importance whatever.' Atkinson also read from St Paul's First Epistle to the Corinthians, xv, xx. The bamboos of the tent were taken out, 'and we then collapsed the canvas upon them and built a large snow cairn over it',* one of history's most majestic interments.

When all was done, 'the sun was dipping low above the Pole, the Barrier was almost in shadow. And the sky was blazing— sheets and sheets of iridescent clouds. The cairn and Cross stood dark against the glory of burnished gold' (Cherry-Garrard). A wide-sweeping search over an arc of thirteen miles was made for Oates. He had vanished, utterly. A cairn was built for him too, surmounted by a small cross. Lashed to the stem of the cross was the written tribute: *Hereabouts died a very gallant gentleman....*

Diaries, letters, personal gear, and Wilson's carefully-hoarded geological specimens from the Beardmore Glacier were gathered up. The search party marched away on 16 November, having made a funerary decision that accorded perfectly with English sentiment, but which was a subject of culturally interesting curiosity among the new-generation Americans established at McMurdo Sound fifty years later. They wanted to know from Sir Charles Wright: Why were the bodies not sledged back?

A large cross of Australian jarrah wood was borne to Hut Point and erected on Observation Hill, a landmark well in sight of the winter base at Cape Evans. There had been discussion of appropriate inscriptions. Then it was remembered that Dr Leeper, in Melbourne, had written some lines from Tennyson in the volume of Browning's poems given to Scott as a parting present. Atkinson had brought the book back from the tent; and there was the quotation from *Ulysses*: *To strive, to seek, to find, and not to yield....* It was carved into the wood of the cross, the lettering picked out in black. The Antarctic, inviolate as yet to all but the oldest form of human communication, was to keep its secret for another three months.

At the annual banquet of the National Geographic Society of America, held that January at the New Willard Hotel, Wash-

* Sir Charles Wright, K.B.E., M.C., M.A., in a letter written to the biographer from the U.S. Naval Antarctic Support Activities Base, McMurdo Sound. 4 November 1965.

ington, Amundsen was the chief guest, Peary the toast-master. The burden of the evening's speeches was: What will such men as Shackleton, Charcot, Amundsen and Peary do next? Popular prejudice being keyed to unqualified success, Scott received scanty mention as the displaced rival for priority at the South Pole.

*

The silliest catch tune ever written, *Yip-I-addy-I-ay-I-ay*—an anaemic imitation of the rip-roaring *Ta-ra-ra-boom-de-ay!* of the 'eighties—was mercifully hushed on the people's lips when, on 12 February 1913, the news of the disaster to Scott's party was made public. The shock wave had as much force as that of the sinking of the *Titanic* ten months earlier and, as with that catastrophe, it was felt beyond the bounds of the far flung British world. Condolence messages streamed in from all parts of the globe.

As a crowning irony, the fates had contrived to give Scott in death a renown that could hardly have been his even had he succeeded in his greatest ambition as an explorer. Its measure could be taken in the newspaper 'morgues', those bulging repositories of *post-mortem* celebrity. They showed that in terms of general esteem, Scott's death ranked him with the leading men of the age. Not all of them were memorialized, as he was, by the publication of a 24-page edition of a national newspaper exclusively given over to him and his career.*

His wife, eleven months widowed, had left for New Zealand with the intention of meeting him on his return there in the spring. She went by the overland route to the Pacific, *via* New York, making notable new friends on the way: Colonel House, who, like her devoted admirer Nansen, was soon to play a prominent role in world affairs; Stefannson, the Arctic explorer; Carl Akely, the American naturalist. When the news of Scott's death was known in New Zealand, attempts were made to get the message to her by wireless. The signals proved to be too weak to reach her ship in mid-Pacific.

Thus she did not know on 14 February that a great memorial service for Scott and his companions of the Polar Party was being held that day in St Paul's Cathedral, where as early as 10 a.m. 'Church Full' notices appeared in front of the portico. The London *Evening Standard* doubted if St Paul's 'ever con-

* *Daily Mirror*, 21 May 1913.

tained in its vast area a congregation so profoundly moved as that which gathered there today,' headed by the King. The 'special correspondent' reporting the event could not forget 'one who is still ignorant of the frightful tragedy, that hapless woman, still on the high seas, flushed with hope and expectation, eager to join her husband and to share in the triumphs of his return. It made one feel that the service was somewhat unreal.'

Similar observances were held in churches and chapels in many parts of the kingdom, and overseas. The villagers of Binton, Warwickshire, had special cause to remember Scott. It was in their church, where one of his Bruce brothers-in-law was rector, that he made his last appearance as a member of the congregation before sailing away in the *Terra Nova* in 1910. Everywhere, flags were at half-mast. Memorial bathos from frustrated poets filled the postbags of local newspapers. At the commemorative service at Estoril, Portugal, where Sir Clements Markham, in his eighty-third year, was spending a winter holiday, it was observed that 'the dear old boy was quite overcome'.

An interview that week with the London manager of the Expedition, G. W. Wyatt, drew from him his opinion of 'the mystery of the oil shortage', referred to as unaccountable in Scott's last message. 'Captain Scott had ample oil. There is an unsatisfactory ring about the whole thing.' The *Daily Express* commented that 'the mystery deepened' after Lieutenant Evans's statement that Scott had enough fuel to last a month beyond the expected date of his return. A leader in the *East Anglican Times* deplored 'the cruel suggestions that the supplies had been tapped'.

On 19 February Kathleen Scott was sitting on the deck of the mail steamer *Aorangi*, 'not feeling very well', when the captain approached her saying that he had a private message for her. He led the way to his cabin. 'It did not occur to me in the slightest what he wanted, but I went. The poor old chap's hands were trembling when he said, "I've got some news for you, but I don't see how I can tell you." I said: "The Expedition?" and he said, "Yes." "Well," I said, "let's have it," and he showed me the message.'

On 21 February she wrote in her diary: 'I played five games of deck-golf and read violently. Anything to get that awful, haunting picture out of my head. It is good that I do not firmly believe in life after death, or surely, surely I would have gone overboard today, and left Peter to Sydney Holland. But I am afraid my Con has gone altogether, except in the great stirring influence he must have left on everyone who had knowledge of him. I think he has made me twice the man I was. Certainly I couldn't have faced this with complete self-control but for his teaching.'

She told herself that she had 'worked, striven, and strained' for his approval, which now she would never have. He had raised her standards, shown her 'what men can be', what he expected her to be. Could she live up to it, she asked herself, now that he was no longer there to applaud her?

All these long, weary days with no more news. Always only his pain, his mental agony, boring into my brain. I sleep, or don't, on the top deck and the nights are beautiful with the moon, and all the different aspects of it come to me, one by one. How one hopes his brain soon got numbed and the weight of his responsibility left him; for I think never was there a man with such a sense of responsibility and duty, and the agony of leaving his job undone, losing the other lives, and leaving us uncared for, must have been unspeakable.

In her sorrow at sea, 'my little friend the Third Officer remains my own stand-by,' for sympathy, 'not advice'. He was 'a dear, clean boy' of 23, who understood little but who, 'like a big dog', sat by her and was sorry. She found out that his quiet watchfulness, day and night, in the last hours of the voyage, was 'because he thought I should throw myself over, not knowing that I did not believe I could find the dead by doing so'.

She was met at Wellington, New Zealand, by her brother Wilfrid; the widow of Dr Wilson; Surgeon-Lieutenant Atkinson; and Lieutenant Evans, who had again taken command of the *Terra Nova* for the voyage south to bring home the Polar Party. 'After dinner, the Evanses, Mrs Wilson, and Dr Atkinson came and talked a great deal of nonsense. Apparently Mrs Wilson is very displeased with the Evanses, who have their knife terribly into Kinsey. I was mollifying and nice to everybody, of course.'

Atkinson brought her Scott's journals. She spent a whole

night reading them, copying one of the last passages into her own diary: 'You must know that quite the worst aspect of this situation is the thought that I shall not see you again.... How much better has it been than lounging in too great comfort at home—but oh, what a price to pay—to forfeit the sight of your dear, dear face.... Oh, but you'll put a strong bold face to the world.' She added her own thought: 'Indeed, indeed he has left a goodly heritage. My Peter now has a great birthright.'

She talked for a long time with Atkinson the next day, 'about $1\frac{1}{2}$ hours. He gave me details of how he found you but not enough. I don't like asking, so I still ache to know more. I am, oh, so grateful it was Atch [Atkinson] who found you, he's so quiet and tactful and reverent.' Mrs Wilson was 'bravery indeed. She was so sweet and gentle and dear. She of course has had more than a fortnight to get used to it, I only a few hours, but we were both very sensible, I think.'

Her brother Wilfrid was 'a dear boy but not much comfort. He doesn't understand me the least in the world.' As for Teddy Evans, 'I don't dislike him, in fact I like him, but he is no sort of stay or assistance to me.'

She returned to London in the middle of April 1913 to find that her husband's Message to the Public had stirred the heart of the nation, which, having shown little enthusiasm for his money-raising activities of three years earlier, was being asked to support a Scott Memorial Appeal Fund launched by the Lord Mayor of London on 14 February. Its purpose was to provide suitable memorials and financial aid for the dependants of those who were lost. Other funds were opened by three London newspapers, and by the *Scotsman*.

At the same time, Lord Curzon publicly announced that money was urgently needed to pay off outstanding liabilities of the Expedition, amounting to close on £30,000. He made it known that both Scott and his wife had pledged their small private resources towards reducing the debt. In the first days, the response was as discouraging as Scott himself had found in his begging campaigns. The Lord Mayor's appeal produced only £3,500 in a week, one-third of which was donated by a single sympathizer. A letter sent to the press by Barrie suggested that people were confused by the number of appeals and the variety of purposes animating them.

Swift official action fused the different efforts into the Scott Memorial Fund, with the King and Queen heading the subscription list. The response from the public was immediate and enheartening. Nearly £30,000 was raised in three days. The final total was £74,509. A Government annuity of £300 was jointly awarded to Scott's mother and sisters; his wife received £100 a year in addition to her Admiralty pension of £200, with £25 a year for her son until he was eighteen.

It was announced from 10 Downing Street that the King was pleased to grant her the rank, style and precedence that would have been hers had her husband lived to be made a Knight Commander of the Order of the Bath, as His Majesty had intended. Obviously the King had acted in that matter on the advice of Asquith, his Prime Minister, who not only continued to call on Kathleen Scott, sometimes staying 'for hours and hours', but wrote her 'long, long letters'. When he told her: 'You have the best brain of any woman I have ever met,' she said: 'Say that again,' and he said it again.

Scott's will was published in May 1913. He left £3,231 12s. 3d., 'as far as at present can be ascertained'. Substantial grants from the Memorial Fund were made to the dependants, from £8,500 to Lady Scott down to £1,250 to the widow of Petty Officer Edgar Evans, whose Admiralty pension for herself and her three children was £48 a year. Scott's mother and sisters received £6,000. The sum of £3,500, administered by the Public Trustee, was provided 'for the maintenance, etc.' of Peter Scott until he was twenty-five, when he was to receive the capital sum.

It was in Kathleen Scott's nature to 'put a bold face to the world', as none knew better than Scott who counselled it in his last letter to her. Doing so, she was at risk of being misunderstood. George Bernard Shaw, to whom she was 'a wonderful woman and a very special friend', totally misread her temperament when he wrote in a private letter: 'She did not seem to feel her loss at all.' For that rash opinion, he was rebuked by one who knew the depth of the grief that she reserved for her diary, and that twice she had to go away, to the Sahara and to Andorra, 'in order to make her self-command secure'.

*

For the rest, her son, her art, her second marriage,* and her friends, were the chief interest of her life, while she long kept in touch with members of the Expedition, and their wives and

* To Edward Hilton Young, M.P., later Lord Kennet (1879–1960).

families, and was active in the affairs of the Scott Polar Research Institute at Cambridge. As for her art, her powers were exclusively centred for months after the tragedy in modelling the life-size figure of Scott in his Antarctic kit that was unveiled by Balfour in 1916 on its site in Waterloo Place, London, S.W. It was one of over twenty memorials in stone, bronze, and stained glass designed to transmit his name and worth to posterity in several countries.

None came near in grandeur to the lonely cairn on the Ice Shelf (Great Ice Barrier). A computation recently made by American scientists at their station in McMurdo Sound suggests that blizzards have driven frozen snow over the burial cairn to a depth of fifty feet, and that the site is now fifteen miles nearer the Ice Shelf edge, whence come the great tabular icebergs that drift away to the north. A leaping imagination foresees a time when the cairn and its Cross are borne by one of them out to the open sea.

*

For epilogue, there is an hitherto unpublished letter. It was written to Scott's widow by Frank Debenham, O.B.E. (1883–1965), of the last Expedition's geological staff, later Professor of Geography at Cambridge, and founder director of the Scott Polar Research Institute. The date is 6 November 1913.

'It seems strange to me now that most of us had few premonitions of possible disaster. I can only account for it by the fact that we all felt that with those five no chain of untoward events could prove more than temporary obstacles. It perhaps sounds as if we thought them superhuman; certainly we were more blind than we should have been.'

Affirming 'the universal pride' of the survivors of the Expedition, Debenham emphasized, 'more than anything', the effect on the younger members, of whom he was one. 'Life has become at once simpler and more real. One realizes that honesty, singleness of purpose, and the duty concept, are all that really matter, since those were the principles by which such lives were led as ended in such deaths.'